The Moral Philosophy of G. E. Moore

THE MORAL PHILOSOPHY OF G. E. MOORE

Robert Peter Sylvester

Edited and with an Introduction by
RAY PERKINS, JR., and
R. W. SLEEPER

Foreword by TOM REGAN

TEMPLE UNIVERSITY PRESS
Philadelphia

Temple University Press, Philadelphia 19122
Copyright © 1990 by Temple University. All rights reserved
Published 1990
Printed in the United States of America

The paper used in this publication meets the minimum
requirements of American National Standard for Information
Sciences—Permanence of Paper for Printed Library Materials,
ANSI Z39.48-1984

Library of Congress Cataloging-in-Publication Data
Sylvester, Robert P., d. 1986.
    The moral philosophy of G. E. Moore / Robert P. Sylvester : edited
and with an introduction by Ray Perkins, Jr. and R. W. Sleeper ;
foreword by Tom Regan.
        p.   cm.
    Includes bibliographical references.
    ISBN 0-87722-645-8 (alk. paper)
    1. Moore, G. E. (George Edward), 1873–1958—Ethics.   2. Ethics,
Modern—20th century.   I. Perkins, Ray, Jr.   II. Sleeper, R. W.,
1925–   .   III. Title.
B1647.M74S97   1990
171'.2—dc20

                                                    89-28661
                                                        CIP

To
Arthur J. Sylvester
and
Alberta L. Sylvester

Contents

Editors' Introduction

The posthumous publication of any author's work must be the result of decisions reached by others. In making such decisions the author's own clear intent to publish, although central to the process, is but one factor. Equally important is the merit of the work itself. Our decision to accept the responsibility of acting as co-editors of this book is based primarily, and equally, on both these factors. What follows is a brief account of the circumstances under which that decision was reached.

Not long after Professor Sylvester died in November of 1986, we came into possession of a copy of Tom Regan's *Bloomsbury's Prophet: G. E. Moore and the Development of His Moral Philosophy*, which had just been published by Temple University Press. We were attending a meeting of the Eastern Division of the American Philosophical Association in December of that year, and the book was being displayed there by Jane Cullen, Temple's senior acquisitions editor, along with *G. E. Moore: The Early Essays*, edited by Regan, which had also just been published by the press.

We had been aware that Sylvester, a long-time friend and professional colleague of us both, had been working on a book about Moore's ethics for some time before his death, a few weeks earlier, in London. We knew it had been Sylvester's intention to spend a few weeks at Cambridge University, studying Moore's papers that had been gathered there, in order to finish work on the projected book and to settle some details concerning a second project that he had in mind. This second project was the publication of a collected edition of Moore's early essays that Sylvester felt had been neglected in the critical literature on Moore's ethics, and that he saw as having had a direct bearing on Moore's 1903 *Principia Ethica*, as well as on the book of practical morals that Moore published in Oxford's "Home University Library of Modern Knowledge" series, the *Ethics* of 1912.

Here, then, were Tom Regan's two books, in which the evidence was that he had accomplished at least some of the purposes that Sylvester had intended. Not only had Regan studied the Moore papers at Cambridge, and made extensive use of them in his book, but he had also published an edition of Moore's early papers. Mention to Jane Cullen of Sylvester's twin projects, and their apparent parallel (or congruence) with Regan's, stimulated her to ask for permission to see Sylvester's work with an eye to the possibility of posthumous publication. As we had not yet had a chance to study Sylvester's manuscript, or Regan's books for that matter, it seemed best to defer any response to her request beyond a promise to convey her interest in Sylvester's project to his wife and colleagues at New England College.

It soon developed not only that all concerned were very pleased at the interest in the manuscript, but that a number of problems needed to be resolved before the manuscript could be put in shape for presentation and review.

The manuscript was incomplete in at least two respects. Although it seemed clear that Sylvester had planned a concluding chapter and had listed it in a table of contents, none was to be found. A second problem arose from the fact that what was obviously the latest draft of the book was peppered with penciled corrections, emended wordings, and in some cases what appeared to be minor, but still substantive, revisions.

The latter problem was at least partially resolved by arranging for a clean copy to be prepared, suitable for review, which incorporated as many of Sylvester's penciled corrections and emendations as could be readily deciphered. Some months later that clean copy was submitted to Jane Cullen at Temple University Press for evaluation and review. The problem of the missing chapter of conclusions was eventually resolved when we came to realize that the present Chapter VIII—the final chapter of the book—would serve handsomely in place of the unwritten chapter.

The publisher's reviewers, David Pears of Oxford University and Lynd Forguson of the University of Toronto, found sufficient merit in the work to warrant publication, but agreed that there was still a need for extensive editing of the manuscript. The manuscript was also examined by Tom Regan and several of our own colleagues, including Abraham Edel, and by John McDermott, from whom we have received a number of helpful editorial suggestions. After considerable discussion it was finally agreed that, acting as co-editors of the projected book, we would undertake the necessary editing, and a contract for publication was entered into with Temple University Press.

The editing of the manuscript proceeded very slowly, owing to other publishing commitments on the part of both co-editors, and because a certain amount of research in the Moore literature was required. Although we in no sense attempted to duplicate Sylvester's own research, we did feel the necessity to become familiar with his sources. While we have made extensive use of Sylvester's own library, including his liberally annotated copies of the works cited in his bibliography, we also felt the need to consult the small number of works that either had been published subsequently to the last date at which Sylvester had worked on his manuscript or had not been available to him. Neither of the co-editors, it should be said, had any expertise in the development of Moore's work in the period with which Sylvester was concerned, although one of us (Perkins) had long been interested in the development of Bertrand Russell's philosophy, which in many respects paralleled Moore's for some years.

As the project began to mature, we became convinced that some means should be devised whereby we could make available to the reader of Sylvester's book some of the background material that he was working with but makes no direct reference to in either the body of his text or the notes. Some of this consisted of historical and bibliographical background material contained in his extensive notes, but a larger part consisted of annotations in Sylvester's copies of Moore's works and the works of his critics. We felt that the brief bibliography he had prepared should be greatly augmented, as it consisted exclusively of works he had made direct reference to in the manuscript, omitting much of the material he listed in the bibliography for his doctoral dissertation on Moore at Northwestern University in 1962, as well as additional material subsequently consulted in the preparation of the present work.

Accordingly we have supplied a critical bibliography in the form of a brief essay for each of Sylvester's chapters. Much of the content of these essays is the result of our own effort to deepen and broaden the historical background context in which Sylvester's reading of Moore's ethics is embedded. While we have tried to include as much bibliographical information as Sylvester actually had at his disposal, we have not limited the essays to that material, but have tried to suggest comparisons between Sylvester's treatment of problems in the interpretation of Moore's work and the interpretations of others. In this respect we have paid special attention to comparisons with works published since the date at which Sylvester was compelled to cease work on his book owing to the illness that clouded the last years of his life. The emphasis we have placed on comparisons with such recent books as those by Tom Regan, Dennis Rohatyn, and John Hill is meant to point up the differences between their several treatments and Sylvester's, not as criticism in any other respect.

It should be emphasized that we have not rewritten Sylvester's manuscript; the style is his. Nor have we tried to annotate the text by the use of notes of our own. At a few points in the body of the text where we felt it would be particularly useful to insert a reference we have enclosed that reference in square brackets, [thus].

While Sylvester appears to have modeled his style upon Moore's own in *Principia Ethica*, that model was not followed consistently. Where Moore divides each of his chapters into many brief and numbered sections, Sylvester followed the model; but he added brief section titles as well. While this addition tends to break up the flow of the text to a far greater extent than Moore's unadorned numbers do, it is obvious that Sylvester intended his section titles to guide the reader's attention and focus it upon the specific content of each section as the argument of the chapter was developed. After considerable hesitation we have decided to allow the section titles to stand; they clearly represent the author's intention in the matter.

Sylvester, following Moore's "Victorian" habit, capitalized substantive words such as "good" and "ethics" in the manuscript, but did not do so consistently. We have dropped that form of capitalization altogether. Instead, we have relied on the context of the sentence as sufficient guide as to whether a word—such as the key word 'good'—is being used substantively or, for example, adjectivally. To distinguish the mention of a word (as above in the case of the word 'good') from its use, single ('scare') quotes are employed for such mention. When a word is quoted from another text or referred to as in some special usage—as above in the case of "Victorian"—double ("blare") quotes are used.

We have checked the accuracy of Sylvester's references for page numbers and source, as well as the internal references that are made within the text. The author's Preface, which follows, is given exactly as we found it, including the line indicating the date. This is the date at which he had effectively completed the manuscript that we have worked with throughout. The Dedication page, also, is given exactly as we found it.

While we have tried to remain as faithful as possible to Sylvester's intentions in editing the text itself, we make no such claim with respect to our remarks in the critical biographies; whatever is said there, for better or worse, is our responsibility and ours alone.

We want to express our gratitude to Audrey Sylvester, who serves as executor of Sylvester's estate, and to Jane Cullen, of Temple University Press, for their unstinting patience and support over the many months that it has taken us to complete our assigned task. We are also especially grateful to the publisher's reviewers, David Pears and Lynd Forguson, for their many valuable suggestions as to editorial matters in connection with the preparation of this work for publication. We also owe a considerable debt of gratitude to the officials of both New England College and Plymouth State College for their generous offer of assistance in duplicating material and for clerical assistance. To Gail Greenly, who prepared the initial clean copy of the manuscript and recorded it on computer disks, our debt is truly incalculable and our gratitude unbounded. Without that first step, nothing!

> Ray Perkins, Jr.,
>   Plymouth State College, USNH
> R. W. Sleeper,
>   Queens College, CUNY (Emeritus)

Foreword

Robert P. Sylvester's *The Moral Philosophy of G. E. Moore* is first and foremost a work of discriminating scholarship. Its publication would gratify even Moore's severest critic—Moore himself. For like Moore, Sylvester is steadfastly determined to say *exactly* what he means or, as is often the case, *exactly* what Moore means. Such dedication has not always characterized Moorean scholarship. Heralded in his later years as the defender of common sense, Moore had a less well-known and appreciated attraction to speculative metaphysics in his youth. Those who would understand Moore's moral philosophy, especially his groundbreaking *Principia Ethica* (1903), are well advised to mine his metaphysical past. In Moore's case, as in others—though perhaps especially in his—everything he means is what it is, and not another thing. And what he means in his moral philosophy is certain to be misunderstood if, as is usual, interpretations are offered that fail to appreciate the metaphysical grounding Moore had in mind. One of the many merits of Sylvester's book is that he does more than recognize this. He insists upon it.

Here is one example among many. In *Principia*'s opening chapter Moore attempts to persuade his readers that good is indefinable. Does he mean the word 'good'? Or does he mean something else? Sometimes Moore himself is not clear, a failing that has led at least one commentator to state that "this confusion is not very important." Sylvester knows better. Moore's sustained exploration of the concept good (or what we might better term *goodness*) is of a piece with his other metaphysical writings of this period, including "Freedom" (1898), "The Nature of Judgment" (1899), and "Identity" (1900–1901). To understand the ethical part, one must understand the metaphysical whole. Among Sylvester's most important contributions is the way he explicates Moore's famous and frequently misunderstood declamations about good within this broader metaphysical perspective.

No less important is Sylvester's attempt to explain the interrelationships between, and the unity of, Moore's writings in moral philosophy. "G. E. Moore" and "the naturalistic fallacy" are all but synonymous to students of contemporary ethical theory, and yet Moore himself, after *Principia*, ceased to explore or invoke this famous "fallacy"—even when one would naturally assume that he would, in his *Ethics* (1912) and in "The Conception of Intrinsic Value" (ca. 1916), for example. How is this change to be understood? To what degree, if any, does it signal Moore's abandonment of *Principia*'s views of good's indefinability? And if these earlier views are abandoned, what does it mean to speak of Moore's moral philosophy? It is to Sylvester's credit that he not only understands the need to ask these questions; he also offers insightful, plausible answers to them.

There is much else in this book that guarantees its enduring importance. Why Moore's understanding of the naturalistic fallacy is logically distinct from the fallacy of deriving an 'ought' from an 'is,' and what role *Principia*'s motto ("Everything is what it is, and not another thing") actually plays in this work, are but two of many other areas where Sylvester's discussions will help shape future Moorean scholarship. We owe him much, including the restrained passion he brings to his task. In a review of a book about the Belgian painter René Magritte, Tom Stoppard writes that the author "is always interesting, lucid and, best of all, mad about Magritte." It goes too far to say that Sylvester is "mad about Moore." It does not stretch the truth to say, he *believes* him—if not always, at least most of the time. Such sympathy in philosophy is as rare as it is pleasant to find.

Earlier I said that Sylvester's book is first and foremost a work of discriminating scholarship. It is this, surely. But it is more than this. That it should see the light of day at all is a gift of love to him, after his death, from two of his friends, Ray Perkins, Jr., and R. W. Sleeper. The particular circumstances surrounding its posthumous publication are summarized by the editors in their Introduction. True philosophers that they are, they sought and, lucky for us, found a novel way to make a philosophical contribution of their own. This we find in their critical bibliographies at the close of the several chapters. In each we are helped to better understand how Sylvester's views differ from those of other Moorean scholars, both past and present, and where—and how—Sylvester may be closer to the truth. Along with Sylvester's, the views of Perkins and Sleeper are certain to have currency among the next generation of Moore scholars. One must assume Sylvester would be pleased.

Questions of philosophical merit to one side, it seems especially fitting that friendships should combine to make this book. It is not maudlin to discern something beautiful in the warmth and loyalty with which the editors have paid homage to a departed friend. Especially fitting, as I say, since the Moore we find in *Principia* believes that the enjoyment of beauty and the pleasures of friendship are the best things in the world. How much better still, then, when we find them, as we find them here, joined together. Such wholes would be good, and no less good, even if they existed quite alone.

> Tom Regan,
> North Carolina State University

Author's Preface

Almost everyone recognizes that G. E. Moore has had a profound influence upon twentieth-century moral philosophy. Even in those studies that no longer see his views as important enough to contest, the very questions developed are the questions set for debate by Moore's work. There are, furthermore, some issues that seem to have been granted a permanent place in thought concerning value and are directly attributable to Moore, for example, the "naturalistic fallacy" and the "open question."

It is not easy to grasp Moore's general doctrine by studying the massive body of criticism of his work. This is true, of course, for any philosopher who commands critical appraisal. But in Moore's case it is sometimes quite inexplicable, since one does not encounter problems of mistranslation or lack of explicitness on the part of Moore. After all, almost everyone who comments on Moore *must* have read at least the first four chapters of *Principia Ethica*.

I think that a great deal of critical analysis of Moore comes from familiarity with the general body of criticism. Let me cite one of the most common judgments about Moore's moral philosophy, which seems incredible, yet is all too familiar. Many have treated Moore as if his "intuitionism" is an intuitionism of obligation, and he is regularly refuted on the ground that we can't have ethics without reasons. The fact that Moore does not hold that type of intuitionism is one matter, but the fact that he explicitly and repeatedly denies that he is an "intuitionist proper" is some evidence that Moore *himself* has not been consulted on his own view.

Like many others, I read Moore through the eyes of others—I studied Moore with others and under the guidance of others. Occasionally I was disturbed by uncomfortable anomalies, but I supposed that Moore and his odd doctrine were the prime source for my discomfort. Finally I resolved to find out for myself, with the help of some who seemed to me to look at Moore directly, what G. E. Moore was actually doing.

The present examination is one that hopes to set the theory in one piece. It is not often presented as if it is a whole. Many do not see how Moore's notion of intuition fits with his "ideal utilitarianism." Some don't care, since both intuitionism and utilitarianism are "fallacies" so clearly perceptible that anyone who accepts either, much less both, need not be listened to in polite circles. I think the doctrine is a systematic whole, although Moore is correct when he says we should regard *Principia Ethica* as a mere prolegomenon to any future moral theory.

In order to get at Moore's views I have attended to the works that Moore published from 1898 to 1920. These include three book-length volumes: *Principia Ethica* (1903) and *Ethics* (1912), of course; but also the course of lectures delivered in 1910–1911 and published much later (1952) under the title *Some Main Problems in Philosophy*. I refer to works later in Moore's bibliography as well. Schilpp's *The Philosophy of G. E. Moore* in *The Library of Living Philosophers*, [which contains] Moore's "Autobiography" and the "Reply to My Critics," is especially important. The essay "Is Goodness a Quality?" (1932) is also used. These works are helpful in shedding light on the theory that is worked out in *Principia Ethica* and *Ethics*.

When I refer to the moral philosophy of G. E. Moore, then, I have in mind the era I have designated; namely, 1898 through 1920. Remarks in the "Reply" [1942] are helpful, as I have suggested, to clarify the early views.

As I see Moore's work in ethics, the 1903 *Principia Ethica* and the coupled works, *Ethics* (1912) and "The Conception of Intrinsic Value" (1916), are a consistent whole. Moore himself found *Ethics* to be the best and clearest statement of his doctrine of moral behavior, probably because it was able to state in a more extended and systematic way his notion of what we ought to do. *Principia Ethica* jammed practical ethical questions into one single chapter, entitled "Ethics in Relation to Conduct." The title of Chapter 5 of *Principia* has seemed strange to some on the very plausible ground that ethics seems analytically to entail conduct. In *Principia Ethica* Moore uses the term "ethics" to mean all the

issues and problems gathered under the three separate questions:
(1) What is good? (2) What things are good? and (3) What ought
we to do?

Principia Ethica begins with the analysis of "good." The first
four chapters represent systematic discussion of the proper analysis; they provide an explanation of the view that good is a simple
and an unanalyzable, an objective and a unique, object of thought.
They offer extended criticism and refutation of current and competing theories of the meaning of good. It is not until Chapter 5
that Moore's own practical ethical theory is stated, as I mentioned
above.

Ethics, the 1912 publication, is a six-chapter argument for *Principia*'s Chapter 5—Moore's brand of utilitarianism. *Ethics* ends
with the substitution of "intrinsic value" for "pleasure" in the
utilitarian schema. It is not until Moore writes "The Conception
of Intrinsic Value" in 1916 (or thereabouts—surely no later than
1917) that the analysis of intrinsic value is completed. The essay
does for *Ethics* what the four initial chapters of *Principia Ethica*
do for the practical ethical theory found in "Ethics in Relation to
Conduct"; namely, analyze the cardinal concept in ethical theory.

The two works present a consistent moral theory. The central
concept is "good," a simple unanalyzable concept, which, when it
becomes exemplified in things and events in the world, makes
those things and events intrinsically valuable. It is the task of practical ethical activity to bring good into existence, to make the
world have more intrinsic value.

The present book is sectioned into six parts, although I have
taken eight chapters to make the presentation. Chapter I gives an
overview of the scope of the value predicate good. I show that
good is the central concept in Moore's value theory. Chapters II
and III are given over to the several issues involved in Moore's
notion of and use of intution, or self-evident truth. Chapters IV
and V take up the question of value judgment; especially with
respect to the 1899 theory of judgment and the nature of concepts. Chapter VI, following on the doctrine of concepts, grounds
Moore's moral philosophy in an almost classical ontology gleaned
from the early essays and *Principia Ethica*. Chapter VII involves a
discussion of fact and value in the moral philosophy of G. E.

Moore. This chapter takes up *Principia*'s use of the naturalistic fallacy. It reviews William Frankena's justly famous article and uses the paper as a foil for understanding Moore's root view about the existence of value in the world. Chapter VIII argues for a positive notion of the moral self, the being who chooses to act morally.

It should be no surprise that the works I have consulted are the early writings. Moore does not publish in ethics after "The Conception of Intrinsic Value" except for the more popular lecture "The Nature of Moral Philosophy," and it was given before the publication of *Philosophical Studies* in 1922, in which it appeared. What may be of surprise is my heavy use of the early papers, most of which have not been reprinted in a volume of their own. I hope that in the near future they will be collected and published. I believe they are of intrinsic worth, but I am sure they help clarify Moore's moral philosophy in obvious ways.

The book is one I began as part of my doctoral dissertation, a part that would not leave me. In its early stages I was guided by the late Robert Browning, my friend and teacher. Others who have been influential in the formation of parts of the book include Professors Herbert Hochberg and Gustav Bergmann. Three of my own former students stand out as important in the development of the study, Professor Lynd Forguson, Bruce Nyland, and the late David Heishman. I want also to mention in appreciation some friends and colleagues who have assisted in all those ways that may seem to them so little, but are so large in my memory. I profoundly thank Ray Perkins, Johathan Westphall, Frank Birmingham, Ralph Sleeper, Tony Skillen, Richard Norman, Val Dusek and Paul Brockelman, Timothy Duggan and Bernard Gert.

Special thanks should go to the Department of Philosophy of the University of Kent, Canterbury, England. I presented five lectures at Kent under the department's sponsorship on Moore and the topics that are included in the book. The lectures were presented in the summer term 1974. I thank the Department of Philosophy at Dartmouth College for providing me the time and place to complete the writing. They appointed me to a research associateship, January through June 1980.

Finally, my deepest gratitude to Dr. Erwin A. Jaffe, friend, most valued colleague, philosopher.

> Robert P. Sylvester,
> Bradford, New Hampshire,
> July 1980

The Moral Philosophy of G. E. Moore

I

Good:
The Value Predicate

1. The Problem: What Is Good?

G. E. Moore initiated a major revolution in moral philosophy by proposing that its central concept is an indefinable, non-natural object of thought. The word 'good' names this unique and simple object, Moore held, and it is the being of this object that, on certain occasions, qualifies things and events in the world of existences, rendering them of intrinsic value. This extraordinary proposal was systematically developed in *Principia Ethica*, Moore's first book-length publication, in 1903. Nine years later in his second book, *Ethics*, Moore expressed the same general view but argued the case in somewhat different terms. The later work stressed the importance of good's capacity for endowing objects and events with intrinsic value but rather neglected the matter of good's simplicity. However, since 'good' and 'intrinsic value' are alternate terms for the same concept, in Moore's view, differing only in that 'intrinsic value' refers to the quality of good *in* things and events, the position that Moore develops in *Principia Ethica* may safely be said to be consistent with the later expression of that position in the 1912 *Ethics*.

In the opening pages of *Principia* Moore lays out the strategy for the analysis and argument that follow. He claims that confusions have arisen in the history of moral philosophy because the basic questions of the enterprise have not been clearly articulated. He distinguishes these fundamental questions from one another and indicates that there are three quite separate lines of inquiry that constitute the subject matter of ethics. They are indicated by the following questions:

(1) What is good?
(2) What things are good and in what degree?
(3) What ought we to do?

The first line of inquiry is directed at answering the substantive question of the nature of value, or of *good* itself, and how it is known. The second is aimed at determining what things are qualified by good; that is, what things possess the quality of *being* good, and how good is experienced in them. The third takes up the problems of normative ethics; that is, the basis of moral obligation and the standards by which moral behavior is to be judged.

It is ironic that many of Moore's critics have completely overlooked the careful delineation of these issues, which he worked so assiduously to clarify, with the result that his views are often misconstrued. One especially annoying blunder is the fact that he is often misrepresented, even by friendly critics, as holding an 'intuitionist' position with respect to his theory of obligation, although he takes great pains to disassociate his views from intuitionisms of both duty and right, carefully limiting his intuitionism to the substantive question of good's intrinsic character. I return to this confusion below, and mention it here only to give early warning to the reader against just this sort of confusion. As Moore himself says in the opening words of the Preface to *Principia*:

> It appears to me that in Ethics, as in all other philosophical studies, the difficulties and disagreements, of which its history is full, are mainly due to a very simple cause: namely to the attempt to answer questions, without first discovering precisely *what* question it is which you desire to answer.

Accordingly, I make every effort to keep the three lines of Moore's inquiry as distinct from each other as possible, although, of course, I must also show how Moore links them up with each other.

In this chapter I begin with a discussion of the question 'What is good?' as Moore explores it in the first four chapters of *Principia Ethica*. The point is to show the centrality of good, and to indicate how Moore connects the other two lines of inquiry in ethics to the substantive reality of good itself. Later chapters examine questions (2) and (3) above, each in its own terms, but this chapter is given over to a presentation of Moore's basic view of good as directly and as accurately as possible, without much criticism or debate. With but one exception, no effort is made to meet the standard criticisms of Moore's views in the present chapter. The central question is, what did Moore have in mind in claiming that good is a simple object of thought that makes possible the predication of value? I begin, then, as Moore began, with the question 'What is good?'

The question 'What is good?' is the (logically) first question in moral philosophy. In fact it is Moore's claim that until we come to grips with what the word 'good' means (that is, what value *is*) we cannot move forward at all in the solution of the traditional problems of ethics. The inquiry into the meaning of, or the definition of, 'good' belongs *only* to ethics and to no other field of investigation. "My business," Moore tells us, "is solely with that object or idea, which I hold, rightly or wrongly, that the word ('good') is generally used to stand for. What I want to discover is the nature of that object or idea." [1]

2. *The Definition of 'Good'*

Good is good. As is well known, that is Moore's answer to the question, "What is good?" In other words, 'good' cannot be defined. It is a simple notion, a simple object of thought. It is a 'non-natural' object, in Moore's characterization; a claim that concerns us at length in a later chapter, but must remain unexplained in detail here. But it can be said that 'good' is *not* the name of a natural object. Nor is it a complex of other notions; it is incapable of division or of definition. Since it has no conceptual parts, it cannot be analyzed into parts. A complex idea, such as is denoted by the word 'horse,' for example, can be defined, Moore tells us, because it "has different properties and qualities, all of which can be enumerated." Horse, then, is an example of a complex object. Good is like yellow, however, not complex. Moore writes that "yellow and good, we say, are not complex: they are notions of that simple kind, out of which definitions are composed and with which the power of further defining ceases." [2]

Good is something, furthermore, that is exemplified in the world. Good is in the existing universe, independent of any or all observation. One judges that a *thing* is good, because the thing *has* good as one of its objective properties. We are directly acquainted with things that are good. It is a *fact* that things are good. Where can good be found in the world? In things that *are* good. What is the *property* good that allegedly is in the thing? *It*, the property itself, cannot be defined, as has been shown. Good, the *property*, is a basic ontological entity.

One further issue needs clarification before moving on. To judge that something is good in the world is not to judge that some action is called for. To say "This is good" is not to say "I ought to do thus and so." That a thing is good is a matter of fact, but that something ought to be done *because* that thing is good is quite another matter. Moreover, as we shall see in this chapter, that something is *beautiful* is due to the fact that the thing in question possesses good as a property. This is yet a third matter.

Finally, if the good were never exemplified in the world, if there were no simple, non-natural object that can be called good and that qualifies things and events, Moore holds that no judgments of value, moral or aesthetic, could ever be ontologically grounded. The unique presence in things of the element named by 'good' is a necessary, but not a sufficient, condition for correct *practical* moral and/or aesthetic predication. [The importance of distinguishing the direct 'intuition' of good from the making of 'practical' judgments of duty and obligation is explained in Section 4.]

3. One Consequence of Good's Exemplification in the World

Moore holds that the question of good's existence in the actual world of things and events is an objective matter. As has already been indicated, Moore's view maintains that good is actually present in the world quite independently of any awareness of it; that is, good is independently real. [So there is a sense in which Moore's view of good both reflects Plato's doctrine of ideas or forms and anticipates the contemporary position in ethics known as moral realism.] I want to be clear about Moore's doctrine on this point, for it is of the utmost importance in grasping the ontological foundations of his conception of ethics. Moore argues that (1) good is a concept, an object of thought. However, as a concept it is not to be identified with any individual's *idea*; rather, good is real and has being, as an abstract entity, *qua* concept. Moreover, (2) some things in the existing world *are* good; that is, they exemplify the intrinsic quality of being good quite independently of any cognition of those things. In order for practical ethical judgments—that is, judgments that an action is right or one's duty—to be made in human experience, there must be some act (or acts) of awareness 'in commerce with' exemplified value in things or events. Precisely what the phrase 'in commerce with' is to indicate is clarified below. Its full meaning is developed in several ways in various of Moore's ethical writings from *Principia Ethica* on. At this moment let 'in commerce with' imply that some person is either (a) presently aware of a thing, things, or events that has or have value, or (b) was at some previous time aware of a thing, or things, or events, which had value; or (c) both. By "has value" I mean, of course, has (or exemplifies) the non-natural property named by the term 'good.'

4. *The Notions of Practical Ethics and Aesthetics*

Before moving ahead with the exposition of the centrality of the notion of good, I want to remind the reader of a terminological observation mentioned, but not discussed, in Section 1. Moore uses the term 'ethics' in *Principia Ethica* generically. He says that ethics includes inquiries into the three major questions historically garbled by confusion. In this study I refer to the general question 'What ought we to do?' by the name 'practical' ethics. Moore often does so as well; but I'm afraid not always. (The 1912 *Ethics* is an extended discussion of the problems involved in practical ethics.) If I diverge from this usage, I clearly indicate that I am doing so.

Moore has not considered the question of aesthetics extensively in his publications. Whenever he has, it has *not* been for the sake of the discipline itself. He offers a definition of the concept of beauty in *Principia* that is interesting, puzzling, and illuminating, and this is examined in Section 10 of the present chapter. I study the definition of the concept of beauty simply in order to point up the centrality of good, for Moore, even in aesthetics.

Good, in Moore's view, is the non-natural and unique concept that makes possible the predication of value. Good becomes exemplified in the world, and, as has been said, qualifies things, actions, and events. Things that *are* good are things that have intrinsic value, for the terms 'intrinsic good' and 'intrinsic value' are names that refer to the conceptual entity called good.

The vocabulary of Moore's usage may become awkward. Moore is led into some regrettable oddities and confusions that might have been avoided with some clarification. Considered by itself, good is a simple concept or, as we have said, 'object of thought.' But even when good is predicated of a thing and really modifies some existing object, the word still refers to the concept good. [The reader may have noticed that the definite article 'the' is not generally employed in referring to good as a conceptual entity or object of thought; this is Moore's style and is adopted here as well.] When good becomes exemplified in a thing, the thing may be said to be 'intrinsically good' or to have 'intrinsic value.' Thus if someone wonders, 'intrinsic to what?' the proper answer is, 'intrinsic to the thing (or event) in question.' Having the simple property good, then, is what makes the thing 'intrinsically valuable.'

To refer to the simple notion of good as 'intrinsic good' or 'intrinsic value,' Moore uses terms that make sense in their proper context, but in a manner that Moore himself does not make particularly clear. When he uses the term 'good' as the name of the concept, property, or object *good*, Moore uses the word 'good' as a noun. But it is also Moore's habit to use the word 'good' adjectivally as well. The adjectival use, of course, typically occurs in predication. But even when he is using the word 'good' as an adjective it is clear that the word being used to predicate value refers to the simple concept good. Thus the sentences 'Some pleasures are intrinsically good' and 'Good is a simple concept' exhibit correct usage of the word 'good,' according to Moore; first as an adjective, then as a noun.

Moore holds that *a thing or event* that has intrinsic value is something of which it can be said that it *ought* to exist "even if it existed *quite alone*, without any further accompaniments or effects whatsoever."[3] The fact that a thing has intrinsic value, and therefore ought to exist, as the sentence quoted above claims, does not *by itself* entail that it is anyone's duty to do anything to make it exist. Merely knowing that it should exist, or ought to be, does not place an obligation on anyone. The terms of practical ethical importance are defined, not merely by taking cognizance of 'good' as 'ought-to-be,' but with other considerations as well. Chapters 7 and 8 are concerned with 'ought-to-be' and 'ought-to-do' in more detail.

We should be clear about the context in which the adjectival use of the term 'good' can be used as equivalent in meaning to the phrase 'intrinsic value,' such that calling something intrinsically valuable may be understood to mean that it would be a good thing if it existed quite alone. The context is ontological, not (primarily) epistemological, nor is it primarily a practical question of moral behavior. If a thing is good, has intrinsic value, and ought to be, it simply *is* good. The thing's mode of being, in Moore's terms, is that 'it would be a good thing if it existed quite alone.' But nothing in the nature of moral obligation is entailed.

5. *Practical Ethical Predicates Defined*

Practical ethics, for Moore, is not primarily concerned with the question 'What ought to be?' although it is not indifferent to it. Practical ethics inquires into 'What ought we to *do?*' Moore writes: "it asks what actions are *duties*, what actions are *right* and what *wrong*."[4] Duty is defined as "that action which will cause more good to exist in the Universe than any possible alternative." The terms 'right' and 'morally permissible' mean actions "which will not cause *less* good than other possible alternatives."[5] There is a definitional relationship here between actions understood as *causes*, and intrinsic value, or good. [Perhaps it might be well to say here that Moore holds that there is a 'causal relation' between actions and the presence of good as a property. This point emerges as very important in practical ethics.] In any event, it is important to bear in mind that these definitions are drawn from the 1903 *Principia Ethica*.

In *Ethics* the definition of 'right' is reaffirmed, but Moore articulates his view more carefully. He stipulates that there is a characteristic that belongs to every action that is right, but not to any action that is wrong. This characteristic is the amount of value found in the total actual consequences of an action that is right. The total actual consequences must have as much value as the total (actual) consequences of any possible alternative action(s) open to the agent that could have been chosen by him. Although the investigation of this formulation must be postponed until later, what I want to emphasize here is that there is a fixed relationship between right and good. An action is said by Moore to be objectively right if its total actual consequences bring as much good (or intrinsic value) into existence as any other action the moral agent could have chosen instead.

One other important practical ethical predicate is defined in similar fashion. 'Obligation' is defined in terms of the fixed relationship we have been discussing. Moore says: "to assert that a certain line of conduct is, at a given time, absolutely right or obligatory, is obviously to assert that more good or less evil will exist in the world, if it be adopted, than if anything else be done instead."[6]

By this means Moore determines the context of practical ethics. The goal of practical ethics is to bring into existence as much value as the agent is capable of through the choices of actions that are open to the agent.

Moore's practical ethical theory assumes the existence of a moral agent who has the power to exert a causal influence on the course of events in the world. The moral agent can become aware of value. The agent can become aware of the causal laws of the world; can understand that some actions may exclude good from existence. Finally, the moral agent will become aware that he is obliged to choose actions that will bring more good into existence than other possible actions.

As Moore fully understood, this theory of practical ethics is a version of utilitarianism in which the moral value or rightness of actions is determined by their consequences. In Moore's version, however, it is the consequences of actions in increasing or decreasing the amount of good exemplified in the world that determines the obligations in question, as the next section shows.

6. *Duty: Ideal and Practical*

Moore's version of utilitarianism has an unexpected consequence that must be acknowledged at the outset. Moore holds that our duty is to strive for an ideal that we may, he admits, never know we have realized. Let me repeat, Moore acknowledges that we may never know when, or if, we have actually done our duty. In any given choice context we may fail to have all the information required to determine the appropriate action. Moreover, we can never *know* for certain what the actual consequences of our action will be. No one can predict the future with certainty, either in science or in practical ethics. Often we may never actually know how much intrinsic value came about because of an action we performed. And, finally, there can be no way of precisely determining the consequences of actions we have rejected. Nonetheless, according to Moore in both *Principia Ethica* and *Ethics*, our obligation is to do our duty.

It should be noted that Moore allows for some actions we are permitted to do that are not strictly speaking our duty. In any given circumstance it may be that two or three quite different actions will cause an equal amount of good to exist. It is morally permissible to choose any one of the them, provided that the good brought into existence by means of the chosen action is the most good possible—in other words, provided that there is not a further action open to the agent, one that he sees as possible, that is in his power to actualize, and that brings more good into the world than the other actions.

I discuss the issues involved in our ignorance of actual consequences more fully in Chapters V and VIII, but here we should recognize that the fact that we cannot be certain of future events, and can never be certain our actions will have the consequences we believe they will, is a matter for theoretical as well as practical concern. Moore has some suggestions for dealing with the practical problem, but I leave the discussion of the issue aside for now by saying that as moral agents we can be sure of the *criterion* for right actions, for duty and obligation. We can make our moral choices with that criterion before our minds; even if we cannot be sure we have succeeded, we know what it means to fail—to do wrong, to fail our duty and our obligations. We *can* have a moral ideal before our minds as a guide for our practical efforts, even though we cannot know of the moral success of those efforts in advance.

7. *The Notion of 'Intrinsically Better'*

Insofar as actual choices are concerned, moral agents find themselves in real situations in which they must choose one course of action among several possibilities. In such situations moral agents must find one course of action that promises, or *at least seems* to promise, consequences that are intrinsically better than those of any other action. In *Ethics* Moore indicates what the notion of 'intrinsically better' means. It refers to a characteristic that reflects a fixed relation either to good, or to evil. According to Moore, the notion of 'intrinsically better' can be developed in terms of pleasure and pain, and he does so in the initial chapters of *Ethics*.[7] However, in paraphrasing Moore I develop the notion of 'intrinsically better' in terms of good and evil.

Consider two possible actions, A and B; and further suppose they are the *only* options open:

1. A may bring about good, and B may bring about good. But if A brings about more good than B, then A is the better act, and it is our duty to do A.
2. A may bring about good, and B may bring about no good at all. In this case A is better than B, and it is our duty to do A.
3. A may bring about good, and B may bring about badness or evil. Then A is better than B, and it is our duty to do A.
4. A may bring about no good at all, but B may bring evil into existence. Then A is better than B, and it is our duty to do A.
5. A may bring about evil, but B may bring about more evil than A. Then A is better than B, and it is our duty to do A.

This shows that it is a consequence of Moore's definition of practical ethical terms in *Principia* and *Ethics* that the context for practical ethical choice can define a hierarchy of action options. Thus given a situation where five different actions are posed for a moral agent—A, B, C, D, E—let us grant that A would bring about great good, B would bring about some good, C would bring about a predominance of neither good nor evil, D would bring about some evil, and E would bring about a great amount of evil. A value hierarchy is thus defined in which the notion 'intrinsically better' implies the relational notion of 'better than.' A is the morally required action, as we know, but B is better than C. So if the moral agent chose B, knowing that A is better than B, his choice would be morally wrong. If a moral agent thought of A, B, and C, but *did not have the power* to do A or B, then C would be the morally required action. It seems that Moore would say that even if, owing to an agent's lack of information, a certain better action was not done, the action would nevertheless be a duty or obligation although the agent would be held blameless. [This matter is discussed more fully in Chapter VIII, but see also *Ethics*, pp. 118–21.] In any event, what may be taken from this discussion of both the notion of 'better than' and the definitions of 'duty,' 'obligation,' and 'right' with the hierarchy of action options, is that Moore supposes his theory to provide an *objective* backdrop in terms of which practical ethical choices can be ranged and cognitively evaluated.

8. *Rightness: Not an Irreducible Property*

It should be evident from what has been said in the last two sections that practical ethical predicates do *not* refer to indefinable properties of things, or of events, or of actions. 'Rightness' does not name a simple irreducible or indefinable property of things. Nor does 'obligation' refer to a unique object of thought that has no parts and is unanalyzable. 'Duty,' the 'morally permissible,' and the 'better than' relation are defined terms; they are defined by means of the value term 'good'—as designating the unique concept good—*as well as* by a choice context requiring causal information. Practical ethical disagreement cannot be seen as a disagreement over the being of an intuitively perceived non-natural quality called 'rightness' or 'oughtness.' Practical ethical disagreement is a disagreement over whether this action or that action ought to be performed. The questions of practical choice involve the assessment of consequences which are likely to follow as a result of the choice. Anticipating the consequences of an action requires some degree of sophistication concerning the way the world works. One must have some idea about what sorts of actions cause what sorts of things to happen. Moore also holds that practical ethics involves an ability to judge the comparative value of outcomes. For example, suppose one is aware that a child will be swept over a waterfall while floating down a river on an inner-tube, and that such an eventuality is bad; and one is also aware that the child could be pulled to the shore before she reaches the edge of the falls, and that the result of carrying out such a rescue would be good; *and* that the latter is better than the former. In such a case it would be right for such a moral agent to perform an action to bring the child to shore. As the example shows, some knowledge of the materially causal factors in any morally problematic situation is just as much needed as strictly moral knowledge. The information involved in a judgment of rightness or obligation must include such causal factors as may either be present in the practical situation, or be anticipated in calculating consequences.

It is very possible that some critics have been misled into thinking that 'duty' and 'obligation' are to be determined solely by 'intuition' or 'self-evidence' by one of Moore's remarks in *Ethics*. Moore, as we have seen, defines 'duty' and 'obligation' in the *Ethics* as that which will produce the best effects on the whole, or will produce the (total) consequences of the most intrinsic value. These definitions are the same as in *Principia Ethica*. In the 1912 book, however, Moore tells us how he *knows* that duty is to be so defined: "It seems to me quite self-evident that it must always be our duty to do what will produce the best effects upon the whole, no matter how bad the effects upon ourselves may be and no matter how much good we ourselves lose by it." [8] But it is clear from this passage that Moore is not claiming that the moral agent 'intuits' any *particular* action to be one's duty. For what he claims to be self-evident is merely that one's duty is whatever action will produce the best consequences "upon the whole." The matter of the role of intuition in Moore's ethics, as well as his analysis of self-evidence are studied in the next two chapters. But for the moment the reader is alerted to the fact that Moore does *not* hold the view that obligation (or duty or rightness) is an indefinable, simple, or irreducible quality or property of actions.

What *is* indefinable, simple, and irreducible is the intuitive object of thought, the entity that Moore calls 'good' and that is an indispensable constituent of the notion of obligation or duty.

9. *Practical Ethical Disagreements*

Practical ethical disagreements, moral disagreements, are not captured by the simple form 'N ought to be' as opposed to 'No, M ought to be.' As Stephen Toulmin has suggested in his critique of intuitionism in ethics, moral disagreements follow the form, "N is right" and "No, not N but M" where N and M represent alternative actions.[9] In preferring N to M, preference is stated in causal terms. If N is done, what consequences may be expected? As we have seen, Moore stresses the causal question. He also emphasizes, as we know, that the consequences chosen by an agent must be (morally) justified. Moore provides the justifying criterion—that the best possible consequences must follow from the action—and it is clear that this criterion determines which of any possible alternatives ought to be chosen. Moore's point is just that the criterion that determines duty is *not* an intuited property that one alternative has and the others lack. Good, indeed, may be expected to follow from *all* the alternatives facing a moral agent, and so it cannot by itself be the criterion for choosing among them.

As we have seen, Moore's practical ethical doctrine allows for disagreement and argument. But the question remains as to what *kinds* of disagreements count as moral and are legitimately the subject of moral debate and argument. There is a very wide range of matters that are subject to error, or moral disagreement, and an equally wide range of the kinds of reasoning and evidence that may be necessary in correcting moral error and resolving ethical disagreements. I shall suggest only some of them.

Let us suppose that two disputants, Smith and Jones, are in disagreement over which action, M or N, ought to be done in a given situation; call it situation Z. *First*: Both must be clear that they have situation Z under analysis. It is a common error for disputants to be unclear as to what the situation actually is that is evoking disagreement. Smith may have Z in mind while Jones, saying he is judging Z, is actually noticing Z^1. Supposing, however, that both have Z as the object of their judgments, the scope for error is still very considerable. Smith and Jones may agree, for instance, that consequence O represents the best possible outcome. However:

(a) Smith believes act N will produce consequence O, while Jones believes act M will produce O. Several errors in this case can be seen to be possible: (i) Smith may be wrong about N's actual consequence, and Jones may be correct about M's. (ii) Jones may be in error concerning M's actual consequence, and Smith correct about N's. (iii) Smith and Jones may both be wrong. Act L brings about consequence O; act M and act N are both mistaken. (iv) Smith and Jones may both be in error when they think that consequence O is the best possible consequence. Consequence U is the best. (v) Smith and Jones may be mistaken *not* about the consequence; O let us say, represents the best consequence possible. They may both be correct, act M produces O *and* act N produces O. The error comes in each thinking the other action wrong. (vi) Smith and Jones may both be correct, act M is right and act N is right. Each is in error in thinking the other to be mistaken. But they are also both mistaken when they think that O is the best possible consequence and that act M and act N produce O. Consequence U is the best possible and both M and N produce U.

The set of possible errors becomes more complex when:

(b) Smith believes act N will produce consequence O and Jones believes act M will produce consequence U. In this disagreement context Smith holds consequence O to be the best possible while Jones opts for consequence U as the best possible. The laundry list of possible errors cited above can be worked out for such a disagreement context.

The incomplete catalogue of error possibilities above is suggested simply for the purpose of demonstrating some of the number of ways in which, according to Moore's theory, disputes and disagreements may arise. The point is just that Moore's theory requires a very careful assessment of possible actions for their causal, hence moral, suitability. It suggests further than an intellectually (and therefore morally) honest person must be careful to make the series of distinctions necessary to be clear as to precisely what he is to judge, and in what moral context. There is *no scope* in this doctrine for any kind of moral absolutism that may be present in some traditional kinds of intuitionism. Insofar as Moore can be called an intuitionist at all, it is clear that the label is not applicable to such matters as his treatment of moral obligation, the morally right and dutiful actions we must perform in our capacity as moral agents in the world. I have an occasion to underscore this point in the last section of the present chapter.

10. *The Aesthetic Predicate: Beauty*

In the last chapter of *Principia Ethica* Moore gives us his account of the aesthetic predicate 'beautiful.' As is true with practical ethical terms, the aesthetic predicate is fixed to the value concept good. 'Beauty' is defined as 'that of which the admiring contemplation is good in itself.' Moore believes that when we judge something to be beautiful, the judgment is made in a specific situation in which one is actually related to an object *that is taken to be* beautiful. The situation is an 'organic whole,' or an 'organic unity,' to use Moore's terminology. It is the unity, the whole, that is 'an intrinsically valuable whole,' and the question "whether it is truly beautiful or not," Moore tells us, "depends upon the *objective* question whether the whole in question is or is not truly good."[10]

Suppose someone is viewing a painting that he finds to be beautiful. Moore calls the experience, as already indicated, an organic whole. When the whole is intrinsically good, beauty is realized. Four aspects of this whole may be distinguished: (1) an object, in this case a painting, that must have (2) intrinsically good qualities that must themselves be (3) admiringly contemplated by (4) a person or subject.

Let's consider (2) first, the intrinsically good qualities. In the eyes of some critics Moore appears to involve himself in a circular argument by defining these qualities in terms of beauty. To obviate such a reading I quote from *Principia Ethica* and give what I hope is a clear and coherent interpretation of Moore's thought:

> When, therefore, I speak of the cognition of a beautiful object, as an essential element in a valuable aesthetic appreciation, I must be understood to mean only the cognition of *the beautiful qualities* possessed by the object, and not the cognition of the other qualities of the object possessing them.[11]

Moore also says, in another way of stating what he takes to be the same point, "when it is said that the picture is beautiful, it is meant that it contains qualities which are beautiful." Those who suspect circularity in Moore's thought are (quite rightly) puzzled by the characterization. Can it be legitimate to define 'beautiful' in terms of beautiful qualities? The problem of circularity appears to haunt Moore's remarks. But I suggest that when we put Moore's view more carefully, the appearance of circularity is not sustained.

What is cognized when one notices that a painting (or any object) is beautiful? Moore claims it is good, or value, that is judged to be present in the object. Certain qualities of the painting exemplify value, and it is these qualities that are grasped *as beautiful*. The qualities in question are certain natural properties of the painting and provide natural grounds into which good *ingresses*. The process of ingression is explained more fully in Chapter VI, but let me say here that Moore's claim is that on the occasion of a person's noticing a painting that has been crafted so that the natural properties are receptive to value, good becomes exemplified. The viewer grasps the value exemplified. That occasion, plus certain other conditions (upon which I remark presently), is one in which beauty may be experienced.

The first analytical step has been fulfilled when the viewer has completed a cognitive act—the grasping of value in the object. The next step is as follows: For beauty to appear it is necessary that an emotive response to the value in the object be had. The experience involves, then, both a cognitive act and an emotional response to an object's qualities. Thus it is natural for Moore to refer to the qualities that call for such a response as 'beautiful qualities.' I take Moore *not* to have been defining the word 'beautiful' in terms of the words 'beautiful qualities.' But what *was* he doing?

As remarked above, *cognition* of the qualities that exemplify value in an object is not a sufficient ground for saying that beauty has been experienced, although it is, of course a necessary one. Moore argues that there must *also* be feeling. The feeling must be an emotional response appropriate to the qualities that exemplify good. When the appropriate emotion is present, the whole becomes intrinsically good, and beauty may then be correctly predicated of the whole. Here is how Moore puts it:

> It is not sufficient that a man should merely see the beautiful qualities in a picture and know that they are beautiful, in order that we may give his state of mind the highest praise. We require that he should also *appreciate* the beauty of that which he knows to be beautiful—that he should feel and see *its beauty*. And by this we certainly mean that he should have an appropriate emotion towards the beautiful qualities he cognizes.[12]

The reader may still encounter uneasiness. Despite what I have said by way of interpretation through restatement of his position, Moore may seem to have referred to seeing and feeling beautiful qualities as if beauty was there, itself, *qua* beauty, in the thing. The text reads as quoted, and I appreciate whatever uneasiness remains. Moore does *nonetheless* explicitly say that beauty is a *defined* notion, and is defined in terms of the simple *undefined* and unanalyzable substantive concept named 'good.' I refer once again to *Principia Ethica*:

> It appears, at first sight, to be a strange coincidence that there should be two *different* objective predicates of value, 'good' and 'beautiful' which are nonetheless so related to one an-

other that whatever is beautiful is also good. But if our definition is correct, the strangeness disappears; since it leaves only one *unanalyzable* predicate of value, namely 'good,' while 'beautiful,' though not identical with, is to be defined by reference to this, being at the same time, different from and necessarily connected with it.[13]

11. *Beauty and Good: Further Remarks*

As I read Moore, in a genuine aesthetic experience it is not enough just to see (and recognize) the value that is in the object in order for the predicate 'beautiful' to be correctly ascribed. There must be, as we have seen, an appropriate emotional response to the value exemplified as well. There must be (4) a subject who (3) has an appropriate emotional response toward (2) the intrinsically good qualities, which the person cognizes in (1) the object. When these four conditions are met, the organic unity of the experience itself, the *whole* thus indicated, is intrinsically valuable. It (intrinsic value) is located in (2), which is part of (1) the intrinsically good qualities of the object. Beauty, unlike good itself, is *not* independent of either the object or the experience of the object, but is in the whole situation, the organic unity of which is achieved when the four conditions are met. Beauty is *not*, like good, an irreducible entity.

Moore does not further examine the notion of appropriate emotion, but not because he overlooks the question. He thinks it is incapable of further explanatory analysis. He observes that different types of emotional responses seem appropriate in accordance with differences in the types of objects experienced. There seems to be wisdom in his observation. A response to the ballet *Swan Lake*, or a series of responses to that complicated object, seems to differ from a response to the *Guernica* as a painting, as would be expected from a difference in an experience in a dance studio and an experience in an art gallery. A response to a musical experience seems different in kind from that of an experience in the visual arts. Perhaps the issue should not be left with these minimal remarks, but I am not going to investigate it for its own sake here.

My purpose has simply been to show the centrality of good, for Moore, even in his account of aesthetic judgment.

12. *Errors in Aesthetic Predication*

Moore's analysis of beauty is consistent with discussion, criticism, and argument in relation to matters of aesthetic judgment. An aesthetic controversy is not to be understood as settled by 'agreeing to disagree,' as the popular cliché about matters of 'taste' would have us believe. Just as there are mistakes in practical moral judgment, so there may be mistakes in aesthetic judgment; in neither realm does the presence of an intuitive factor in the experienced presence of good in the whole situation entail that such judgments are incorrigible. Moore does not hold a doctrine of the incorrigible aesthetic perception, just as he does not hold a doctrine of the incorrigible perception of value in practical moral decisions. In fact Moore outlines two types of errors that can be committed in aesthetic contexts roughly parallel to similar types of mistakes that occur in making moral choices.

(1) One might notice an object and be mistaken about the properties of the object. One might suppose that certain properties were part of the object that were not in fact actually present. Thinking that the absent properties were there, one might have an emotive response that would have been entirely appropriate if the imagined properties had been present. Moore calls an error of this sort an *error of judgment*. The fact that Moore cites errors of judgment as important errors, which can occur, indicates why Moore was insistent upon referring to the beautiful *qualities* of the object and not to the beauty of the object *as such*.

(2) One might see the qualities of the object clearly and grasp the value that is exemplified through them correctly. Still one might have an emotional response that is inappropriate. Moore refers to an error of this type as an "error of taste."[14]

I should suppose that aesthetic criticism would generally consist in discussion and debate over the context in which errors of judgment are made or are likely to be made. I should also suppose that aesthetic education, or education in any of the art forms, would be concerned with issues of cognition. But, and I emphasize the fact once again, Moore does not, with any frequency or consistency, pursue questions of aesthetics in his subsequent work. In the one instance that he does so, several years after both *Principia* and the *Ethics* were written, a view is expressed that clashes with the one we have just been explicating. I turn to that view in the next section.

13. *An Alternative Analysis of Moore's 'Beautiful'*

Moore does not follow up the discussion of the two orders of error, as outlined above, in further elaboration, nor does he turn to aesthetic theory for its own sake. The remarks on beauty in *Principia Ethica* must therefore be interpreted almost entirely as adjuncts to the general theory of value articulated there. That this is not always accepted by Moore's critics is, however, worth noticing.

In Moore's 1916 essay, "The Conception of Intrinsic Value," Moore speaks of beauty as if it were a type of intrinsic value on its own. Because of the remarks I quoted at the end of Section 10, in which it is stated that analysis "leaves only one *unanalyzable* predicate of value, namely 'good,' while 'beautiful,' though not identical with, is to be defined by reference to this, being at the same time, different from and necessarily connected with it," [15] and because of my analysis of Moore's views, I take it that Moore's 1916 notion of beauty *is* in fact different from the *Principia* view. But there is a critical interpretation of *Principia Ethica*'s concept of beauty that differs from the one I have suggested, and I want to air it here. Austin Duncan-Jones suggests that Moore thinks the *Principia Ethica* thesis calls for the existence of a great number of "pulchrific qualities." These qualities, it is suggested, attach themselves to objects. Each of the pulchrific qualities "is such that the appropriate kind of admiring contemplation of it would be intrinsically good." Duncan-Jones adds, "The distinction between pulchrific qualities, and other qualities which are involved in the subject terms of value generalizations, lies in their being ingredients of certain wholes of which another element is the admiring contemplation." [16]

As far as I can see, nothing in Moore's published works faintly suggests the being of simple particular particles of beauty. Moreover, if there were such particulars, the distinction between natural and non-natural properties of things would collapse. For, as we shall presently see, good as a quality is not a simple particular that is constitutive of a thing, as natural properties are. [This has to do with the fact that good is always a *supervenient* property of objects in which it is exemplified, a complex matter to be taken up later.] Duncan-Jones's suggestion is intriguing, however, for it shows how important it is to recognize why Moore insists that there be only *one* unanalyzable predicate of value, and that—however puzzling the analysis may turn out to be—'beauty' will have to be defined in terms of it. Duncan-Jones's analysis requires beauty to be located in discrete value particles, qualities that are unanalyzable on their own account. Moore, however, holds that there is only *one* unanalyzable predicate of value: good itself.

It may well be that Austin Duncan-Jones was trying to square the *Principia* view of the beautiful with Moore's statements in "The Conception of Intrinsic Value," where beauty *is* said to be a kind of intrinsic value. But the two views collide. Of course the *Principia* analysis must be made consistent with itself, as shown in Section 10 above, but there is no further requirement that it be made consistent with the essay that Duncan-Jones cites. And it seems clear that the *Principia* analysis is the one we should be exhibiting here, and that it must be understood in its *own* terms and not those of the later essay. Even so, we are not yet finished with the matter.

14. *Organic Unities and Beauty*

Each and every object that is good in the world of human experience, Moore tells us, is an organic unity constituted by diverse natural elements. If such an object, as an organic whole, is so constituted that good *may* become exemplified in the whole, then good *necessarily* will exist in that object. Epistemically, we can have no a priori insight into precisely the grounds for any instance of value entry into the world. But if a certain object *is* intrinsically good, then, in Moore's ontology, anything just like it will also be intrinsically good.[17] [Again, this notion is the foundation of the doctrine called supervenience in subsequent moral theory. It is mentioned here in application to aesthetic theory, however.] It is useful to see how Moore treats the presence of good in an aesthetic object of beauty.

Beautiful objects are like any other existing object in that they are conceived by Moore as organic unities. They are wholes, he tells us, consisting of many parts. Any particular part may have no value at all. Some parts may have minimal value. In fact, an object of great value may have diverse parts, each of which may have little or no value in itself. Yet when the whole is grasped in its unity, the object's beauty becomes experienceable. Moore calls this the 'principle of organic unities' and holds that it governs value's exemplification in the world. The principle, which Moore articulates in the first chapter of *Principia Ethica* and explicates at various points throughout the book, is also an essential notion in the *Ethics*. It requires that we assess the value in each whole *as* a whole, and that we refrain from assuming that the value of the sum of the parts of a whole equals the value of the whole. Each and every whole is a thing with its own intrinsic integrity; it is never to be judged as the mere conjunction of other wholes, its elements.

I do not want to be misunderstood in my review of Moore's notion of beauty. I have not said, for instance, that *Principia Ethica*'s view was his final word on beauty. In fact, I said that the later essay, "The Conception of Intrinsic Value," elevates beauty to the status of an intrinsic value. I also said I thought Duncan-Jones may have allowed the later view to have influenced his analysis of Moore's *Principia* doctrine. I do say, however, that the essay is inconsistent with *Principia Ethica* if it implies, as it seems to, that there are *two* indefinable, unanalyzable predicates of value. Accordingly, and for the purposes of the present chapter, we may leave aside whatever controversy may arise over the question of the meaning of Moore's remarks about beauty in "The Conception of Intrinsic Value."

15. *Final Remarks*

The task of the present chapter has been to set the main features of Moore's view of the centrality of good—the simple, indefinable, unanalyzable, non-natural, and unique object of thought—in value theory. I have shown that Moore claims that good, alone, is the simple and unanalyzable predicate of value. I have shown that practical ethical predicates—such as his notions of duty, obligation, right, morally permissible—are defined (in part) by reference to good. I have shown that the aesthetic predicate beautiful gets its content by reference (in part) to good.

It is my contention that *Principia Ethica* and *Ethics* present a remarkably consistent moral theory. The two texts agree as to the cardinal role that good, or intrinsic value, plays in ethics. The two texts define the practical ethical terms in identical ways.

I have indicated that Moore *defines* 'beauty' in *Principia Ethica*, thus marking out a way in which beauty and good are different. But there is no occasion for Moore to deal with the aesthetic predicate in the *Ethics*. It has been suggested that there may be a difference between the view that Moore takes in the 1903 *Principia Ethica* and in the later essay on "The Conception of Intrinsic Value" in 1916 with respect to beauty, and that if Moore had continued to study problems of aesthetics, perhaps there would be more to say about the difference. What is important about the study of beauty, from the point of view that this chapter has presented, is that in *Principia Ethica* the analysis of good, the value predicate, shows it to be the pivotal concept in Moore's value theory, whether in moral practice or in judgments of beauty. It is in fact a singular feature of Moore's philosophy of value that both aesthetic and moral judgments turn upon the same simple concept. It is the concept of which Moore has this to say:

> If I am asked 'what is good' my answer is that good is good, and that is the end of the matter. Or if I am asked 'How is good to be defined?' my answer is that it cannot be defined, and that is all I have to say about it. But disappointing as these answers may appear, they are of the very last [sic] importance. To readers who are familiar with philosophic terminology, I can express their importance by saying that they amount to this: That propositions about good are all of them synthetic and never analytic; and that is no trivial matter. And the same thing may be expressed more popularly by saying that, if I am right, then nobody can foist upon us such an

axiom as that 'Pleasure is the only good' or that 'The only good is the desired' on the pretence that this is 'the very meaning of the word.'[18]

CRITICAL BIBLIOGRAPHY

Prefatory Note on Citations

References to Moore's works in the main text and notes are to the editions used by Sylvester, as noted in his manuscript. These editions are given below in the chronological order of publication favored by the author of the manuscript. References to Moore's early essays are made by the author to their original sources of publication, a practice he continues in the text and notes, and retained by the editors.

However, in the period since the author was compelled to interrupt his work on the manuscript by an illness that proved terminal, the republication of many of these essays in Tom Regan, ed., *G. E. Moore: The Early Essays* (Philadelphia: Temple University Press, 1986), has made it possible for the editors to add page references to the new edition below as well as to the text and notes. The page numbers of the Regan edition are given in square brackets following the original page numbers. Square brackets are also used to indicate the editors' insertions of alternative sources, where available, to the editions of Moore's works used by the author.

References to, and quotations from, other works are to the editions referred to by the author in his notes where such references were available; otherwise to such editions as were available to the editors. In all cases, both quotations and citations have been checked by the editors for accuracy.

Works by Moore: Author's List

The following books, articles, and reviews are the main sources for the present study. I have abbreviated some of the citations for use in the notes and, occasionally, in the text.

"Freedom," *Mind*. n.s., 7 (April 1898), pp. 179–204 [Regan, pp. 25–57].

"The Nature of Judgment," *Mind*. n.s., 8 (April 1899), pp. 176–93 [Regan, pp. 59–80; cited as "Judgment"].

"Necessity," *Mind*. n.s., 9 (July 1900), pp. 289–304 [Regan, pp. 81–99].

"Identity," *Proceedings of the Aristotelian Society*. n.s., 1 (1900–1901), pp. 103–27 [Regan, pp. 121–45].

"The Value of Religion," *International Journal of Ethics*. 12 (October 1901), pp. 81–98 [Regan, pp. 101-20; cited as "Religion"].

"Mr. McTaggart's 'Studies in Hegelian Cosmology,'" *Proceedings of the Aristotelian Society*. n.s., 2 (1901–1902), pp. 177–214 [Regan, pp. 147–84; cited as "Cosmology"].

J. Mark Baldwin, ed. *Dictionary of Philosophy and Religion*. London: Macmillan, 1902 (see entries "Real" and "Truth").

Principia Ethica. Cambridge: Cambridge University Press, 1959 (first paperback edition) [originally published 1903].

"Experience and Empiricism," *Proceedings of the Aristotelian Society*. n.s., 3 (1902–1903), pp. 80–95 [Regan, pp. 185–200; cited as "Experience"].

"Mr. McTaggart's Ethics," *International Journal of Ethics*. 13 (April 1903), pp. 341–70 [Regan, pp. 201–32].

"The Refutation of Idealism," *Mind*. n.s., 12 (October 1903), pp. 433–53 [reprinted in *Philosophical Studies*, New York: Harcourt Brace, 1922, Chapter 1; cited as "Refutation"].

Review of Franz Brentano, *The Origin of the Knowledge of Right and Wrong*, in *International Journal of Ethics*. 14 (October 1903), pp. 115–23 [cited as "Brentano Review"].

"Kant's Idealism," *Proceedings of the Aristotelian Society*. n.s., 4 (1903–1904), pp. 127–40 [Regan, pp. 233–46].

"The Nature and Reality of Objects of Perception," *Proceedings of the Aristotelian Society*. n.s., 6 (1905–1906), pp. 68–127 [cited as "Objects of Perception"].

Lectures at Morley College, London, 1910–1911, published under the title *Some Main Problems of Philosophy*. London: Routledge, 1953 [cited as "1910–1911 Lectures"].

Ethics. London: Oxford University Press, 1958 [originally published in 1912].

Symposium: "Are the Materials of Sense Affections of the
Mind?" by G. E. Moore, W. E. Johnson, G. Dawes Hicks,
J. A. Smith, and James Ward, *Proceedings of the Aristotelian
Society*. n.s., 17 (1916–1917), pp. 418–58 [cited as "Affec-
tions of the Mind"].
"The Conception of Intrinsic Value," as reprinted in *Philo-
sophical Studies*. New York: Harcourt Brace, 1922, Chapter
8.
Symposium: "Is Goodness a Quality?" by G. E. Moore,
H. W. B. Joseph, and A. E. Taylor. *Aristotelian Society, Sup-
plementary Volume* 11 (1932), pp. 116–68 [reprinted in
Philosophical Papers: G. E. Moore. London: Allen & Unwin, 1959; paperback edition, New York: Collier Books,
1966].

General Bibliography

A serviceable bibliography of the writings of G. E.
Moore, compiled by Emerson Buchanan and G. E. Moore, is
contained in the Library of Living Philosophers, vol. 4, *The
Philosophy of G. E. Moore*, edited by P. A. Schilpp (Evanston,
Ill.: Northwestern University Press, 1942). Sylvester obviously
worked over this bibliography, as the marginal notes in his
own copy of the volume are extensive, indicating by a series of
markings that he had checked out virtually all the documents
listed. He also marginally annotated most of the articles contained in this volume, although not all of them deal with the
subject-matter of Moore's ethics.

In his manuscript Sylvester almost always refers to the aforementioned volume simply as "Schilpp"; and we have retained
that practice for publication. (It may be noted that Sylvester
worked with Professor Schilpp on more than one occasion in
the capacity of indexer for volumes in the Library of Living
Philosophers series.) In any case, the Schilpp volume on Moore
is as good a place as any to start looking for background material helpful in understanding Moore's project in ethics. It
contains Moore's only autobiography, for example, as well as
a generous sampling of expert criticism of Moore's ethics to-

gether with an extensive essay by Moore, "A Reply to My Critics."

Although the Schilpp volume contains much more than just criticism of Moore's ethics, we mention here only those critical essays apposite to Sylvester's thesis. Among them are "Moore's 'The Refutation of Idealism,'" by C. J. Ducasse; "Moore's Theory of Moral Freedom and Responsibility," by A. Campbell Garnett; "The Logical Structure of G. E. Moore's Ethical Theory," by Abraham Edel; "The Alleged Independence of Goodness," by H. J. Paton; "Obligation and Value in the Ethics of G. E. Moore," by William K. Frankena; "Moore's Arguments Against Certain Forms of Ethical Naturalism," by Charles L. Stevenson; and "Certain Features in Moore's Ethical Doctrines," by C. D. Broad.

It is perhaps a sign of both the richness of Moore's works on ethics and their difficulty that there is little overlap in the criticisms made in these essays. All are important, though not equally so for Sylvester's treatment. In developing his own reading of Moore's ethics, not all of these critics make important points that Sylvester wants to incorporate into his own view or test his own view against. Judging from the marginalia in Sylvester's copy of Schilpp, he was most bothered by the essays of Stevenson and Frankena. It seems that he found fault with the reading these philosophers give to Moore's famous doctrine of the naturalistic fallacy—a finding he airs in several places in the manuscript.

There are two collections of essays on Moore's work, published subsequent to the Schilpp volume, that Sylvester consulted extensively: *Studies in the Philosophy of G. E. Moore*, ed. E. D. Klemke (Chicago: Quadrangle Books, 1969); and *G. E. Moore: Essays in Retrospect*, eds. Alice Ambrose and Morris Lazerowitz (London: Routledge & Kegan Paul, 1970). Although neither collection focuses exclusively on Moore's ethics, both volumes contain important critical essays, including previously published material on the naturalistic fallacy and other contested points of Moore's account of the subject, which were annotated by Sylvester. Reference to both volumes is made with some frequency in the chapter bibliographies that follow.

The most useful and up-to-date bibliography of works critical of Moore's ethics that the editors have discovered is in Dennis Rohatyn's *The Reluctant Naturalist* (Lanham, Md.: University Press of America, 1987). Although this could not have been used by Sylvester, it is mentioned here as a convenience to the reader who may wish to compare Sylvester's interpretation of Moore's ethics with the readings given by Moore's many critics since the publication of the Schilpp volume. Rohatyn's own reading of Moore is, as his title indicates, very different from Sylvester's since he argues that Moore's *Principia Ethica* can be given a naturalistic interpretation.

The only book-length study of Moore's entire philosophical work of which the editors are aware is Alan R. White's *G. E. Moore: A Critical Exposition* (Oxford: Blackwell, 1958). White devotes only a single chapter to Moore's ethics, however, so his treatment is less valuable than can be found in several books that are devoted mainly to Moore's ethics. We have already mentioned one such book above. Tom Regan published another simultaneously with the publication of his edition of *The Early Essays*; it is *Bloomsbury's Prophet: G.E. Moore and the Development of His Moral Philosophy* (Philadelphia: Temple University Press, 1986). While the intent of Regan's interpretation of Moore's ethics is best captured in the main title of the book, the subtitle indicates that Regan's interest in the importance of the early essays in approaching an understanding of Moore's ethics is parallel to Sylvester's. Although he neglects the profound reciprocal influence due to the relationship between Bertrand Russell and Moore in the years leading up to *Principia*, his account of other influences on Moore in the period is accurate and valuable.

In the end, it is clear that Regan's interest in Moore's impact on the so-called Bloomsberries is allowed to outweigh his interest in the details of the development of Moore's thought. As a consequence, his treatment of the connections and changes between the 1903 *Principia Ethica* and the 1912 *Ethics* is relatively light and lacking in detailed analysis. It is also the case that Regan pays little attention to Moore's influence in the development of subsequent ethical theory, emotivism and noncognitivism in particular.

Unlike Tom Regan's treatment of Moore's ethics, or that of Dennis Rohatyn mentioned above, the reading given in John Hill's *The Ethics of G. E. Moore: A New Interpretation* (Assen, Netherlands: Van Gorcum, 1976), parallels Sylvester's in a number of respects, particularly in terms of his emphasis on the importance of the early essays in the development of Moore's thought. But Hill gives a very different interpretation of the role of the naturalistic fallacy argument, departing rather sharply from that given by Sylvester, despite the fact that Hill seems to share Sylvester's view of the importance of Moore's ontology in respect to the role of the fallacy in the development of Moore's position.

The editors return to the comparison of Hill's and Sylvester's views in the bibliographical comments for the appropriate chapters as the author's argument is developed.

As mentioned in the Preface, the author's treatment of Moore's ethics is quite obviously a development of some ideas worked out in his doctoral dissertation at Northwestern University some years before he commenced the present work. The publication date of Hill's book, 1976—it was submitted as a doctoral dissertation at the Pontifical Gregorian University at Rome in 1973—and its availability in the library at Dartmouth College, which Sylvester used with some frequency, indicate that he might have been familiar with Hill's thesis, yet there is no evidence of that fact in the manuscript or notes. The editors believe that the many parallels between the two interpretations, and the fact that both writers differ rather sharply with mainstream interpretations of Moore's ethics, indicate that *had* Sylvester been familiar with Hill's work, he would have made use of it, by *some* reference at least. We have concluded—tentatively to be sure, for there can be no certainty in such matters—that the two readings were developed in complete independence from each other. The fact that, in many respects though not in all, they tend to reinforce each other's views should not be at all surprising.

Of some interest in relation to the early Moore, Paul Levy's *Moore: G. E. Moore and the Cambridge Apostles* (New York: Holt, Rinehart & Winston, 1979) deals less with Moore's philosophical development than with that of his personality.

Most of the important content in Moore's early papers and unpublished material that Levy deals with is treated again in *Bloomsbury's Prophet* to greater philosophical advantage.

James H. Olthius develops an account of Moore's ethics in *Facts, Values and Ethics: A Confrontation with Twentieth Century British Moral Philosophy, in Particular G. E. Moore* (New York: Humanities Press, 1968). However, as the subtitle indicates, his approach is far more confrontational than helpful in critically interpreting Moore's work.

The last volume to be included in this general bibliography, although largely devoted to a consideration of Moore's ethics, is not merely a critical interpretation but an attempted refutation as well. It is Richard J. Soghoian's *The Ethics of G. E. Moore and David Hume: The Treatise as a Response to Moore's Refutation of Ethical Naturalism* (Washington, D.C.: University Press of America, 1979).

Critical Bibliography: Chapter I

As indicated in his Preface to the manuscript, Sylvester acknowledges an essay by Herbert Hochberg as of special significance for the development of the thesis sketched in this chapter. It is "Moore's Ontology and Non-natural Properties," which appeared in *Review of Metaphysics* (15, 3 [1962], pp. 365–95; reprinted in E. D. Klemke, ed., *Studies in the Philosophy of G. E. Moore*, 1969). It was this essay, Sylvester indicates in his doctoral dissertation (Northwestern University, 1963), that opened the way to the reading of Moore's ethics, which he developed there and which is equally important for the present thesis.

Sylvester's insistence upon the importance of Moore's tripartite division of the general subject-matter of ethics is nearly unique in the literature. Though sometimes acknowledged by Moore's more sympathetic interpreters, it is generally disregarded by his critics. Compare Sylvester's treatment with Nicolai Hartmann's, for example, in Hartmann's "The Definition of Good: Moore's Axiomatic of the Science of Ethics" (*Proceedings of the Aristotelian Society*, 65, [1964–1965], pp.

237–56), or with that of John Hill (cited in the General Bibliography above), as well as the very different versions of Regan and Rohatyn. Only Regan seems to share Sylvester's sense of the import of this threefold division, but he makes far less of it than does Sylvester, who takes it that Moore's analysis of the three distinct tasks of ethics is the sine qua non for a structural understanding of how the various elements of Moore's ethics hang together.

Hill takes the position that Moore was working backward from the problems of duty and obligation, through the problem of what things are, toward the conclusion that good is an in definable property. Owing to his sense that this was Moore's actual procedure, almost completely reversing the order in which the chapters in *Principia* present these problems, Hill treats the indefinability of good as a *result* of Moore's arguments in the later chapters rather than as a premise (or presupposition) upon which they are based. Accordingly, Hill's treatment of Moore's conception of the *ontological* status of good is very different from Sylvester's. Hill's procedure compels him to rely less upon Moore's early essays that led to the writing of *Principia* than Sylvester does, and far less on the close similarity between Moore's early Platonism and that of Bertrand Russell.

There are several essays on Moore's efforts to present his view of good as an indefinable property that fail to recognize the difference between good as a concept and its exemplification in the world—a distinction that Sylvester finds to be at the very foundation of Moore's thinking. See, for example, Panayot Butchvarov, "That Simple, Indefinable Nonnatural Property, *Good*" (*Review of Metaphysics*, 36 [1982], pp. 51–75). On the other hand, critics who approach Moore with a grasp of the relationship between Moore and Russell, particularly during the early Platonistic period of Russell's work on mathematical logic, have no difficulty in seeing the import of the distinction. Thus Ronald Jager, "Analyticity and Necessity in Moore's Early Work" (*Journal of the History of Philosophy*, 7 [1969], pp. 441–58; see also the same author's *The Development of Bertrand Russell's Philosophy* [London: Allen & Unwin, 1972]).

As Sylvester indicates, it is a common failing of most analytic treatments of Moore's ethics to neglect the fact that Moore and Russell adopted rather similar and Platonistic ontologies in their efforts to shake themselves free from the Cambridge idealism of their mentors. John Passmore gives a useful historical account of their work in this period in his *A Hundred Years of Philosophy* (London: Duckworth, 1957). For the idealism from which both Moore and Russell were escaping, the classic sources are F. H. Bradley, *Ethical Studies: 1876*, 2d ed. (Oxford: Clarendon Press, 1935); Henry Sidgwick, *The Methods of Ethics*, 7th ed. (London: Macmillan, 1907); T. H. Green, *Prolegomena to Ethics*, 5th ed. (Oxford: Clarendon Press, 1906); C. D. Broad, *Five Types of Ethical Theory* (London: Kegan Paul, Trench, Trubner, 1930); A. J. Ayer, *Russell and Moore: The Analytical Heritage* (Cambridge: Harvard University Press, 1971), esp. Chapters 8 and 9, "The Fruits of Analysis" and "Moore's Treatment of Abstract Entities."

The importance of abstract entities in Moore's early philosophy is well documented in a study by David O'Connor in his *The Metaphysics of G. E. Moore* (Dordrecht, Netherlands: D. Reidel, 1982). Unfortunately for our purposes, O'Connor develops that importance for Moore's epistemology and neglects its importance for his ethics.

II

Intuition (I): A First Look

1. *The Problem*

How do we know what things are good in the world? A preliminary analysis of what Moore means by the concept good is given in Chapter I, for it is necessary, according to Moore, to clarify the proper meaning of 'good' before turning to other questions of ethics. Moreover, until good's ontological status can be determined, other questions, including the one posed above, tend to become confused with the question 'What is good?' We now know that Moore's answer to 'What is good?' is that good is a simple, unanalyzable object of thought; that good's ontological status is independent of any and all knowledge of it; and that it is objectively real. We also know that it is a simple and unanalyzable quality that is sometimes exemplified by things in the world. Things that are good, however, are not simple entities, they are not unanalyzable, nor are the value terms that we assign to them indefinable. At this point it is important to work out how it is that Moore can claim we know something that exists is good, when it is good.

In order to get at this question there is yet another possible ambiguity in the use of the word 'good' to which we must attend. The issue of knowing which things are good involves being able to tell which entities in existence have the alleged property that Moore calls good. There is a use of the word 'good' which suggests that a thing may be good, not simply as it exists, but rather as a means to something else. Sometimes this sense of 'good' is referred to as an 'extrinsic good,' in order to contrast it with a notion of 'intrinsic good.' Moore does not make use of the term 'extrinsic.' He is interested in the notion of 'good as a means,' however, for it is this usage that he wants sharply distinguished from 'good,' the name of the concept of intrinsic value. Let us

35

mark the distinction, then, for it is important in subsequent discussion. The question raised in this chapter, however, is: 'How do we know what things are intrinsically good in the world?' The answer that Moore gives us is that we are directly acquainted with intrinsically good things. We notice good things through acts of intuition.

2. *Intuition: A First Glance*

There are many things that are good in the world. We come to know some of them, and we do so by finding them in our experience; it is through the experience of direct acquaintance with objects that are good that we even come to suspect that there is value in the world. Moore tells us that it is a matter of fact that some things are good. So all actual judgments of value in things are 'synthetic' and are thus on an epistemological par with other factual judgments. If, for instance, I tell someone that a particular thing I have experienced is good, and am asked why I believe the thing is good, my answer is that I have noticed that it is good as matter of direct and immediate experience. (I would respond in similar fashion if I were asked why I said that some object that I have experienced is yellow.) That it is good is a definite feature of my cognitive awareness of that particular thing. Let us go through the imagined dialogue a step at a time:

I say, "X is good."
Someone says, "Why do you say 'X is good'?"
I say, "Because I am aware of goodness in X."
My interrogator says, "What evidence do you have that X is good?"
I say, "I have no evidence other than X having the property I notice and call good. I cannot deduce X's goodness from some other facts true about X, or from some theory about X's being, or from anything else whatsoever except X's goodness being manifest to me."

In what follows I call the experience of 'being manifest to me' by the name 'intuition.' Moore hardly ever uses the term 'intuition' when he is seriously discussing how we come to know that things in existence are good. As I move forward in the present chapter I explain how Moore works out the issue in the texts. It is sufficient to remark here that intuition in Moore's moral theory is not equivalent to a mysterious power, or any so-called sixth sense that may put us in contact with some divine, or other, transcendent source of moral authority. Its presence in Moore's theory is, however, evidence of his acknowledgment that if one does not experience the encounter with good in existence, one cannot find it at all.

3. *The General Scope of Moore's Intuitionism*

Since we are said to become acquainted with good in the world through acts of direct awareness, it is crucial that we do not read more into the role of intuition than Moore himself allows. At root, I have said, the intuition of value for Moore is the exercise of direct cognitive awareness of value in something that exists. [Perhaps it may help to clarify the point by saying that we learn the meaning of the word 'good' by ostention; that is, by experiencing things that are good in themselves.] Such direct cognitive awareness (intuition), however, conveys no information about what actions ought to be done. No question of the form 'What actions ought I to do?' can be answered by a simple appeal to intuition. In the Preface to *Principia Ethica*, and again in Chapter 5, "Ethics in Relation to Conduct," Moore explicitly warns the reader not to confuse his views with those philosophers whom he calls intuitionists proper. Philosophers in that category hold that we can have intuitions that infallibly reveal that certain actions ought to be done or to be avoided. Moore does not merely deny that he is in agreement with such views, but claims that in his theory actions that ought to be done are capable of a degree of proof by means of evidence that goes far beyond the appeal to intuition alone.

Moore's own view of practical ethical choice among alternative courses of action clearly involves much more than the intuition of value as such. It should be clear by now that the question 'What ought I to do?' is answered after reflective thought, deliberation, calculation, and whatever other tools one has at one's disposal for coming to an understanding of the way the world will likely become as a consequence of the choice one makes. The more accurate the factual and causal information at the agent's disposal, the more likely it is that the agent can know that one action is more likely to be the right one than any other action. Granted, the approach to comparative value judgments is strictly inductive (we cannot deduce them from a priori principles), but it is as far from a mere intuition as one could wish to get. In any event, Moore's explicit point is that questions of practical ethical importance are not to be answered by intuitive acts alone. Intuition can never be a substitute for reasoning, he argues, and we reason to practical ethical conclusions.

It is therefore a plain mistake for anyone to classify G. E. Moore as an intuitionist with respect to obligation, duty, or the rightness of an action. Despite Moore's explicitness on the question of practical ethical choice and the necessity for reasoning in assessment of what ought to be done, there are a number of critics who deal with Moore's theory as if he never took pains to disassociate himself from philosophies that hold that obligations, or duties, are known by means of intuition alone.[1]

4. *Santayana's Criticism of Moore and Intuition*

There is a historically important criticism of Moore that must be discussed here, since it is an example of the mistaken reading of Moore on intuition mentioned above. It is the critique leveled at both Moore and Bertrand Russell by George Santayana. Although the critical argument that Santayana constructed was primarily directed at Russell, it is clear that it was also meant as a criticism of Moore's theory of obligation. It had a profound effect on Russell, according to Russell himself, and helped cause him to reject the account of the objectivity of value that he once held in common with Moore.[2] [In his 1910 essay "Elements of Ethics," Russell says that his views are "largely based on Mr. G. E. Moore's *Principia Ethica*." See Russell's *Philosophical Essays* (New York: Simon and Schuster, 1910 and 1968), p. 13.] In any event, Santayana argues that reasoning and self-criticism are of crucial importance in moral discussion, and that the Russell-Moore appeal to intuition [or knowledge by aquaintance] prohibits all such discussion. We have seen, in Section 9, Chapter I, that Moore agrees with the necessity of such discussion in practical ethics. But Santayana thinks that Moore and Russell hold a doctrine that makes such moral reasoning impossible. The doctrine that Santayana is concerned to score is, as we might expect, the intuitionism he mistakenly ascribes to both Russell and Moore.

It is Santayana's contention that intuitionism in ethics, and the Moore-Russell version specifically, conceives things to be "dead good and dead bad" and that Moore and Russell are in danger of becoming shouting moralists. Such a stance is out of place in philosophy, he observes. A philosopher who thinks that "X is (dead) good" is (self-evidently) true will not be inclined to debate, discuss, or reason as to whether some action ought to be performed. Here is Santayana's parting shot at the Russell-Moore view:

> When a man has decided on a course of action, it is a vain indulgence in explicatives to declare that he is sure that his course of action is absolutely right. His moral dogma expresses its natural origins all the more clearly the more hotly it is proclaimed; and ethical absolutism, being a mental grimace of passion, refutes what it says by what it is.[3]

It seems clear that Santayana's critique does not confront Moore's view at all. Moore is as critical of those doctrines of moral intuitionism that entail the absolutism that Santayana's derision is directed against as is Santayana himself. Moore agrees that there can be no actions that are morally justified by an appeal to a simple intuition as an absolute. Moore is not an absolutist, of any stripe.

5. Intuition and Self-evidence

Santayana's critique gives us an opportunity for a more explicit examination of Moore's reliance on intuition. I want to indicate what intuition is capable of revealing, according to

Moore, and what order of evidence it is able to present to us. Will intuition guide us in any important ways? If it is the way we discover good to exist, then clearly it is of importance. If intuition cannot tell us what we ought to do in a given instance, how does it function in moral reasoning?

In Section 2 of this chapter it is pointed out that if a claim is made on the grounds of direct awareness that X is good, for example, then X's goodness must be (or must have been) manifest to the person making the claim. I now want to take up that notion for more detailed comment. Put briefly, that X's goodness is manifest to someone implies, for Moore, that the person who asserts the proposition 'X is good' has no independent evidence for asserting that X is good beyond the evidence given in the proposition itself. Moore claims that the truth of a proposition asserting the goodness of a thing or event is self-evident—at least to the person asserting it—although the logical form of the assertion itself is held to be synthetic. Moore acknowledges the awkwardness of this claim as follows: "By saying that a proposition is self-evident, we mean emphatically that its appearing so to us is not the reason why it is true; for we mean that it has absolutely no reason."[4] Moore seems to be holding that if an assertion such as 'X is good' is true, its truth is evident to the one who notices that it is true, but no further evidence that X is actually good can be given independently of the awareness of X's goodness itself. The reasons that one judges X to be good cannot be stated, other than to say that the proposition's truth is manifest to the person experiencing X's goodness.

Perhaps an analogy of the sort Moore was fond of providing will be helpful in presenting the point. Suppose one notices something that has several properties, among them both yellow and good. One judges that X is yellow. Can it be proved that X is yellow? Are there reasons for asserting 'X is yellow'? One can of course point to X, direct attention to its color, and compare it ostensively with a standard color chart. But still the only evidence that X is yellow is given in actual visual acquaintance and recognition. [The use of a scientific measurement of the color's wavelength as compared with the wavelength of the standard yellow does not alter the fact that the direct experience of the color as yellow is required at some point for the truth of the assertion 'X is yellow' to be claimed.] Using Moore's 1899–1903 way of speaking, one cites the evidence given in direct acquaintance of X's being yellow for the claim that the proposition 'X is yellow' is true. Moore believes that the same argument pattern holds for good. One judges that X is good because the truth of the proposition 'X is good' is evident and is given in the proposition.

Whatever strangeness may strike the reader concerning Moore's doctrine on this point can perhaps be neutralized in a short discussion of Moore's view of propositions held in the 1899–1903 period. Moore has no hesitation in calling 'the object of experience' a proposition. In 1903 Moore is unable or unwilling to distinguish an object that is experienced—in other words, the X that is yellow and good—from the cognition 'that X is yellow and good.' The point is not made in *Principia Ethica*, but it is quite clearly stated in the February 1903 paper read before the Aristotelian Society entitled "Experience and Empiricism," and the passage I now quote from that paper says it directly:

> It may seem strange to some that the object of an experience should be called a proposition. But such an object may undoubtedly be "the existence of such and such a thing," and it seems impossible to distinguish the cognition of this from the cognition "that such and such a thing exists." The object of experience, moreover, is undoubtedly true, both of which properties seem to me to be characteristics of propositions.[5]

So for Moore, although there is no independent evidence available to prove that 'X is good' is true, since truth is held to be a characteristic of the object of experience (which is the proposition, or which cannot be distinguished from the proposition), truth is (somehow) a definitive trait of the proposition 'X is good.' And so it must be that if one notices (correctly) X and experiences (correctly) X's properties, or characteristics, one grasps the experience, so to speak, propositionally, so that the truth of the proposition is grasped as integral to the experience itself.

The point to underscore is that Moore denies that, when propositions are cognized, we exercise any special gift. Humans have no psychic power, no unique intuitive insight. There is no ethereal intuitive faculty that permits us to pick out value. All we have are the usual mundane and fallible faculties and ways of judgment that any empirically persuaded philosopher would acknowledge. In fact, Moore emphasizes, "I hold, on the contrary, that in every way in which it is possible to cognize a true proposition, it is also possible to cognize a false one." [6]

In the Preface to *Principia Ethica*, and even before Moore begins to articulate his views, the reader is told that self-evidence cannot guarantee that a proposition is true. To have the 'intuition' that X is good is only to cognize a self-evident proposition. And "in every way it is possible to cognize a true proposition, it is possible to cognize a false one." The criterion of self-evidence is a far weaker measure than Moore has generally been thought to have suggested. Yet its role in Moore's epistemology of value is as explicit as it is crucial. Intuition of, or the self-evident truth of an assertion concerning, or direct experiential acquaintance with, objects that have value are the only ways we come to know what things are good, and in what degree. As we have seen in Chapter I above, according to *Principia Ethica* the question of what things are good, and in what degree, is the second of the three general questions that the enterprise of ethics, or moral philosophy, must successfully answer. However, it should be clear that intuitions of the sort I have been discussing indicate a more fragile element in Moore's moral theory than has often been recognized. For the successful resolution of most moral questions, it seems safe to say, requires much more than just intuition. Moreover, Moore goes out of his way to deny the cognitive incorrigibility of intuitions of value. The epistemic certitude of value judgments cannot be justified, but that does not diminish the fact that all such correctly made judgments are instances of objective knowledge.

6. *Moore's Intuitionism; Evidence and Proof*

It follows from Moore's remarks on self-evidence that those philosophers who are in search of a grounding for moral theory that guarantees the truth of intuitions will not find it in G. E. Moore. Moore holds, as we have seen, that good is met in the world of experience as a matter of fact. The evidence for good's existence in an object of experience rests solely on the experiencing of value through acts of cognitive awareness, or in other words, through direct empirical acquaintance. The doctrine of self-evidence, or intuition, is the epistemological grounding for knowing value to be in existing things. More must be said, however, about the notions of proof and evidence. I begin with an example of their use:

One person can prove to another that there are three misprints on a page. The sense of proof indicated here is straightforward. B opens the page in question and shows A by pointing and saying, 'Here's one misprint, and here's another, and here's a third.' I call this sense of proof ostensive proof. If A grasps what B points out, no additional proof is necessary.

There is a second sense of proof that must be discriminated; a more weighty and, Moore would say, a more rigorous sense. Reasoning used in logic and mathematics makes use of proof in this sense. When a conclusion is shown to follow from true premises in the required (logically valid) manner, the proof is said to be rigorous.

Moore holds that the presence of good in a thing cannot be proved to exist in either of these senses.

It may appear from what is said in Section 5 above that one could prove to someone that something is good in the ostensive sense. Someone might claim that a particular action is good and point out, to a skeptic, precisely the action in question that is claimed to be good. The skeptic might, having followed the description of the action given, agree that he now 'sees' and acknowledges that the action is good. It may appear that this case is similar to the example of the misprint case given above as an instance of ostensive proof. Yet a moment's reflection shows otherwise.

If B points to the misprint and says, 'here's one,' and A says, 'nonsense,' there is an independent way to resolve the dispute. B goes to the library shelf, picks out a dictionary, finds the proper entry in the authoritative text, and indicates to A that the misprint really is a misprint. In the case of value disagreement, however, when the skeptic disagrees, there is no rule book, no referee, no independent judge who can function as an authority. Only the thing that has, or does not have, value is available for consultation. And it can only be consulted by means of an act of (cognitive) awareness. The thing as it is actually encountered, in direct awareness, furnishes the only possible evidence.

In practical ethical terms, when one performs an action and attempts to justify the action, justification lies in the claim that the action brings about more good than any other action available to the agent. Suppose A wrestled B to the pavement on the grounds that the action prevented A from stabbing C, and that this outcome was the best possible. Suppose further that A was correct; the wrestling prevented the assault and brought about more value than any alternative. If a fourth person took issue with A, claiming that the wrestling outcome was less valuable than some other action outcome, such as speaking coolly and rationally to the potential assailant, there is a clear disagreement over the moral correctness of the action. If the disputants are able to articulate the actual outcomes and present them cogently to each other, and if there is still disagreement over the comparative value, there is a significant problem in resolving the moral issue.

Moore's doctrine of obligation requires the one who wrestled the potential assailant to the pavement to do the act, since he has correctly judged its consequences to be the best possible. Intuition is the agent's ultimate ground, and it is plain that the agent may very well be mistaken about it in the opinion of others, as in the example given. The self-evident truth of the value in the outcome was his reason, and his only reason, for the justification of the action. [The dispute here is *not* about alternative consequences but about their respective value.] Intuition, Moore tells us: "can only furnish a reason for *holding* any proposition to be true; this however it must do when any proposition is self-evident, when, in fact, there are no reasons to prove its truth."[7] There is no independent proof that will help in value disputes. And yet there may be alternative courses of action, of which a moral agent may be unaware, that might indeed be morally preferable to an action chosen by the agent, if only the agent had stopped to consider them. But Moore is realistic enough to realize that there is not always sufficient time available in order for the moral agent to consider all the options that are available. And there is always a time when the intuitive self-evidence of some proposition or other to the effect that X is good must suffice; a point we come back to in what follows.

7. *Truth, True Belief, and Evidence*

It is far from easy to locate Moore's precise view of truth in *Principia Ethica*. It would indeed be helpful to have a clear notion of Moore's view in the matter of truth, since one might then be in a better position to grasp the place of self-evidence and its role in finding truth in propositions. Moore was very open in his remarks about the function of self-evidence and of intuition in its role in relation to self-evidence, including the fact that intuition is a fallible power. But precisely how self-evident truth is to be reached by means of intuitive awareness is never made clear beyond Moore's insistence that truths reached by such means are never merely 'analytic' or 'a priori' in nature. [All value assertions are, remember, expressed in synthetic propositions.]

Some may feel that Moore's self-evidence is too weak a criterion to be allowed to play the crucial role it must in Moore's practical ethical theory [or that synthetic propositions are never self-evident]. My own view is that his use of self-evidence puts good in no better, but no worse, a position epistemically than any other alleged simple property of things found in the world. For example, one may make a mistake in judgment when one thinks that the pencil is yellow because it appears so. Perhaps it really is grey, but under the strong morning sunlight and placed as it is on the table, it merely looks yellow. As Moore does make clear, one may substitute 'good' for 'yellow' in an appropriate context; the role of self-evidence given in moral experience is similar [as when we say such things as 'I thought X was good at the time, but looked at in the cold light of dawn, I saw I had been mistaken'].

Leaving such errors in value judgment aside, what can be said about truth in *Principia Ethica*? Can a theory of truth be found in Moore in 1903? In 1899 Moore had some things to say about truth. He held, for example, that truth was a simple concept. Truth was an immediate property of a combination of concepts; these concepts Moore called propositions. The position is stated in

"The Nature of Judgment," [8] an essay published in *Mind* in 1899, when Moore was already hard at work on the writing of *Principia Ethica*. The 1903 essay, "Experience and Empiricism," from which I quoted in Section 5, echoes the earlier paper's themes—especially with respect to the analysis of propositions. In "The Nature of Judgment" Moore does not produce a fully developed theory of truth, but he does make some serious claims about what he calls truth for its own sake. Moore says things such as: "truth is itself a simple concept; that it is logically prior to any proposition" and "we regard truth and falsehood as properties of certain concepts, together with their relations—a whole to which we give the name of proposition" [9]

While these remarks concerning the nature of truth were little more than tantalizing hints, in 1902 Moore contributed several entries to Baldwin's *Dictionary of Philosophy and Psychology*. One of his contributions was on truth. In the course of his discussion Moore dealt with a theory of truth called correspondence or agreement with reality. Propositions, he said, were held to be true or false "in virtue of their partial similarity to something else, and hence that it is essential to the theory that a truth should differ in some specific way from the reality, in relation to which its truth is to consist, in every case except that in which the reality is itself a proposition." [10] [Note Moore's apparently casual assumption that a proposition is a reality.]

However, in the Baldwin article, Moore claims that it is impossible to find the required difference—"a truth should differ in some way from the reality"—and so the correspondence theory cannot be maintained. Moore offers three arguments to support his view.

The second of these arguments is designed to cast doubt on the correspondence theory of truth by directing attention to its claim that the proposition is a "mental copy of the reality, or an idea." The view falls short, Moore tells us, because it makes the "almost universal error" of making the object of a belief or idea to be an attribute or content of the belief itself, and thus to be dependent upon the mind. [Moore's escape from such an 'idealist' account of truth had already taken place by 1902.] The third argument rejecting the correspondence theory hinges on the second. Moore is satisfied that the mental copy theory is refuted, and so, since no other difference between the proposition and reality has been suggested, Moore remarks:

> Indeed, once it is definitely recognized that the proposition is to denote, not a belief or form of words, but an object of belief, it seems plain that a truth differs in no respect from the reality to which it was supposed merely to correspond: e.g., the truth that I exist differs in no respect from the corresponding reality—my existence. So far, indeed, from truth being defined by reference to reality, reality can only be defined by reference to truth: for truth denotes exactly that property of the complex formed by two entities and their relation, in virtue of which, if the entity predicated be existence, we call the complex real—the property, namely, expressed by saying that the relation in question does truly or really hold between the entities.[11]

The passage suggests that in judgments whose objects exist in the world, truth and reality are convertible. That is, if it is true that the pencil is yellow, then yellow is real; in other words, yellow has being and can be said to exist as a property of the pencil. [To 'have being' is to be real as an 'object of thought' or concept; 'to exist' is to be in the world, not just as an 'object of thought,' but also 'in the world' of existing things.] The pencil is really and truly yellow. It is so. It is a reality. That the pencil (really) is yellow is true. The passage above says, "the truth that I exist differs in no respect from the corresponding reality—my existence."

It is difficult to tell if Moore's remarks on truth in Baldwin's *Dictionary* are a product of the very same view found in "The Nature of Judgment." Three years elapsed between the two publications, and Moore's thought seems to have been in transition in some respects. The earlier view and the 1902 remarks seem to be consistent insofar as each passage invites the same interpretation, but there is no general systematic doctrine set forth by Moore to which we might appeal for confirmation.

In his 1910–1911 lectures, later published in *Some Main Problems in Philosophy*, Moore refers to a theory of truth that he had held at one time, probably around 1899, but we cannot be sure of this. In any event, a brief look at it may put the views we have been considering into perspective. The 1899 view runs as follows: To believe truly that 'It is good that Smith helped Jones to the hospital' there must be (*a*) a cognizer, who believes (*b*) a proposition, in this case 'It is good that Smith helped Jones to the hospital,' and believes that the proposition in question is true. Furthermore its truth is a simple property.

To believe falsely that 'It is good that Smith helped Jones to the pub' there must be (*c*) a cognizer, who believes (*d*) a proposition, in this case 'It is good that Smith helped Jones to the pub,' and who believes that the proposition has truth as a simple property; but in this case the proposition does not have truth as a simple property. Moore writes of this theory, in 1910:

> But the difference between a true and false belief [the theory says] consists simply in this, that where the belief is true the proposition, which is believed, besides the fact that it is or 'has being' also has another simple unanalyzable property which may be called 'truth.' 'Truth,' therefore, would, on the view, be a simple unanalyzable property which is possessed by some propositions and not by others. The propositions which don't possess it and which therefore we call false, are, or 'have being'—just as much as those which do, only they have not got this additional property of 'truth.'[12]

Moore tells us, in these later lectures, that he can find no conclusive reasons for denying this theory of truth as a simple property. [Russell is known to have held this view in 1904 but relinquished it by 1906. It is probable that Russell was influenced by Moore at the time. In any case, Moore's theory seems to treat truth in much the same way that good is dealt with in 1903, in *Principia Ethica*.] On the other hand Moore also says that he does not accept it. This appears to show that his views on truth in the 1910–1911 period, the same time frame in which he was working on the *Ethics* (1912), remained unsettled. In the *Ethics*, the reader should recall, I have said that Moore does not deal with finding good in the world and does not mention either intuition or self-evidence in that context.

It is not a certainty, then, that Moore still held the earlier theory of truth at the time that he was writing *Principia Ethica*. He does tell us in *Principia* : "No truth does, in fact, exist" [p. 111]. But he says this in a context in which he is referring to what he calls metaphysical ethics and is saying that such truths as that 'two and two are four' are about objects that, like truth, "do not exist either." [He says that such truths as these have been called universal truths and that they have "played a large part in the reasonings of metaphysicians from Plato's time until now."] Truth, he tells us, is not a constitutive property of a thing or an event in the world. Truth is a property of propositions, which have being but do not exist. The least that can be said concerning all this is that Moore does not seem to buy into the correspondence theory of truth at the time that he is working on *Principia*.

On the other hand, it is patently clear that Moore does hold the view in *Principia* that we can and do discover things and events in the world that are [truly] good and that have [real] value. He holds that the discovery of value involves a cognitive act. Cognition is propositional. For Moore, in 1903, "the object of an experience should be called a proposition." The discovery of value comes in immediate and direct acquaintance with the object (of experience) that is good. The proposition, which articulates the experience, is the self-evidently true and, surprisingly, synthetic in logical form. In "Experience and Empiricism" Moore says, "The object of experience is undoubtedly true." Acquaintance with value is as direct as acquaintance with any other property of things in experience.

Whatever the actual texture of Moore's thought was, as he wrote *Principia Ethica*, it remains the case that independent evidence for the truth of any intuition of value is not possible. Moore, in stressing the self-evidence of the experience of good, acknowledges that awareness of value, our knowledge of what things and event are good, is both experientially direct and epistemologically fragile.

8. *Pepper's Mistake*

Moore's theory of moral philosophy is often categorized as an intuitionist version of ethics, despite the very limited role that is ascribed to the intuition of value by Moore himself. Indeed, the claim is often made that Moore's ethics must stand or fall on the adequacy of his account of intuition. Consider, for example, the following criticism of Moore's position by Stephen Pepper:

So, in the end, Moore's argument rests on the question as to whether the claim for such an intuition can be justified. Moore obviously believes he has such an incorrigible intuition. He is on very weak ground, however, when he claims that every man has it. He offers no positive evidence for this claim, but he does suggest an explanation as to why many people may fail to get the intuition. It may be due to lack of expertness in the proper sort of discrimination. . . . Of course, Moore can say that when such a claim is based on incorrigible intuition, questions of empirical evidence are irrelevant to even one such intuition. Here the empiricist makes his regular answer that claims for incorrigible modes of cognition— whether of self-evidence, intuitive certainty, or indubitability of immediate data—have so often proved false or doubtful that this type of justification ceases to have any claim for creditability. . . . Men have often been deceived by claims of incorrigible cognition. So Moore's appeal to intuition in support of his simple quality good need not be taken very seriously.[13]

It is doubtless true that some philosophers who adopt an intuitionist approach in ethics hold that intuitions are incorrigible. And it may be that some hold that incorrigibility implies certitude. Again, some philosophers may hold the notion of self-evidence to mean that the truth of a self-evident statement is guaranteed by means of intuition. But it should already be clear from what we have seen so far that Moore does not think of intuition in this way at all. Moreover, as has been emphasized, Moore takes great and explicit pains to deny that he holds such a view. Moore's notion of intuition does not guarantee truth, nor does he ever speak, as Pepper implies, of anything at all like 'intuitive certitude.' Insofar as the passage above implies that *Principia Ethica* makes use of intuition in order to dispense with other sorts of empirical evidence in support of value judgments, Pepper is mistaken about that as well. To be sure, intuition does play a crucial role in such judgments, according to Moore, but that does not mean that intuition is the sole means by which such judgments are reached. I have recounted Pepper's critique of Moore in order to show how such misreadings of Moore arise and how they should be treated. It seems clear that Pepper misreads Moore owing to his assumption that, since he is (according to Pepper) an intuitionist in ethics, he therefore must make all the mistakes that intuitionists always make!

But is there, for Moore, any sense at all in which an intuition that something is good can be said to be incorrigible? If one has an experience where one finds value, and one says 'X is good,' and one is further asked to justify the claim, then the claim of self-evidence is the ultimate (and only) claim that Moore allows. For if one has such an intuition, one has it. But that is far from being the end of the matter. As Pepper reminds us, there have been all too many instances where such intuitions have proved to be mistaken. We have ample reason to be wary of intuition, especially as a measure of certitude. Moreover, in *Principia Ethica*, Moore actually makes this same point himself. It is only in an extremely narrowly defined sense that an intuition might be said to be incorrigibly what it is, and Moore himself does not even use the word. Moreover, it is a sense in which there is clearly no certitude about it at all. For Moore, any and all intuitions of value are epistemically contingent, no matter how convincing they may be from a psychological standpoint. They are immediate experiences of value awareness that are, indeed, what they are. But every such experience may be, and often is, succeeded by subsequent and quite different experiences altogether. So no such experience in itself, be it as self-evidently true as it may be, carries with it anything like a sense of absoluteness.

In Chapter 5 of *Principia Ethica*, when Moore takes up the question of self-evidence, or intuition, in relation to practical ethical choices, he denies that normative judgments can be self-evidently true, or that intuitions can offer any definitive proof of them. In the course of his argument he points up the limited part that intuitions play in the making of practical moral decisions. He writes: "We must not therefore look on Intuition as if it were an alternative to reasoning. Nothing whatever can take the place of reasons for the truth of any proposition: intuition can only furnish a reason for *holding* any proposition to be true: this however it must do when any proposition is self-evident, when, in fact, there are no reasons which prove its truth."[14] In such passages as this Moore seems to be suggesting that self-evident propositions have a role to play in moral practice, but they are scarcely the whole story. The passage given here is hardly clear as to what the other supporting reasons may be, and we have occasion to return to that question in another chapter.

9. *The Place of Intuition in the* 1912 Ethics

I have been examining Moore's doctrine by reviewing his thoughts as he set them forth mainly in *Principia Ethica*, reserving any detailed look at *Ethics* for a later chapter. That is as it should be. For the question that required Moore to discuss such matters as self-evidence and intuition in detail was, 'What things are good?' *Ethics* discusses that question in a different fashion entirely. In fact, the main concern in *Ethics* is a systematic effort to argue for Moore's own brand of utilitarianism—an answer to the third question of *Ethics*; namely, 'What ought we to do?' Quite remarkably, Moore does not mention intuition in the 1912 *Ethics* at all.

It is true, however, that Moore invokes the concept of self-evidence in the later work [suggesting, of course, that self-evidence and intuition are practically equivalent]. In Section 8 of the first chapter, above, I warned that Moore's use of the concept of self-evidence may have misled some critics into thinking that Moore believes that obligation, or right, may be a simple and irreducible notion. Moore says it is self-evident (to him) that it must always be our duty to do the act that will maximize the good. Moore does not, however, explain in *Ethics*, as he does in *Principia*, what self-evidence is. But there is no reason I can find to believe that Moore changed his mind about the role of self-evidence in his moral theory in the time elapsed between the writing of the two books.

A final comment will close this chapter. The fact that Moore does not discuss the question of intuition in *Ethics* should be instructive for anyone tempted to think of his doctrine as if it allowed an intuitionism of right, obligation, or duty. *Ethics* is an attempt at a systematic practical ethical theory. It tries to clarify the concepts involved in action in the world. It presents an analysis of right and wrong. Answers to questions with practical ethical implication depend upon reasoning, calculation of cause and effect, and knowledge of the way that the world is likely to be in the future. No answer to any specific question of duty or obligation can be arrived at by intuition alone, a fact that renders the use of 'intuitionism' as a general label for Moore's ethics somewhat dubious at best and at worst a serious blunder.

CRITICAL BIBLIOGRAPHY: CHAPTER II

There is considerable significance in the fact that Sylvester chooses to devote *two* chapters—this one and the one that follows—to the clarification of Moore's use of the term "intuition" in his discussion of the basic concept of ethics. As the present chapter shows, sufficient clarification of the matter enables us to avoid the error of classifying Moore as an intuitionist in any of the usual senses, as well as in the specific readings set forth by Nowell-Smith, George Santayana, and Stephen Pepper. (See the author's notes for references.) Moreover, by means of his clarification of just what Moore intends by the use of "intuition" Sylvester blocks the kind of criticism of Moore's epistemology of value that became the stock in trade of the non-cognitivists and emotivists in ethics.

It is a commonplace move by the defenders of emotivism to argue that, since there is really no basis for Moore's claim that intuition is any help in giving us reliable (or scientific) knowledge of values, values are therefore some how generically different from facts. Coupled with the naturalistic fallacy argument, this becomes the ground of the non-cognitivism principle commonly adopted by emotivists in ethics such as Moritz Schlick, A. J. Ayer, and C. L. Stevenson. See Schlick, *Problems of Ethics*, tr. D. Rynin (New York: Prentice Hall, 1939); A. J. Ayer, *Language, Truth and Logic* (London: Gollancz, 1936; 2d ed. 1946); and C. L. Stevenson, *Ethics and Language* (New Haven: Yale University Press, 1946).

In the light of this purported consequence of Moore's intuitionism—the alleged failure of intuition to establish a scientific basis for ethics—it is striking that neither of the most recent book-length treatments of Moore's ethics affords us more than a passing glance at the issue. Regan, for example, spends nearly a chapter on "The Nature of Judgment"—in which Moore struggles with the problem of the knowledge of truth and its indefinability—yet fails to connect it with Moore's account of the knowledge of value in *Principia*.

See *Bloomsbury's Prophet*, Chapter 7, "The Autonomy of Ethics," where, in relation to this topic if at all, Regan might have acknowledged the empirical character of Moore's approach to knowledge of value. Rohatyn likewise neglects to examine Moore's use of intuition as a means of empirical access to value owing, perhaps, to his eagerness to undermine the cogency of Moore's arguments in the naturalistic fallacy defense. (See especially *The Reluctant Naturalist*, Chapter 5, "A Guided Tour of *Principia Ethica*, Chapter I.") The difficulty with Rohatyn's thesis is that, without examining the matter of Moore's account of the knowledge of value that is critically implicated in his use of intuition, he concludes: "Most crucially, here, Moore sharply distinguishes between fact and value" (p. 36). While it is surely correct that Moore does distinguish between fact and value in *some* respects, it is *not* the case that the non-cognitivity of value is one of them.

The knowledge of good that Moore ascribes to intuition is indeed parallel to the knowledge of truth that he was trying to work out in "The Nature of Judgment" (1899), which closely preceded *Principia*. Not only is there a parallel in respect of the fact that, for Moore, to know that X is good is to know that the proposition ('X is good') is true, but also in that both truth and good are simple concepts knowable intuitively, by acquaintance.

Moreover, in the case of truth it is clear that Moore was not dealing with an object but with a concept and that his procedure here anticipates the one adopted by Bertrand Russell in the same time frame. A quote from Russell's 1903 *The Principles of Mathematics* (Cambridge: Cambridge University Press, p. xviii) helps to show the importance that Russell attached to Moore's distinction between conceptual entities such as propositions and existent things:

> On fundamental questions of philosophy, my position, in all its chief features, is derived from Mr G. E. Moore. I have accepted from him the non-existential nature of propositions (except such as happens to assert existence) and their independence of any knowing mind; also the pluralism which regards the world, both that of existents and that of entities, as composed of an infinite number of mutually independent entities, with relations which are ultimate, and not reducible to adjectives of their terms or of the whole which these compose.

Both Moore and Russell, in their protest against Bradley's thesis that concepts are mental abstractions from ideas or empirical impressions, were asserting the realist claim of the independence of universals. Hence concepts are viewed by them as independent entities; they are independent of *other* entities, thus denying Bradley's doctrine of internal relations, as well as being *mind*-independent, thus denying the *esse est percipi* of idealism.

While it is true that in 1899 Moore was not entirely clear about the metaphysical status of concepts, he was already prepared to claim that they are cognitively apprehended directly in the process of judgment. It was this process of apprehension, as Sylvester shows, that he later called intuition. Russell, perhaps sensing that Moore's use of the disputed term "intuition" in *Principia* had opened a Pandora's box of confusion, settled on a distinction between knowledge by acquaintance and by intuition in his 1912 *Problems of Philosophy* (London: Williams and Norgate). There he reserves "acquaintance" for the "immediate knowledge of things" and "intuitive knowledge" for "judgments" of "*self-evident* truths" (p. 109).

It seems clear that Russell, as well as Moore, wanted to link his new-found realism with empiricism as well as with the ancient tradition of Platonism in mathematics. Thus in the years after 1903, when Russell's *Principles* and Moore's *Principia* were published, we find both philosophers working more and more on the empirical foundations of their extreme realist view of conceptual entities. Russell's 1911 essay "Knowledge by Acquaintance and Knowledge by Description" was followed in 1914 by "On the Nature of Acquaintance" (the first published in the *Hibbert Journal* and reprinted in the collection *Mysticism and Logic and Other Essays* [London: Longmans, Green, 1919]; the second published in the *Monist* and reprinted in *Logic and Knowledge: Essays 1901–1950*, ed. R. C. Marsh [London: Allen & Unwin, 1956]).

Moore in the same time frame was of course famously abandoning his use of the term "intuition" in favor of the far more widely acceptable term of his later work, "common sense." (See the Schilpp volume as well as Moore's *Some Main Problems of Philosophy*.) It is often overlooked that Moore and Russell were not the first British philosophers to make use of "knowledge by acquaintance" and "intuitive apprehension" in their efforts to get away from Kant's "a priori forms of intuition" and the need for "transcendental deductions" in establishing them. As early as 1865 John Grote had used the phrase "knowledge by acquaintance" in his *Exploratio Philosophica* (Cambridge: Deighton, Bell), and Shadworth Hodgson had used it for self-evident propositions in his monumental four-volume *Metaphysics of Experience* (London: Longmans, Green, 1898). It is also of significance that Russell acknowledged, though Moore did not, the use that William James made of "acquaintance" as contrasted with "knowledge about" in the context of his two-volume *Principles of Psychology* (New York: Holt, 1890). Though Moore failed to acknowledge James's distinction, the use that James makes of it is close to that which Moore adopts in *Principia*. Although James uses the example of the color blue and Moore the color yellow it seems clear that both are concerned with the indescribable character of certain qualities that we nevertheless meet up with in experience. Thus in the first volume of his *Principles* James tells us:

> *About* the inner nature of these facts or what makes them what they are, I can say nothing at all. I cannot impart acquaintance with them to anyone who has not made it himself. I cannot *describe* them, make a blind man guess what blue is like, define to a child a syllogism, or tell a philosopher in just what respect distance is what it is, and differs from other forms of relation. [p. 221]

While Russell eventually abandoned "knowledge by acquaintance" in favor of the non-relational and non-cognitive term "sensation," and Moore gave it up in favor of "common sense" in his later work, James had already relinquished the phenomenalist roots of the distinction in favor of pragmatism by the time Russell and Moore were using it in the early 1900s.

It may not be particularly apposite to Sylvester's thesis on Moore's ethics, but it is noteworthy that both Russell and Moore were influenced in this same time frame—and in 1913 especially—by the work of Ludwig Wittgenstein, Russell's brilliant pupil of the period. Wittgenstein was working in the direction of what was to become the first of the two works published in his lifetime, the famous *Tractatus Logico-Philosophicus* of 1921, trans. David Pears and Brian McGuiness (London: Routledge & Kegan Paul, 1961). It was in preparation for this work that Wittgenstein was trying to show Russell that knowledge by acquaintance wouldn't work for the purposes that Russell envisaged; that is, for analysis of judgment and logical form. Wittgenstein argued that these are not, as Russell held, anything like primitive constituents of our experience but are instead what "has to be shown." The impact of this criticism, which took form in the *Tractatus*, was quite possibly what drove Russell to abandon "sense data" in the direction of neutral monism. It is at least equally plausible that the effect of this same line of criticism pushed Moore in the direction of the common sense empiricism that he worked out in the years following his exposure to Wittgenstein's lectures at Cambridge. (Russell and Moore were the sole examiners when Wittgenstein finally sat examination on the *Tractatus* for his doctorate at Cambridge.) And it is equally noteworthy that, long after he had abandoned the position of the *Tractatus*, Wittgenstein returned to the question of Moore's common sense empiricism in the studies with which he occupied his final days, published posthumously as *On Certainty*, eds. G. E. M. Anscombe and G. H. von Wright (Oxford: Blackwell, 1969). An account of Wittgenstein's early criticism of Russell's use of knowledge by acquaintance is given in Merrill B. Hintikka and Jaakko Hintikka, *Investigating Wittgenstein* (Blackwell, 1986), especially Chapter 3, "The Objects of the *Tractatus* as Objects of Acquaintance." See also David Pears, "The Relation Between Wittgenstein's Picture Theory of Propositions and Russell's Theories of Judgment," *Philosophical Review*, 86 (1977), pp. 177–96.

III

Intuition (II): A Second Look

1. *The Problem*

The varieties of intuitionism in ethical thought have given rise to several misunderstandings of the meaning and function of intuition in Moore's moral philosophy. As we have seen in the preceding chapter, one mistake comes about from the erroneous assumption that Moore gives an unqualified intuitionist answer to all three of the central questions of ethics that Moore himself distinguishes. Another seems to be the result of reliance upon a general criticism of intuitionism that misses its target altogether when applied to Moore's unique version. Both mistakes might have been avoided had Moore's critics attended to the important distinctions between different types of intuitionist doctrine; distinctions that Moore himself did much to clarify in *Principia Ethica*.

At the same time, it is also quite possible that some critical misreadings of Moore's views are due to points of apparent ambiguity or inconsistency in Moore's own work. As we saw in Chapter I above, Moore's views did sometimes change over time, and there have been attempts to read his early work in *Principia* in the light of views that he expressed at a much later date. Moreover, it must be acknowledged that there are some points in *Principia* itself where Moore's account of the role of intuition in making practical moral choices is not entirely clear. While the main line of Moore's thought in both *Principia* and the *Ethics* is remarkably consistent and unambiguous, there are certain fine points of detail where Moore's arguments rest upon points that are more implicitly embedded than explicitly discussed. It is my purpose in this chapter to single out some of these points for clarification.

59

My procedure so far has been to consider some of Moore's uses of intuition in which its role is explicitly discussed in some detail, and I continue in that fashion in the present chapter insofar as that is possible. Moore's discussion of the role of intuition with respect to the virtues, which I deal with presently, is a case in point. But some of the topics discussed are approachable only by studying the implications of Moore's general doctrine as they apply to specific problems that Moore himself does *not* discuss directly. As we saw in Chapter II, for example, Pepper's assumption that Moore's use of intuition is equivalent to the claim of incorrigibility, or even of epistemic certainty, is wrong on its face, even though Moore himself never directly confronts these issues. However, since Moore holds that self-evidence is the only evidence possible in a whole range of cases, it may appear—and apparently does so appear to Pepper—to be implicit that debate in cases of opposed intuitions is pointless. And yet, as I have already suggested, that is not what is to be implied at all.

I want to show in what follows that it is plainly evident that Moore allows ample and decisive room for debate in resolving problems of moral choice and practice. What Moore stresses, in fact, is that the role of intuition in deciding hard cases in ethics is of far less importance than critics like Pepper or the non-cognitivists imagine. For the bulk of moral argument, Moore contends, is not concerned with the issue of intuition at all, but with the uses of factual and causal information, as well as in the employment of our general knowledge of the way the world works, as such information and knowledge bear upon the moral problem at hand. It is convenient, however, to commence the discussion of Moore's general conception of moral argument and debate with an examination of his own argument against his fellow intuitionist in ethics, Henry Sidgwick.

2. *General Principles in Moore's Use of Intuition*

It has puzzled a number of Moore's critics that he should have devoted so much attention in *Principia Ethica* to the refutation of Sidgwick's intuitionist claim that pleasure alone is good. Indeed, for many critics of intuitionism in ethics, Moore's

criticism of Sidgwick's version of intuitionism is of little consequence precisely because it can be taken for granted that, since
Moore and Sidgwick are fellow intuitionists, any disagreement between them must be of purely parochial interest. What is not recognized is that the extended criticism and refutation of Sidgwick's
intuitionist claim that pleasure alone is good is the chosen vehicle
for the full development of Moore's *general* theory of moral judgment and his assignment of the proper role of intuition within that
theory.

In the previous chapter I dealt with Moore's account of the role
of intuition in the making of *particular* judgments [such as 'this X
is good'], but that account left the role of intuition in the making
of *general* judgments [such as 'all X's are good'] unexamined and
unexplained. For it cannot be assumed, on the account Moore
gives, that because 'this X is good,' therefore 'all X's are good';
nor does Moore even hint at the possibility of such an inference
from the (intuited) particular case to the general rule or principle.
On the other hand, according to Moore, the making of such an
inference is just what is required by Sidgwick's formulation of the
general rule implied in the claim that pleasure alone is good, even
though Sidgwick himself thinks otherwise and bases his claim on
intuition alone.

As Moore sees it, the proposition that pleasure alone is good
cannot be based upon intuition alone. And he bases this claim
upon his own and *counter*-intuitive claim, his own intuition,
which tells him that Sidgwick's claim is false. "I shall try," Moore
says, "to show you why my intuition denies it, just as his intuition
affirms it. It may be true notwithstanding; neither intuition can
prove whether it is true or not."[1] The problem to be resolved,
then, is whose claim is correct, if either is, for they cannot *both* be
objectively true no matter how vividly each claims to intuit the
validity and truth of his own claim. It is a problem, obviously,
that cannot be resolved by intuition alone. Resort *must* be made
to argument and debate, to causal information and knowledge of
the way the world works.

Moore begins his refutation of Sidgwick's claim [though not of
Sidgwick's *intuition*, it should be noted] by arguing that the formulation 'pleasure alone is good' can be shown to be faulty on its

face. He puts the matter this way: "Our question is: is it the pleasure as distinct from the consciousness of it, that we set value on? Do we think the pleasure valuable in itself, or must we insist that, if we are to think the pleasure good, we must have consciousness of it too."[2] And he continues his attack on Sidgwick's claim by means of an extended citation from Plato's *Philebus*, the famous dialogue in which Socrates is shown refuting the hedonistic claim of Protarchus. Here is the conclusion that Moore draws from the line of argument that Plato causes Socrates to develop:

> Socrates, we see, persuades Protarchus that Hedonism is absurd. If we are really going to maintain that pleasure alone is good as an end, we must maintain that it is good, whether we are conscious of it or not. We must declare it reasonable to take as our ideal (an unattainable ideal it may be) that we should be as happy as possible, even on condition that we never know and never can know that we are happy. We must be willing to sell in exchange for the mere happiness every vestige of knowledge, both in ourselves and in others, both of happiness itself and of every other thing. Can we really still disagree? Can anyone still declare it obvious that this is reasonable? That pleasure alone is good as an end? [*Principia,* p. 89]

What *does* appear obvious, to Moore, is that at least some types of disagreement between value intuitions *are* resolvable in some such fashion as this. They are capable of being resolved by appeal to rational argument concerning concepts and states of affairs that can be, and are, known quite independently of intuition.

The method for dealing with such disputes, Moore tells us, is really quite simple. As the first step, one clarifies, or brings before the mind, the meaning of the intuited proposition that is claimed to have general (or even universal) import, for example, 'pleasure alone is good.' One must attend to the meaning of the concepts involved in the proposition. Since concepts, for Moore, *are* logical ideas or meanings themselves and, as such, are objective and independent of the mind, the exercise is one of reflective analysis and reasoning concerning propositions containing them. (I study

Moore's view of concepts and propositions and their roles in judgments in Chapters IV and V. Here it must suffice to say merely that judgments must reflect the accurate understanding of concepts as well as knowledge of states of affairs, or matters of fact.)

In the second step, one considers some propositions that follow logically from the clarified general proposition in dispute. The propositions thus obtained—as in the example of the *Philebus*—may then be shown to conflict with the truth of other general propositions that the proponent accepts. [In the *Philebus*, Protarchus is led by Socrates to see a contradiction between the claim that pleasure is the *sole* criterion of value and *knowing* that one is pleased. The latter—while distinct from merely *being* pleased—is a thing of yet *more* value than merely *being* pleased.] By use of this method, Moore concludes, one may sometimes be able to show an opponent that an appeal to self-evidence is misplaced. He writes: "Following the method established . . . I claimed that the truth of the proposition was not self-evident. I could do nothing to *prove* that it was untrue. I could only point out as clearly as possible what it means, and how it contradicts other propositions which appear to be equally true."[3] As in the *Philebus*, Moore's method is the classic one of *reductio ad absurdum*. But we should also take note that Moore does *not* take the *reductio* as proof that pleasure alone is not the sole good.[4]

Two brief remarks are in order here: First, it seems clear that Moore's analysis of conceptual thought supposes the intellect to be capable of grasping the logical meaning, or concept, 'pleasure' and the meaning, or concept, 'consciousness' quite independently of each other. Second, it will be well to remember that one of Moore's philosophical motives in his work, at the turn of the century, was his intent to contest a set of crucial issues against the views, prevailing at the time, of the idealists. The proper analysis of consciousness was just such an issue, and Moore wanted to show that idealism is badly mistaken in its failure to distinguish between the *object* of value and the *consciousness* of that object. In criticism of Sidgwick's version of hedonism (hedonistic utilitarianism), as we have seen, Moore does not think that pleasure apart from consciousness carries value; that is, qua pleasure alone. He does think that consciousness of pleasure not only *may* but surely *does* carry value, as the instance of consciousness of a beautiful object (which we have already discussed) shows quite clearly. It is not consciousness as such, but the organic *unity* of consciousness and pleasure that, is valuable *as a unity*. (The nature and importance of organic unity is discussed in more detail in a later chapter.)

Moore is not particularly worried over the fact that we cannot *prove* a principle, said to be self-evident, to be false. It should, he tells us, cause no real uneasiness, and he gives us an example designed to set the issue in proper perspective. Try to prove to a madman, he says, that this is a chair alongside the desk. "We can only persuade him by showing him that our view is consistent with something else which he holds to be true, whereas his original view is contradictory to it." [5] This is of course just another way of showing how the *reductio* works; it can be a useful, though not a definitive, procedure for resolving the differences between competing intuitive claims and alleged self-evident truths. No matter how peculiar the intuition, the method is a way of clarifying the terms of the dispute.

3. A Conceptual Disagreement

This is not the place to begin a full-scale discussion of Moore's theory of judgment, but one feature of that theory must be noted here, for it bears directly on the problem of moral disagreements. In his discussion of judgment Moore draws an important distinction between *concepts*, or *logical* ideas, and what he calls psychological ideas. These psychological ideas are entertained as contents of the minds of existent persons, but do *not* exist independently of those minds. Concepts (logical ideas) are *not* dependent in this way. Concepts, then, are what we properly make use of in judgments; *not* psychological ideas. Pleasure, qua concept, is—that is, has being—independent of any pleasant experience had by any subject. A pleasant experience, by contrast, cannot be independent, or exist independently, of any thinking that the person having the experience may do about that particular experience. [The point here is just that psychological ideas such as having pleasure and feeling good cannot go about by themselves—

as concepts can—for they are dependent on conscious subjects; they are mind-dependent.] Similarly, and as I have mentioned, the concept of consciousness *is* independent from any consciousness of *it*. Moreover, as Moore makes clear, he holds that both pleasure and consciousness, as distinct concepts, are independent of the concept 'good.'

Moore's argument concerning the way moral disagreements may be resolved rests upon the fact that we are able to reflect upon such notions as pleasure and consciousness [when they are considered as concepts] independently of the psychological experience of either. As a consequence we are in a position to see that pleasure, all by itself and isolated, is simply itself; that is, an objective concept that is independent of the simple concept 'good.' It is different from the concept 'good' and not reducible to it. Good does not ride along with it. Yet Moore thinks the proposition is true that 'consciousness of pleasure is good.' Good *does* go along with the *complex* concept 'consciousness of pleasure'; and we know this by reflective analysis of the complex concept in question.

A complex concept makes a connection between concepts, and it is the seeing of such a connection that may amount to seeing that the complex concept is *necessarily* true or, as Moore says in some cases, is self-evident. [Not all necessary truths are held to be self-evident, for some complex concepts may be necessarily true but not self-evident to judgment. Independent complex concepts, or ideas, when they involve predication, are called propositions by both Moore and Russell. In 1903 both believed propositions to be objects that have reality independently of mind or consciousness, and are (sometimes) necessarily true by virtue of the connections, analytic *or* synthetic, among the concepts themselves; for example, in what are sometimes called synthetic a priori propositions.] And Moore *does* hold that 'consciousness of pleasure is good' is a complex proposition that is self-evident; in other words, it is necessarily true owing to the relations between the meanings of the independent concepts 'pleasure' and 'good.'

The point to be stressed is that Moore's argument does not maintain that pleasure exists someplace, alone and unexperienced. It is the *concept* of pleasure that is independent of both the (psychological) experience, or consciousness, of pleasure, and the *concept* of consciousness. And both concepts are independent of the concept good. Once we have grasped the sense of all three concepts *as* independent and objective *meanings*, we can then grasp the uncertainty of the complex concept involved in the proposition 'pleasure alone is good.' In the *Principia*, he puts the argument as follows: "*Either* pleasure by itself (even though we can't get it) would be all that is desirable, *or* a consciousness of it would be more desirable still. Both of these propositions cannot be true; and I think that it is plain that the latter is true; whence it follows that pleasure is *not* the sole good."[6] In rational argument we use concepts that are the meanings of words. We know the meaning that the word 'pleasure' stands for, and we know the meaning that the word 'consciousness' stands for, and we can see that the things that are pleasures are not significantly valuable—or at least we can doubt that they are—apart from consciousness of them. That is, we can see that they are not, apart from consciousness of them, intrinsically good. We can also see that pleasures *alone* are not, by any logical stretch of their meaning, intrinsically good. That is to say that pleasure as a concept is neither identical with, nor included in, the concept good. [Moore also makes this point differently by means of the open question argument, which see.]

The disagreement we have been considering has concerned the truth or falsity of the general proposition 'pleasure is the only good.' Neither Sidgwick's intuition nor Moore's—the one finding truth, the other finding falsehood—can be found capable of independent proof. Moore, as we have said, does not claim to prove that Sidgwick's *proposition* is false; merely that its truth is not self-evident.

But Moore also considers a possible revision of Sidgwick's view expressed in the complex proposition: 'It is self-evidently true that consciousness of pleasure is the only good.' Moore subjects the amended proposition to the same treatment as the original. Let us suppose that 'consciousness of pleasure is the only good' is true. It follows that any two situations will be equally valuable, *provided only* that both have the exact amount of conscious pleasure in them. If this is so, then, as Moore tells us in the *Ethics*, the drunkard who is immensely pleased with breaking crockery is in a state of mind just as valuable in itself "as that of a man who is fully realizing all that is exquisite in the tragedy of King Lear, provided only that the mere quantity of pleasure in both cases is the same."[7] In this passage Moore was not explicitly targeting the amended version of hedonism that might be offered by a defender of Sidgwick's position, but rather a cruder version that held that the amount of intrinsic value of a thing is always proportional to the amount of pleasure. But clearly, what the argument shows is still a *reductio* of the amended version, provided that we take 'pleasure' to be 'consciousness of pleasure' and we stipulate that the drunkard is conscious of the fact that he is 'immensely pleased.' And it is surely clear that Moore would so regard it.

Of course, Moore admits, the revised proposition may still be true. And yet anyone holding that view must provide some independent argument for its truth. In any case, the claim of self-evidence for the truth of either the original proposition or the revised version has been shown—by means of the *reductio*—to be subject to reasonable doubt.

4. *Self-evidence and the Definition of Duty*

We have seen in Chapter I that Moore defines the crucial terms employed in practical ethical contexts in terms of the simple unanalyzable concept, good. 'Duty,' for example, was defined as the doing of the action that will cause more good to come into existence than any other action open to the agent. In *Principia Ethica* Moore supposed that this quite openly utilitarian principle could be strictly demonstrated. He supplied an argument, but the argument, as we shall see, was merely a restatement of the position rather than a demonstration. Perhaps Moore was aware of this, for he turns the entire argument in the 1912 *Ethics* over to making his own version of the utilitarian position in ethics more secure. Moore does, of course, still claim that his utilitarian principle—the principle that lies behind all practical ethics including right action as well as duty—is self-evident. He writes: "It seems to me quite self-evident that it must always be our duty to do what will produce the best effect *upon the whole*, no matter how bad the effects upon ourselves may be and no matter how much good we ourselves may lose by it."[8] The self-evident intuition that he refers to is of a general, or universal, proposition. Three comments should be made concerning such propositions.

First, in the final chapter of *Ethics* Moore confronts the claims of egoism as possible grounds for practical ethical choice, and he defends his version of utilitarianism against this rival view. Egoism stands, he thinks, as a substantial alternative to utilitarianism, and the choice between them cannot be shown to be without "practical importance" on traditional Platonic grounds; i.e., on the grounds that, according to Plato, all actions maximizing the general good will, ipso facto, maximize the agent's own good. All argument to prove this point, Moore thinks, must fail. But this leaves both the egoist and the utilitarian bereft of an answer to the fundamental question as to whether it may be one's duty to sacrifice one's own good for the general welfare.

Moore, facing the necessity of justifying his preference for the utilitarian view, responds to the egoists in this way:

> If any person, after carefully considering the question, comes to the conclusion that he can never be under any obligation to sacrifice his own good to the social good, if they *were* to conflict, or even that it would be very wrong for him to do so, it is, I think, impossible to prove he is mistaken . . . (but) for my part, it seems quite self-evident that he is mistaken.[9]

If, as Moore claims, the egoist *is* mistaken, it may very well be that it follows, reasonably, that 'Our duty is to do that action which will produce the best effects on the whole,' just as Moore claims.

The disagreement between the egoist and the utilitarian should remind us of the disagreement between Moore and Sidgwick. Moore agrees that the egoist's alleged self-evident principle—maximize the good for oneself—cannot be proved false. But Moore can, and does, match the egoist's principle with his own utilitarian one.[10] He does not engage in debate with the egoist, as he does with Sidgwick, however. Instead he gives over the entire *Ethics* to argument for the version of utilitarianism he espouses. The point I make is that Moore gives prolonged argument and explanation, dialectically, for what he calls ideal utilitarianism and the definition of 'duty' that it requires. Its plausibility does not rest on the mere assertion of intuition or self-evidence. Reasons are given and arguments are supplied.

The second comment is this: In articulating the principle of duty—'*Our duty is to do that which will produce the best effects upon the whole*'—Moore produces a general moral principle. It may sound odd to emphasize something that is clearly obvious. But I do it for good reason. Moore does not propose that his principle of duty stand as a claim that the concept of duty is unanalyzable. Duty is not a simple concept, as good is. Duty is analyzable into constituent elements. Duty is a complex concept. The same is true of the concepts of right and obligation. I mention this because some philosophers seem to have been misled by Moore's suggestion that the principle of duty is self-evident. Notice the following passage, taken from A. C. Ewing's *Ethics*:

> There are indeed these alternatives: (a) we may hold good indefinable and define ought in terms of it . . . (b) we may hold that good and ought are both indefinable; (c) we may regard ought as indefinable and define good in terms of ought. Moore took the first view in *Principia Ethica*, but the second in his later work *Ethics*.[11]

The self-evidence of the truth of the principle of duty is indeed held by Moore, but the indefinability of 'duty' or 'ought' is quite another matter. Ewing may have confused the two, and he is not the only one. Mary Warnock in her *Ethics Since 1900* says, "in his later book, *Ethics*, Moore was inclined to treat 'obligation' as another indubitable property." The sentence appears on page 58; and following it, on pages 59 and 60, she adds, "In his later book, *Ethics*, he regarded the apprehension that something was a duty as separate from the apprehension that it was good, and equally irreducible." Separate from, yes; Moore always held duty and good to be separate concepts. Equally irreducible, no. I think Warnock has also been thrown off in supposing that the self-evidence of the general proposition about duty, which Moore holds, is self-evidence that some particular action here and now is a duty. Both Ewing and Warnock appear to have confused the notion of self-evidence with the very different notions of irreducibility and indefinability. Moore never deals with duty, obligation, and right as if they are indefinable, unanalyzable, or indubitable simple concepts. *Ethics* is at least as clear about the complexity of such concepts as *Principia*, if not even clearer.

The third and last comment is this: Moore claims, in *Principia Ethica*, that 'duty' is to be defined as "that action, which will cause more good to exist in the Universe than any possible alternative." [Compare with his definition of the morally permissible: "what will not cause less good than any possible alternative."] He claims also that this definition is not merely stipulative but can be demonstrated. (The text of this definition and its purported demonstration appears on pages 147 and 148, Chapter 5, of *Principia*.) However, the alleged demonstration is nothing but a reiteration of the principle: "It is plain that when we assert that a certain action is our absolute duty, we are asserting that the performance of that action is unique in respect to value." Moore claims this as demonstration on the grounds that, 'unique in respect to value' *means* 'the whole world will be better if it be performed, than if any possible alternative were taken.' In summing up the argument he concludes with the following expression, "It is in fact, evident that" the sum of goodness would be greater if we do one act—the dutiful one—as opposed to any other. But this is hardly a demonstration.

The point emphasized in this section is that, in the *Ethics*, or even in *Principia Ethica*, Moore does not either prove or demonstrate, despite his claims to the contrary, that 'duty' ('obligation' or 'right') is what he defines it as. On the other hand, in both books he gives a variety of arguments and reasons for holding the views that he does about the definition of the practical ethical predicates. He does not rest content with appeals to intuition or self-evidence, even though he believes his definition of the principle of duty to be self-evident. Rather, Moore advances cogent reasons and mounts substantial arguments to defend his position and to show the falsity of the views of his opponents. In any event, it is surely not right to claim that Moore is an intuitionist with respect to practical moral judgments and prescriptions. On the contrary, he argues *against* those who hold such views.

5. *Intuition and Moral Laws*

No moral law, according to Moore, is self-evident. Nor does Moore hold an intuitionist doctrine with respect to the self-evidence of moral prescriptions. Views claiming that we are able to grasp certain general rules for action as self-evident are views that Moore takes explicit pains to argue against. He does not deny that we make immediate judgments that certain actions are right or wrong in a *psychological sense*.[12] He affirms that we do. But as I emphasized at the outset, a major task that *Principia Ethica* sets for itself is the delineation of the three separate categories of moral philosophy. Moore wants to avoid confusions of the sort that result from mixing up mere psychological certitude [commonly referred to, somewhat confusingly, as moral certitude] with the result of rational methods of judgment with respect to matters of duty and right. We must never confuse moral generalizations, which are merely probable at best, with allegedly indubitable moral laws.

Moore argues that answers to the question 'What ought we to do?' are to be found in investigations of proper evidence and require that we have appropriate causal information at our disposal. We discover such causal information by means of empirical investigation; we look to the world of scientific and social fact. We consult history, geography, sociology, and biology. Our sources are empirical and are *not* intuitive in the sense that our apprehension of good is. But empirical knowledge is very limited. We cannot, with any confidence, lay down any universally applicable moral precepts. We cannot say that obeying such a maxim as 'Thou shalt not bear false witness' will always produce the best possible consequences. The same is true for any, and indeed all, proposed moral law.

In saying that we cannot hold any moral law as absolute or certain, Moore is not arguing that we are morally justified in holding all moral law to be exceptionable. It is rather that moral law is always held to be subject to the utilitarian ideal, and we can never be intellectually certain about the exact and precise application of that ideal to any concrete case. Moore argues the quite conservative view that we must obey the well-founded rules of society because the rules define the very grounds of our social experience, and we breach them at our peril.

Moral laws, then, or what some refer to as the moral rules, can never be known or held with certitude. Their truth can never be given in acts of intuition, or as self-evident truths. Nor can they be stated even as the principles of duty and right were stated. The most exalted status that a moral law can aspire to, Moore tells us, is that of a widely accepted empirical generalization. And even then, as the condition 'widely accepted' indicates, whether such moral laws should be followed depends upon the empirical fact of general societal acceptance as one of the well-founded and useful rules in the given society. More is said about the concept of well-founded rules in society in Chapter V, Section 6, but I pass now to certain common generalizations and Moore's way of dealing with them.

6. *Kindness Is Good*

Consider a general proposition such as 'kindness is good.' Does Moore believe that a proposition of this type can be self-evident? The question is, I think, not clearly answered in Moore's work. He does not discuss the question as I have put it. Nevertheless, with the help of Moore's theory of simple and complex concepts, we may gain considerable insight into the sort of answer that is consistent with his other and explicitly expressed views.

There are, I suggest, two distinguishable theses—two different ways—that one may approach the question, 'Can we know that the proposition "Kindness is good" is true?' One is in the context of the theory of judgment found in Moore's 1899 article, "The Nature of Judgment." The view there is that truth is a simple and unanalyzable concept (similar to good), which attaches itself to certain combinations of concepts, but not to others. We may call this the a priori thesis. Another way to deal with the question is from the point of view of the discovery of good in a specific situation and the grasping of the general truth through the specific instance. Call this view the a posteriori thesis.

According to the a priori thesis, if kindness really is good, then the pattern of concepts that includes both kindness and good relates them in such a way that when the two are found together in a proposition, the additional property, or concept, 'truth' always appears with them. The proposition that 'kindness is good' is true is, on this thesis, self-evident. But the reader should remember that, even if 'kindness is good' is true or self-evident, and even if every instance of an act of kindness is good, Moore is not committed to hold that in any particular instance an act of kindness is morally required of an agent.

According to the a posteriori thesis, by way of contrast, there may be an actual occasion when a moral agent acts with kindness to another and where an observer sees the act and judges, correctly, that the act exemplifies value. Moore has held, in "The Conception of Intrinsic Value," that if something has intrinsic value, anything exactly like the thing must also have value, and in the same degree. [This is Moore's principle of supervenience: see the bibliographical essay for chapter 6.] Thus the act in question, since it has value (*ex hypothesi*), shows value to be exemplified in acts like it. That 'kindness is good' is true is grasped in this case, is self-evident, and thus can be grasped as true *for all such cases*. As in the a priori thesis, the self-evidence of the truth of the general proposition has no tendency *by itself* to obligate a person to be kind in any particular instance.

Moore seems to be closer to the a posteriori thesis in *Principia Ethica* if, indeed, he can be said to have any opinion about the status of propositions of the sort under investigation. It makes no actual difference, however, for Moore's stress on the *method of isolation* for value assessment indicates that he believes the mind is capable of *knowing* general propositions of the form 'kindness is good' as true. But let us turn to an examination of the method and the related principle of organic unity.

7. *The Method of Conceptual Isolation and the Principle of Organic Unity*

If a person knows that 'kindness is good' is true, then he knows also (is committed to the belief) that whenever and wherever an act of kindness occurs, it must be valuable. Under either the a priori or the a posteriori thesis the above claim is true. For Moore tells us: "Judgments of intrinsic value have this superiority over judgments of means, if once they are true, they are always true." [13] The matter deserves to be carefully stated. If an act of kindness occurs in any situation whatsoever Moore does not teach that the situation in which the act occurs is *itself* necessarily good. A particular occasion, itself intrinsically evil, may have, as one of its parts, a valuable act of kindness. The principle of organic unities, sometimes called the principle of organic relations, holds that the value of a (an organic) whole bears no particular relationship to the value inherent in each of the parts. A given situation may be intrinsically good. It may have within it an act of kindness. For one to suppose that the value of the whole is grounded in the known value in the act of kindness is to neglect the principle. [It would also be to commit the fallacy of composition.] The value of the whole must be judged in terms of the integrity of the whole, qua whole. The act of kindness is merely an element in the whole.

This principle may help clarify Moore's argument directed against Sidgwick's claim that pleasure alone is good. Moore thinks the value that comes about in the experience of pleasure is due to the organic unity, consciousness of pleasure. The value is not due to consciousness by itself (although consciousness may have value), and it is not due to pleasure by itself. In fact, as we have seen, Moore believes that pleasure by itself has little if any value. But even that is irrelevant in the context of the present discussion. The value that is to be assessed is that of the unity, the whole situation of the entity as an entity, and not the sum of any of the parts of that whole.

In order to judge of the value residual in a whole, the mind must be able to grasp the whole *as* a whole. Thus for the mind to judge of the value in a part of a larger whole—in our example, an act of kindness—the mind must be able to abstract that part from the whole. To do so implies the mind's ability to isolate and abstract. Moore writes:

> What things have intrinsic value, and in what degrees? . . . In order to arrive at a correct decision on the first part of this question, it is necessary to consider what things are such that, if they existed *by themselves*, in absolute isolation, we should judge their existence to be good.[14]

It is by means of this method of isolation that we are able to consider the act of kindness divorced from the situation in which it is embedded.

In Section 6 above it was suggested that this method is most appropriate to the context of the a posteriori thesis. Moore clearly supposes that one can prescind from actual occurrences in order to make general value assessments, but it may also be supposed that one could abstract from conceptual complexes generated by the a priori thesis as well. Moore may have had such cases in mind, and the two worlds argument that Moore sometime uses may be confirming evidence of this. To imagine a world immeasurably beautiful is *not* to engage in an act of abstraction. It is, in an unalarming sense, to isolate conceptually in order to contemplate. Thus it seems clear that the method of isolation is compatible with either of the two theses.

Moore intends the method of isolation to be the epistemological counterpart to the so-called principle of organic relations. The mind, by means of the method of isolation, grasps the value that exists when good is exemplified in the world. Goodness *ingresses* into an existing situation, and an agent (knower) becomes aware of the value in the situation when the agent is conscious of (aware of) the organic unity that is the situation. The method of isolation and its counterpart, the principle of organic relations, are accordingly of central import for understanding Moore's value theory in *Principia Ethica*.

It should be clear that Moore intends that, when the method of isolation is used to ascertain the value inherent in a thing or a situation, the mind must be understood to find the value through an act of intuition—by the self-evidence of the truth of the proposition that makes the thing or situation intelligible. Thus in the situation in which kindness is an element, and from which the mind isolates the act of kindness for value assessment, the mind discovers that the proposition 'kindness is good' is self-evidently true. I try to illustrate this process in the next section.

8. *An Example and the Method of Isolation*

I want to construct, in imagination, a complex situation and then apply the method of isolation in order to illustrate Moore's doctrine of intuition. To this purpose I tell a fragment of a story and pick out a feature of it to discuss.

Suppose some hikers are camping and exploring in the north country. While investigating an area one afternoon, the hikers come upon a mountain river. The river is white-watered and churning. The hikers decide to follow the river upstream. Some yards upstream and around a sharp, steep bend in the terrain, the river takes on a lazy, peaceful aspect. The appearance is in decided contrast to the violence of the flow below.

From the point of the sharp bend looking down the mountain the river drops off from a dramatic waterfall, which begins the swirling white water the hikers first encountered. As the hikers move up past the waterfall to the lazy part of the river they become aware of a small child paddling and playing on an inner-tube floating on the river. She and her family have come upon the river from another direction. They are unaware of the dramatic change in the river's course and do not know of the waterfall and of the potential danger to the child. The inner-tube is gathering speed, having been caught up in the current that will bring the child to the brink of the falls. The inner-tube, with the child, moves toward the bank of the river and is about to be carried onward. As the tube sweeps past the embankment, one of the hikers plunges into the water and manages to pull the child to the shore, barely succeeding in preventing them both from being pulled into the main current and over the falls.

As the hiker carries the child up the embankment he suddenly collapses. He is a man who has been recuperating from a heart condition and who has been encouraged by his physician to do the hike as long as his exercise and rest are controlled sensibly. His hiker friends rush to his side and have, now, the problem of getting him the proper medication, attention, and care for his heart condition.

Given the larger whole, one can isolate the saving of the life of the child for a value judgment. From Moore's analysis, at any rate, one will be able to say, "The saving of the life of the child is good." We have picked an element of the whole that is in itself a whole. We can, and do, judge it. Moore's view, furthermore, is that if saving the life of that child was good, then the saving a child's life is *always* good. It is not just this one particular act that is good, but the *kind* of act it exemplifies.

As for the larger whole, is it good? The hiker has collapsed. He is in real danger of dying. Of course, he did save the life of the child. Had he not dived into the river, he might not have collapsed. The act of saving the life helped cause the collapse. Thus an act that is itself good becomes an essential part of a whole that, as a unity, does not exemplify good. The whole is *at least*, and obviously, not *wholly* good. Whether or not it is evil, or bad, is not at issue here. The point to be taken is that whatever may be said of the value of the whole, the value of any part of the whole is irrelevant to the value-integrity of the whole, and vice versa.

In *Principia Ethica* Moore claims that one of the goals of ethics is the discovery of actions that are good wherever and whenever they occur: "So Casuistry aims at discovering what actions are good, *whenever they occur*. . . . Casuistry is the goal of ethical investigation."[15] By the application of the method of isolation a careful investigator might be able to prepare a list of the kind of actions that are intrinsically good. Although Moore does not show that we may become aware of propositions such as 'the saving of the life of a child is good' as self-evident truths, he has stated the obvious grounds whereby one should be able to come to such an awareness. In Chapter V, where the matter of judgments of this type comes in for a more complete discussion, we return to this issue once again.

9. *Virtue and Self-evidence*

Moore does not view virtue, or the virtues, as intrinsically good. He argues that we test virtue (or virtues) for value and ethical content in the same way that we test for duty. Virtue is a *means* to good. In fact Moore defines the notion of virtue as "a habitual disposition to perform certain actions, which generally produce the best results." [16] As Moore sees the role of virtue, it is to be used as part of moral education. Moore agrees, he supposes, with Aristotle, uses the latter's classic definition of virtue as habit (or habitual disposition), and recommends that the habit be well established. Without examining the matter in detail at this point, let it suffice to say that the habits (virtues) that are important are valued for utilitarian reasons. It is not self-evident that a *particular* habit—called a virtue or anything else—is to be cultivated. The virtues promote, or ought to promote, the best possible outcomes by means of their practice. Moore observes: "If it could be shown of a particular disposition, commonly considered virtuous, that it was generally harmful, we should at once say: Then it is not really virtuous." [17]

Moore meets the question 'Are virtues good in themselves?' head-on because he finds that a number of moral philosophers have assumed that the sole good must *be* virtue. But he saves his main discussion of virtues for analysis under the heading "Ethics in Relation to Conduct," the chapter in which he defines 'duty,' since, as we need to remind ourselves, the definition of 'virtue,' for Moore, is nearly identical with the definition of 'duty.'

Moore thinks that those moral philosophers who have considered virtue as the sole good have made the same sort of mistake as the hedonists sometimes make, for they fail to note that intrinsic value is captured in a *simple* and *unique* concept. In short, they have confused ends and means. He writes:

They have discussed, as if it were simple and unambiguous, the question 'What ought we do?' or 'What ought to exist now?' without distinguishing whether the reason why a thing ought to be done or to exist now, is that it is itself possessed of intrinsic value, or that it is a means to what has intrinsic value.[18]

Virtue is not, nor does it have, intrinsic value. Intuition shows that any act done from a habitual disposition will bring about states of intrinsic value.

10. *Final Remarks*

I have discussed some aspects of Moore's doctrine of intuition in this chapter, points that I believe have generally been overlooked or misunderstood. I have done so because I have wanted to clear up some of those misunderstandings, but have also wanted to introduce and show the importance of the method of isolation and its counterpart, the principle of organic unities. As we shall see in the chapters to come, these two principles must be appreciated if we are to gain an accurate understanding of how Moore's ethical philosophy hangs together.

The reader will notice that most of the analysis involved in this and the preceding chapter referred to *Principia Ethica*. By now the reason ought to be clear. The *Ethics* deals with the practical question 'What ought we to do?' and we should by now be well aware of the fact that answers to *that* question are not to be found in isolated acts of intuition or by appeal to self-evidence alone. Explanation of the role of self-evidence can be held to a minimal level in any text that attempts to present a theory of practical ethical import, and Moore does exactly that in the 1912 *Ethics*.

Critical Bibliography: Chapter III

In this chapter the discussion of Moore's intuitionism turns to his differences with Sidgwick, surely the least idealist of his Cambridge mentors. In his efforts to effect an alliance with empiricism in ethics—implicit in his insistence that *Principia* be read as "prolegomena to any future Ethics that can possibly pretend to be scientific" (p. ix)—Moore felt constrained to distinguish two kinds of propositions: those that are self-evident, for which no evidence may be offered, and those representing causal knowledge, for which evidence may be submitted. Because, as he says, he "sometimes followed Sidgwick's usage" (p. x) in calling his self-evident ethical propositions intuitions, Moore found it necessary to distinguish his own usage from Sidgwick's. This is all the more important for Moore because in much else he *did* follow Sidgwick, even to the point of adopting Sidgwick's "hedonistic utilitarianism" as a fair denomination of his own system.

Famously, Sidgwick's system was an attempt to reconcile the two dominant moral views of the Victorian age: the utilitarianism descended from Jeremy Bentham and John Stuart Mill on the one hand, and the intuitionism descended from Reid and the Scottish common sense school through Mill's strongest critic, William Whewell, on the other.

It may not be particularly significant, but in "Memories of G. E. Moore" Morton White reports the following incident from Moore's brief tenure at Columbia University:

> One day a Columbia colleague of Moore's was looking for a book by Whewell—the famous Dr. Whewell who played such a great part in the history of Moore's own college, Trinity. He met Moore as he was looking for the book in the offices of the *Journal of Philosophy*. As his colleague took the book down from the shelves he showed it to Moore, thinking that Moore would certainly know it, and asked him what he thought of Whewell. To which Moore replied without the slightest sign of embarrassment and even a sly twinkle: "You know, I've *never* read Whewell. Should I?" [in Klemke, p. 206]

Whatever Moore may or may not have read of Whewell, he certainly *had* read Sidgwick. Although the period of Moore's and Sidgwick's presence at Cambridge barely overlap—Sidgwick died in 1900—there is little doubt of the immense impact of Sidgwick's monumental work, *The Methods of Ethics*, on Moore and his contemporaries.

First published in 1874 and extensively revised over the years, *The Methods of Ethics* (London: Macmillan) went through seven editions, the last in 1907. The sixth edition of 1901, the last to be revised by the author, contains a brief autobiography. Sidgwick's system, perhaps in Herbert Spencer's glossy "scientific" and "evolutionary" version of it (1907), seemed to many an incarnation and symbol of the moral beliefs of the Victorian age.

Moore may have taken it as such, for his arguments in *Principia* against Spencer's naturalistic ethics move on to blame Sidgwick for supplying the fundamental premise of Spencer's ethics—that is, the misleading idea that egoistic hedonism is *rational,* a conclusion that Sidgwick drew from his apprehension that "pleasure is the sole good" (See *Principia Ethica*, pp. 54, 60). In other words, it was Moore's contention against Spencer's evolutionary ethics that the naturalistic fallacy it embodies is grounded in a misconception of the role of intuition in ethics for which Sidgwick can be held responsible. Sylvester argues that we can grasp the significance of the naturalistic fallacy arguments in Moore's ethics only if we bear in mind how those arguments relate to the problem of self-evident truths and their mode of apprehension.

Sylvester wants to show this, in part, by taking up the discussion of Moore's intuitionism *before* he turns to the question of the naturalistic fallacy arguments. In so ordering his priorities, of course, Sylvester may seem to depart from the ordering that Moore himself suggests in *Principia,* where the naturalistic fallacy question dominates Moore's discussion of Spencer's ethics in Chapter 2 before he moves on to consider Sidgwick's intuitionism in Chapter 4. However, as Sylvester goes on to show, Moore's argument against Spencer's naturalistic ethics—thus the significance of the naturalistic fallacy itself—turns crucially upon what can and cannot be claimed as self-evident truths among the foundations of ethics. As Sylvester approaches the matter, Moore saw that the fallacy of Spencer's naturalistic ethics is invited by Sidgwick's *intuitive* identification of pleasure as the sole good, which in turn invites the fallacious identification of a natural property (pleasure) with a non-natural one (good).

In approaching Moore this way Sylvester's procedure is unique among critics and commentators, who, with few exceptions, tend to dismiss Moore's appeal to self-evidence and intuition as without any foundational significance while at the same time accepting his naturalistic fallacy argument as having independent validity. Thus it is common for critics who accept the naturalistic fallacy as favoring the emotivist or non-cognitivist approach to ethics—Ayer, Frankena, Stevenson—to dismiss the cognitive foundation for ethics that Moore himself supplies by means of intuition and self-evidence without serious examination of Moore's epistemological arguments or the ontology he supplies to back them up.

In so doing, as Sylvester shows in this chapter, they simply miss the point of Moore's intensive and detailed criticism of Sidgwick's system. Moore confines his attack to a single point of Sidgwick's epistemology, the question of how we come to *know* what good is, reserving consideration of the ontological status of the *object* of that knowledge to another context altogether. Chapter 3 of *Principia* is almost entirely devoted to epistemology and consists principally of an examination of Sidgwick's intuitionism. Chapter 4, which is a discussion of the ontological status of value, is conducted by reference to such famous metaphysicians of ethics as Plato, the stoics, Spinoza, and Kant. Sidgwick and intuitionism come into the later discussion only tangentially, the point of the exercise being to show that all metaphysical ethics is based on a mistake.

Moore's criticism of Sidgwick's intuitionist foundation for ethics is highly technical in that it is developed by means of the techniques of conceptual and linguistic analysis. Moore is perhaps even more famous for having introduced them to philosophy than he is for the prolegomena that he was attempting to establish for all future ethics. Indeed, were it not for the exercise of such technical means as these in the process of criticizing Spencer, Sidgwick, and various classical metaphysicians of ethics, we would probably regard Moore simply as having offered a revision of Sidgwick's ethics rather than as inaugurating a new beginning in analytical philosophy and ethics.

Because the foundation of Moore's ethics, like Sidgwick's, consists of non-inferential knowledge that both philosophers held to be self-evident, it should be pointed out that Sidgwick's tests for self-evidence are much less stringent than Moore's. Moreover, they include such tests as that all propositions held to be self-evident must be consistent and that there must be general agreement among experts as to their truth. Such criteria are of course indicative of Sidgwick's continuing allegiance to idealism, despite his utilitarianism and the strong emphasis he placed upon common sense. J. B. Schneewind, in his article on Moore in *The Encyclopedia of Philosophy*, gives a crisply stated account of the four principles that pass Sidgwick's tests for self-evidence:

(1) Whatever action anyone judges right for himself, he implicitly judges to be right for anyone else in similar circumstances. (2) One ought to have as much regard for future good or evil as for present, allowing for differences in certainty. (3) The good enjoyed by any individual is as important as the good enjoyed by any other. (4) A rational being is bound to aim generally at good. [vol. 7, p. 435]

The most solid effort to recapture the history of the period that immediately preceded Sidgwick's voluminous 1874 *Methods of Ethics* is J. B. Schneewind's *Sidgwick's Ethics and Victorian Moral Philosophy* (Oxford: Clarendon Press, 1977). As Schneewind points out, Sidgwick was nearing the end of his life and his service to Trinity College, Cambridge, when Russell and Moore came up to Cambridge and Trinity. He quotes Sidgwick on Russell's dissertation in 1895: "'both Whitehead and I have looked through it,' he said; 'We think it decidedly able'" (p. 16). And on Moore in 1900: "Moore! I did not know he had published any *Elements of Ethics*. I have no doubt they will be acute. So far as I have seen his work, his *acumen*—which is remarkable in degree—is in excess of his *in-*

sight" (p. 17). On the other hand, Schneewind reports that
Moore attended some of Sidgwick's lectures and "thought him
dull" (p. 16). Schneewind provides an excellent bibliography of
nineteenth-century sources as well as of commentary and criticism on Sidgwick's work. Schneewind is also the author of the
Encyclopedia of Philosophy article (quoted above), which
serves as an excellent introduction to Sidgwick. The article on
"Intuitionism" in the same work, by Richard Rorty, should
also be consulted for an account of the many varieties of intuitionism that have graced the history of philosophy.

An excellent bibliography and brief discussion of seven-
teenth- and eighteenth-century intuitionists can also be found
in W. D. Hudson's *Ethical Intuitionism* (London: Macmillan,
1967). Hudson interprets such intuitionists as Shaftesbury,
Price, Butler, and Hutcheson as "taking the view that men, as
such, are endowed with consciences which give them an immediate and unerring awareness of moral values" (p. vii). While
he may be aware that this is not Moore's view at all, Hudson
does point out the linkage between earlier intuitionists and
Moore that consists in their anticipations of the naturalistic
fallacy argument. A similar point is made by A. N. Prior, from
whom Hudson's point derives, in his *Logic and the Basis of
Ethics* (Oxford: Clarendon Press, 1949). Both Hudson and
Prior treat Moore's naturalistic fallacy argument as if the fallacy involved were a matter of logical rather than ontological
bad form. Moore himself, however, as Sylvester points out, understood Butler's maxim—which he takes as the epigraph for
Principia—as making an ontological point that it would be a
fallacy to deny, but *not* the naturalistic fallacy.

Perhaps the best known of Moore's contemporaries to write
both critically and appreciatively of Sidgwick and Moore is
C. D. Broad. His *Five Types of Ethical Theory* (New York:
Harcourt Brace, 1930) was in fact something of a successor to
Sidgwick's *Methods of Ethics* in the role of classroom text.
Broad also included the essay "Henry Sidgwick" in his *Ethics
and the History of Philosophy: Selected Essays* (London:
Routledge & Kegan Paul, 1952). See also Broad's contribution
to the Schilpp volume.

F. H. Bradley, Sidgwick's contemporary and critic, has an important essay, "Mr. Sidgwick on Ethical Studies," in his *Collected Essays* (Oxford: Clarendon Press, 1935). Brand Blanshard, one of Sidgwick's most ardent admirers in the second half of this century, presents an excellent portrait of Sidgwick in his *Four Reasonable Men: Marcus Aurelius, John Stuart Mill, Ernest Renan, Henry Sidgwick* (Middletown, Conn.: Wesleyan University Press, 1984).

Herbert Spencer's two-volume *Principles of Ethics*, first published in 1879, is most widely available in the 1892–1893 edition (London: Williams and Norgate). An excellent brief account of the influence of biological evolutionary theory upon ethics from Darwin to Spencer and beyond is given by Antony Flew in *Evolutionary Ethics* (London: Macmillan, 1967). Flew provides a useful bibliography as well.

Moore's 1898 *The Elements of Ethics*, referred to in the quote from Sidgwick above, was not published in Moore's lifetime. It will be available in an edition edited by Tom Regan and published by Temple University Press.

IV

Value Judgment:
The General Theory

1. *The Problem*

In the autobiographical essay written for the *Library of Living Philosophers* volume honoring his work, Moore reviews the early stages of his career. He points out that from 1896 through 1898 he was working to win a fellowship at Trinity College, Cambridge. The fruits of his studies on Kant's philosophy during this period were eventually published in two issues of *Mind*. But he also points out that during this period he was working through the metaphysical views of McTaggart and Bradley, trying to free himself from his initial acceptance of the idealism that had so long been in vogue at Cambridge.

His election to the Trinity fellowship in 1898 was followed by the publication of the last chapter of his fellowship thesis as a paper entitled "The Nature of Judgment." During the entire period, he tells us, he was thinking about the problems of ethics. "It was in writing the course on Ethics [which he had been asked to teach] that I developed the main outlines of *Principia Ethica*: but *Principia* was almost entirely a new, and was a much longer work, and the latter part of the six years (1898–1903) was mainly occupied in writing it." [1]

It seems sensible to remark that an appreciation of the views published in *Principia Ethica* may therefore be enhanced by some familiarity with the set of mind of the author as he worked on the book. As I have already indicated in the foregoing chapters on intuition, there are features of Moore's thought that were in transition during the period in question, especially his views on the nature of existence and truth. Yet it is possible—and important—to come to grips with the core of his thought in this 1898 to 1903

87

period. I use this chapter and the next to set forth the grounds and the materials that Moore used in formulating his analysis of judgments of value.

We have seen that Moore holds that good comes into existence—ingresses into the world—as an objective feature that is experienced by human beings. It is by means of acts of direct acquaintance—intuition—that good is known to qualify things and events in the world. We have seen that good is not, for Moore, a property of things that requires a special faculty or a magic gift enabling us to experience it. Good is discovered and known in much the same fashion as anything else is discovered and known. We experience it as we empirically notice things or events around us, and as we reflect on and judge of their properties and relations. Good is but one of the properties of things that have this objective, independent status.

Moore holds that such things and events are independent of our judgments about them. Moreover, their properties, qualities, and relations are ontologically independent of our judgments; and good, or value, is just one of the properties of things and events for which he claims this objective status.

In order to come to know *what* good is in the world through an act of intuition, Moore tells us, we may employ the method of isolation. Using this method we are able to hold an existing event in awareness in order to make a reflective judgment of the value that may be exemplified in it. Since the method is that by means of which we come to explicit awareness of value's existence in the world, it is appropriate that we glance briefly at what Moore hopes the method will bring.

The method of isolation is available "to decide the question, 'What things have value, and in what degree?'" To use it we may find that "it is necessary to consider what things are such that, if they existed *by themselves*, in absolute isolation, we should yet judge their *existence* to be good: and, in order to decide upon the relative *degrees* of value of different things, we must similarly consider what comparative value seems to attach to the isolated existence of each."[2] The method seems straightforward. And it is clear that the method supposes a notion of mind and its abilities that is also straightforward.

If the theory of judgment that issues from these straightforward beginnings does not strike us as itself equally straightforward, it is possible to blame the fact that the theory is not explicated in any detail in *Principia Ethica*. The task of *Principia* is not primarily epistemological—or, at least, Moore does not there pursue epistemology for its own sake—but he does tackle the epistemological question as to matters of judgment in two papers published, in 1899 and 1901.

2. *The Nature of Judgment: Concepts*

In the 1899 paper entitled "The Nature of Judgment"[3] Moore claims that when we judge we make use of the *logical* idea. The logical idea is contrasted sharply with the *psychological* idea. The two must not be confused.

A psychological idea, as we have seen, is a contingent entity produced in individual minds by stimuli that are also purely contingent. Truth and falsity cannot be understood in terms of a mere relation of contingent ideas to reality. For Moore maintains that whether or not our individual ideas correspond to things in the extramental world is irrelevant to the notion of truth. Of course, it is important that our individual psychological ideas be in correspondence with reality for us to know whether our ideas *may* be true or false, but that's not the issue.

The issue is the proper analysis of concepts, ideas and truth. The non-psychological idea, the *logical* idea as Moore calls it, is called also by the name 'concept.' Concepts have their own being, and that being is independent from psychological ideas.

Judgments appeal to concepts. Thus in order for judgments to be objective, it is important that we appreciate the fact that concepts cannot be thought to be mental in any sense. If the concept were a mental fact, or any part of a mental fact, judgment would be involved in a vicious circle. We could never come to grasp the nature of what Moore calls identity of content. Moore writes, "Identity of content is presupposed in any reasoning; and to explain the identity of content between two facts by supposing that content to be a part of the content of some third fact, must involve a vicious circle."[4] It is, then, the problem of securing intelligibility—identity of content between the concept and that about which the judgment is made—that prompts Moore to recognize the independence of concepts.

In an act of judgment the knower comes to judge objectively. The use of concepts guarantees that the knower is not merely going over events that have existence in his own awareness alone. The judgment "this tree is oak" or "the saving of a child's life is good" asserts a specific combination or arrangement of concepts. Thus the judgment has an objective ground. The one who articulates a judgment such as "this tree is oak" utters a proposition that he grasps directly as true. Since the proposition is nothing but a complex concept, a synthesis of concepts, the judgment cannot consist of mere subjective ideas. Concepts, since they are said to have being but not existence, have a mode of reality appropriate to being. They are immutable and eternal. Individual psychological ideas, by contrast, change and are temporal. Propositions referring to concepts that are themselves immutable, Moore holds, are immutable as well.

If someone can be said to know (correctly) both (a) this tree is oak and (b) the saving of that child's life is good, then there must *be* (ontologically) a proposition (a) and a proposition (b) for the knower *to know*. Moore explicates:

> With this, then, we have approached the nature of a proposition or judgment. A proposition is composed not of words, nor yet of thoughts, but of concepts. Concepts are possible objects of thought, but that is no definition of them. It merely states that they may come into relation with a thinker, and in order that they *may* do anything, they must already *be* something. It is indifferent to their nature whether anybody thinks them or not. They are incapable of change: and the relation into which they enter with the knowing subject implies no action or reaction. It is a unique relation which can begin or cease with a change in the subject; but the concept is neither cause not effect of such a change. The occurrence of the relation has, no doubt, its causes and effects, but these are to be found only in the subject.[5]

Moore's point is, as we have said, that concepts *are*. They are timeless. They are incapable of change. They do not change because they *cannot* change. This means that they are not *causes* either; for causes must exist, and concepts have being but *not* existence. According to Moore, however, individual minds may, and do, come into contact with them. [They are said to 'come before the mind' or to be 'held before the mind' in mental states of awareness.] Such contact is due to the *existing* causes in the situation in which the individual mind finds itself.

I try to illustrate this by reference to my earlier example of the hiker who comes upon a child floating down a river on an inner tube. If the hiker discovers himself in a situation where the child is about to be carried over the falls, the existing state of affairs may well cause the hiker to entertain certain concepts—life, death, safety, waterfall, and others. If the hiker grasps the proposition "the saving of the life of the child is good," it is no doubt because he is in the contingent situation he is. But it's the situation that causes his response, not the proposition.

The proposition is eternally what it is. Though it may enter into the situation, it neither changes the situation nor is changed by it. According to Moore's 1899 view in "The Nature of Judgment," the act of cognition by means of which the hiker grasps the character of the value elements in the situation is simply the cognition of a complex existential proposition; in other words, a proposition that has, as a part of its constitution, the unanalyzable property of existence as well as the unanalyzable property of good. (It is in this essay that Moore claims that both truth and existence are simple unanalyzable concepts.) So with respect to the hiker's judgment it would appear that for him to be aware of the particular situation as it is—including the presence of value—is for him to cognize a proposition of a certain type. This may be all that Moore intends by his (grammatically odd) remark: "All that exists is thus composed of concepts necessarily related to one another in specific manners, and likewise to the concept of existence."[6]

It is indeed difficult to bring more precision to the view than this. Moore's essay is vague on how concepts that have being but not existence relate to each other and to existents. He says that he follows Bradley in the matter.[7] So perhaps at that stage he has not yet shaken free from the habits of mind that he had picked up from idealism. In any case, Moore's treatment of the question of existence is clarified by the time he writes *Principia Ethica*; clarified at least in the sense that he recognizes the reality of the realm of existence as the natural order.

3. *The Nature of Concepts: In* "*Identity*" *(1900) and* Principia Ethica *(1903)*

Good is clearly a concept, according to *Principia Ethica*. I have been speaking of good all along as if it were a concept, as genuine a concept as any other. It may be unnecessary to emphasize the point, but I do so anyway owing to its extreme importance and the fact that some treatments of Moore's position tend to obscure the fact, or neglect it, in favor of emphasizing that good is a simple and unanalyzable quality.

As I have shown in Chapter I of the present book, the initial chapter in *Principia Ethica* is given over to an analysis of good. The meaning of the term 'good' is grasped by reference to the concept. Moore does not invoke the notion of intuition in claiming that good is simple and indefinable. In Moore's use the reference of 'good' is revealed by philosophical reflection and analysis. In *Principia Ethica* Moore explains that it is a concept, an object of thought. He writes that good "is simple and has no parts. It is one of those innumerable objects of thought which are themselves incapable of definition, because they are the ultimate terms by reference to which whatever is capable of definition must be defined."[8]

In his review of Brentano's *The Origins of Our Knowledge of Right and Wrong*, published in the same year as *Principia*, Moore says, "As regards intrinsic value, his [Brentano's] theory has the almost unique merit in that it defines 'good in itself,' not only as an *objective* concept, but as containing that very concept which is in fact denoted by the words."[9] The italicized term "objective" is Moore's. Good is a concept, an objective notion, an object of thought. It has all the characteristics that concepts have in "The Nature of Judgment"; it is changeless, timeless, and, as such, objective—independent of any subjective awareness of it.

In an essay in the *Proceedings of the Aristotelian Society* for 1900–1901 [entitled "Identity"], Moore again presses forward the view that a concept may be an independent and objective entity. In discussing the meaning of identity, he invokes a traditional metaphysical doctrine to secure his view; the traditional pattern of analysis of the relationship between universals and particulars. The text clearly shows that Moore thinks the traditional analysis to be correct, for he claims that universals may be predicated of particulars, but particulars can be predicated neither of universals nor of particulars. [His account takes on a markedly Platonic flavor here.] He says that particulars exist, but that universals do not. Universals have being nonetheless. Like concepts, they *are*.

The text reads: "it seems certain that this red and that red do exist, but very doubtful whether redness itself does. And equally certain that this red is red; whereas undoubtedly red itself is not this red, nor this red that red." [10] Moore means to argue that "this red" exists—not "this red thing" exists. Although "this red thing" *does* exist, it—the thing—is a composite particular. "This red" is a simple particular. I return to this ontological point in Chapter VI. In the present chapter I am concerned to deal with universals such as redness and good.

Finally, in the 1910–1911 lectures[11] Moore argues once again for the *being* of universals. He says that universals "are" or "have being" and must be distinguished from entities that exist. He argues for the reality of propositions—they too have being, or at least Moore claims they do in one of the lectures. I am not particularly eager to secure Moore's opinion on the status of propositions in 1910. I am, however, in 1903, for that will help us to understand *Principia*. The essay "Experience and Empiricism," which I cited in Chapter II,[12] shows that the *Principia Ethica* ontology remains, in this respect, embedded in the view developed in both "Judgment" and "Identity."

4. *The Existing Universe, Truth and Judgments of Value*

Moore holds that human beings discover value in things in the world. We become directly acquainted with good in things and events. It is through the exercise of acts of cognitive judgment that we can pick out value in things and events. One way for the mind to judge of value is by an act of conceptual isolation where one considers a state of affairs "lifted from" the flux of contingencies within which it exists. How are we to understand what is grasped in conceptual isolation?

In Chapter II, where I discussed the notion of truth, I pointed out that Moore does not discuss it as a concept in *Principia Ethica*. Good is said to be simple and unanalyzable, of course, but truth is not cited as another example of that sort of concept. Numbers are said to be non-natural properties of existing events, like good. But truth is not explicitly included in the category of non-natural along with good and numbers. Moore does claim that there *are* truths, and that truths have being (but not existence), and he may even imply that propositions *that are true* have being.[13]

But the fact is that it is to the entry in Baldwin's *Dictionary* (1902) and to "Experience and Empiricism" that one must turn to discover Moore's view with respect to truth in 1903. I have implied that whether truth is a concept or not makes no effective difference for the dynamics involved in intuiting value in the world. Whether the a priori thesis or the a posteriori thesis is closest to Moore's own view in 1903, it is clear that judgment of the self-evidence of a truth such as that "the child is in the inner tube" can be made.

The mind is capable of judging (the proposition) that the saving of the life of the child is good. The mind is capable of holding a state of affairs—such as that a child is saved from a waterfall—in awareness by means of the proposition 'the child is saved from the waterfall.' This proposition reflects—or, better, is—a complex concept. Moore has told us that a proposition is true if (or when) the state of affairs that it states is identical [or corresponds] with an experienced state of affairs. Moreover, Moore at least *seems* to imply that the truth of such a proposition is self-evident. If truth is a simple and unanalyzable concept, it would seem to be one more component in an even *more* complex proposition.

5. *Value Judgment and Error*

Suppose the hiker pulls the child from the river. Someone judges it to be true that the saving of the life of the child is good. Moore has said that the judgment may be false; one may be mistaken when one makes such a judgment. In every way that it is possible to cognize a true proposition, it is equally possible to cognize a false one. The method of isolation has been proposed, by Moore, to help curtail the possibility of error. The one who judges it to be true that the saving of the life of the child is good arrives at this judgment by examining the proposition and isolating it from contingencies irrelevant to its terms. Is the proposition self-evidently true? Can inspection of it, in isolation, certify that its firmness is more than mere psychological certitude?

No. For, as our discussion of general propositions and self-evidence has shown, one might be able to shake the firmness of a purported self-evident instance of value-ingression. One could fashion a counterexample to the case suggested: find a situation when it is not clear that the saving of the child's life was good. A counterexample would be another conceptually isolated instance and would therefore, be an example of the method Moore suggests.

But let us suppose that after all attempts to manufacture counterexamples fail, the self-evidence in the instance persuades the intellect of the truth of the proposition. What follows, according to *Principia Ethica*?

Accepting the fact that *Principia* and "The Conception of Intrinsic Value" have relevantly similar ontological grounds, it follows that wherever and whenever a child's life is saved, and is expressed by a true proposition, the event is must be—good. [Supervenience again. See bibliographical notes for Chapter 6.]

What can be said about an occasion when a person notes that a child's life has been saved yet fails to discover in the event the goodness that, according to the theory, must be there? The theory stipulates that if the saving of the life of a child is intrinsically good, anything precisely like it would also be good. [Superveniently, we might say.] The person who misses good's existence in the event has made an error. Can error be understood?

We should here point out that Moore's doctrine allows for good to be missed (in a judgment) in two different ways. Granting the truth of the proposition in question, an error could come about as follows. Error 1: The person could fail to see the actual situation. From the welter of contingencies in the situation, the person could have attended to a facet of the whole that did not have value. For example, one of the hiker's companions, knowing of the heart complications, noticed only that his friend plunged into the water to begin vigorously swimming to the child. He rivets attention on the danger to the friend. When he hears another say, "That's good!" referring to the saving of the child, the hiker's companion says, "No, it's not." He means, of course, his friend's act of strenuous exertion. The potential danger to the hiker in the act is what the friend's judgment intends.

Error 2: One might see, correctly, the actual event and discriminate the pattern quite correctly as well, but fail to grasp the goodness. There may be many reasons for missing the value. If, for example, the child who was saved had some days earlier carelessly blinded the son of the person making the judgment, the fact that the observer did not grasp the good in saving *that* child may be understandable, though hardly condoned.

The errors cited are ones that Moore suggested in his analysis of beauty. One could call the two orders of error by the names Moore suggested in the last chapter of *Principia*, thus, error 1 is an error of fact, and error 2 is an error of value. The two types of error have non-value analogues, I think. I indicate what I have in mind as follows.

As an analogue to error of fact: Contrast an experienced bird-watcher with a novice. An experienced bird-watcher has learned to pick out, from the natural patterns of colors and shapes, precisely the colors and shape that is the flicker. In one sense the novice sees what the experienced watcher sees. But in the appropriate sense, the novice fails to see the fact; he does not see at all. Thus the novice commits an error of fact.

As an analogue to error of value: Consider a person who comes to an art gallery to view an exhibition of contemporary paintings. The person is told to be sure to see the series of paintings whose colors move. The viewer goes to the paintings with great anticipation. He does not have the experience that others report having. The shaped colors that to the normal eye seem to move do not affect the viewer. He is able to describe in the appropriate terms the painting and its shapes and colors. He does not see the illusion. He grasps the pattern as do others, but he does not share the motion-of-colors experience.

6. *Concepts and Existence, Once Again*

We saw in Section 2 above that in "The Nature of Judgment," Moore, following Bradley's lead, conceived of existence as a simple and unanalyzable concept. Existence apparently entered propositions—complex concepts—as did good or truth. We have seen that early on (1899) the existing world was nothing but a proposition with the concept of existence included. Precisely how the concept *existence* grounded the existent world so that the world becomes other than concepts I am unable to tell, for the essay does little more than assert the view. I have implied, however, that by the time *Principia Ethica* was published Moore's thought had changed. I meant only that, in *Principia*, Moore distinguishes the being of concepts from the existence of things. In fact, already in "Identity," the 1900–1901 essay, Moore recognizes the existence of simple particulars as distinct from universals that *are*.

In the 1899 paper Moore had argued: (*a*) that concepts are mind-independent, and (*b*) that the *world is formed out of concepts*. The world is formed out of concepts; so much so that there *is* no real difference between the conceptual order and the existential order. Moore writes: "The opposition of concepts to existents disappears, since an existent is seen to be nothing but a concept or a complex of concepts standing in a unique relation to the concept of existence. . . . It now appears that perception is to be regarded philosophically as the cognition of an existential proposition." [14] The difference between being and existence, under this analysis, is only modal. [In other words, things that have being have it necessarily, whereas things that have existence have it contingently.] When the concept existence is conjoined with other concepts in a complex of related concepts (a proposition), then and only then does a thing have existence. When a complex concept has the proper relation with existence, the existential proposition *is* the state of affairs, necessarily.

Principia Ethica gives no such analysis. But in "Experience and Empiricism," an essay that appeared in the same year [1903], there is something that comes close to such an analysis. *Principia* seems to suppose an existing world that has genuine and independent status. And it seems clear that the distinction between natural and non-natural properties—essential to *Principia*—cannot stand up unless there is a natural world of *existence* to be contrasted to a world of *being*.

I return to the problem in Chapter VI, but I want to remind the reader here of a point that Moore articulates [in the early essay on "Identity"] concerning identity. This red *exists*; but red itself does not, it simply *is*. Without this distinction it is impossible to make sense of Moore's position, and yet it is ignored by almost all his critics. [See bibliographical notes.]

In 1905, Moore published a paper entitled "The Nature and Reality of the Objects of Perception." In this piece he held that existence is a concept that "seems to me to be so simple that it cannot be expressed in words, except those which are regarded as its synonyms." He thinks, furthermore, that "the property, we have seen, is neither identical with nor inclusive of that complex one we mean by the words "is perceived." [15] Moore seems perplexed by the notion of existence in 1905. But whatever it means, apparently it no longer is such that we may understand perception to be analyzed simply as "cognition of an existential proposition." The world of existence, the one we perceive, *is there* and is given.

By 1910–1911 Moore seems clearly committed to three distinguishable ontological constituents of the universe: (1) particulars, which exist; (2) universals, which have being or *are*; (3) truths, or facts, which have being. It is not clear, at this point in Moore's development, whether he considers that facts or truths are complex concepts—complexes of universals. However, I think the *Principia* view is closer to the 1910–1911 lectures, for in both, particulars (things) *exist*, and universals (concepts) have *being*. Thus *Principia* seems to accept the being of propositions (which one might call facts; he would call them truths). Moreover, *Principia* presupposes the existence of simple particulars that exist. In any event, we have another opportunity to clarify this whole matter in Chapter VI, which is given over to a thorough examination of the ontological commitments of *Principia Ethica*.

I have been concerned to clarify Moore's views on value judgment in the present chapter. The discussion involved presenting Moore's notion of concepts, their status and their use, in the context of *Principia*'s doctrine. There, as we have seen, concepts or universals are the proper objects of thought. We make use of concepts in logical judgment—judgment properly speaking. In this respect, value judgments are identical to judgments of fact; they are objective. Value judgments, when true, require that a concept be properly part of a complex; that is, part of a complex proposition. And that proposition must be true in a sense that is *logically* independent of existential conditions.

Already in his 1903 review of a book by Brentano, Moore began moving away from his earlier and more extreme conceptualist view. He states in 1903: "truths of the form 'this is good in itself' are logically independent of any truths about that which exists. No ethical judgment of this form is such that, if a certain thing exists, it is true, whereas if that thing does not exist, it is false. All ethical truths are true, whatever the nature of the world may be." [16] So, even before *Principia* was undertaken, Moore had already reached the conclusion that there is conceptual order of being, as well as a natural (existential) order that is ontologically distinct and logically independent.

We come to grasp ethical truths conceptually. Whether a proposition is true—for example, that the saving of the life of a child is good—is not contingent upon the concept 'existence' playing a role in the complex. It may be that a set of contingent existing conditions are such that someone is caused to become aware of the proposition. Indeed, because a person notices a child being pulled from the river he is in a position to intuit the truth of the proposition that the saving of the life of a child is good. That's the epistemological point. The logical point remains secure, namely that the truth of the proposition is independent of the contingent fact; that is, this child being pulled from the river today. [The securing of this logical point by Moore should not be taken as placing the supervenience of true ethical judgments in jeopardy. See bibliographical notes for Chapter VI discussion.]

Judgments of value are propositional. If we know that the proposition 'the saving of the life of a child is good' is true, the self-evidence of the proposition permits us to declare the judgment independently of what actually exists.

Principia Ethica is committed to the existence of a world that is independent of a realm of concepts. If 'existence' is still indefinable and simple, qua concept (in 1903), what it means and how it is to be understood as a concept are not at all clear. In 1903 there seems to be a natural world distinct from a conceptual world. Likewise there are non-natural properties as distinct from natural ones. The natural world exists and concepts do not. Yet concepts enable us to make intelligible factual *and* value judgments concerning the natural world.

It remains for the succeeding chapters to deal with Moore's efforts to resolve the apparent anomalies that these divisions (or categories) present. But some hints as to the shape of those efforts may be gleaned from a discussion of the famous two worlds argument that Moore develops in *Principia*.

7. *The Two Worlds Argument*

I close the present chapter by reviewing one of Moore's most frequently cited arguments. I choose to do so in this chapter, for its force is to be appreciated, I think, in the light of the theory of concepts I have presented here. Known as the two worlds argument, Moore invokes it in hopes of casting doubt upon Sidgwick's intuition to the effect that pleasure alone is good and the supporting arguments that Sidgwick offers. Here is the way that Moore presents it:

> Let us imagine one world exceedingly beautiful. Imagine it as beautiful as you can; put into it whatever on this earth you most admire—mountains, rivers, the sea, trees and sunsets, stars and moon. Imagine these all combined in the most exquisite proportions, so that no one thing goes against another, but each contributes to increase the beauty of the whole. And then imagine the ugliest world that you can possibly conceive. Imagine it simply one heap of filth, containing everything that is most disgusting to us, for whatever reason, and the whole, as far as may be, without one redeeming feature. . . . The only thing we are not entitled to imagine is that any human being ever has or ever, by any possibility, *can* live in either, can ever see and enjoy the beauty of the one, or hate the foulness of the other. Well, even so, supposing them quite

apart from any possible contemplation by any human beings; still, is it irrational to hold that it is better that the beautiful world exist, than the one which is ugly? Would it not be well, in any case, to do what we could to produce it rather than the other?[17]

Several comments are appropriate. First: Moore's analysis of conceptual judgment makes thought experiments of the above sort a matter of course. One surely can imagine a beautiful world and an ugly one. One can conceptualize two such worlds as well, if the notions of imagine and conceptualize indicate two separate acts of awareness, as some have claimed. In Moore's 1898 (and 1903) thought, one can reflect upon propositions—complex concepts—that represent the two worlds.

There have been criticisms of the Moore thought experiment on the ground that Moore banished an observer out the front door only to sneak one in through the rear. One critic says that the very choice of language, the choice of terms that are not purely descriptive, requires human tastes, preferences, likes and dislikes for the meanings involved: "to imagine something as beautiful or ugly, admirable or disgusting, is already 'to react' to it."[18]

Moore's view is, as we have noted, that if a term conveys meaning it *is* a concept—simple or complex. What goes on in any *soma* or *psyche*, what events flow through an individual's existing body or mind, may be important for that individual's search for concepts to make a situation intelligible, but that is a mere contingency. Terms that mean non-descriptive elements in experience are as *bound to concepts* for intelligibility as are descriptive terms. Moore has no difficulty in accepting that emotive notions require certain affective responses from a knower. Moore's analysis of beauty is evidence of his acknowledgment of the place of emotive response and emotive meaning.

Second: The two worlds argument is constructed for a specific purpose. The purpose is to show that a particular intuition of Sidgwick's is not self-evidently true. We have seen, in Chapter III, that Moore suggests a method for dealing with contrary intuitions. The quotation above is preceded in *Principia Ethica* with these observations: "'No one,' says Prof. Sidgwick, 'would consider it rational to aim at the production of beauty in external nature, apart from any possible contemplation of it by human beings.' Well, I may say at once, that I, for one, do consider this rational; and let us see if I cannot get anyone to agree with me."[19]

The use of the argument, then, is philosophical, not experiential. To be used philosophically, in the present context, involves being reflectively critical about concepts. The fact that someone is making judgments about two complex situations—described by different complexes of concepts—and noting that one of the complexes is more valuable than the other is not particularly startling. To judge, further, hypothetically producing one and not the other, because the one is more beautiful than the other, is not surprising. Hypothetically producing the one, if one could, because it was beautiful even if no one ever would see it, know it, or appreciate it does not seem irrational. We can *think* the experiment because we *can conceptualize* what we are asked to conceptualize. If what has been said is correct, then Moore's argument does not depend as much on any special theory of concepts as it does on his general theory of judgment, the theory that has been under consideration in this chapter. Which is to say, of course, that the argument *itself* depends upon meanings, that concepts are meanings that enable our thoughts to reach beyond the contingent (natural) order of things.

Third: Moore stresses beauty in the argument—a beautiful world as opposed to an ugly world. In Chapter I, Sections 10 and 11, I discussed the definition of 'beauty' and showed that Moore defines 'beauty' in terms of good, or intrinsic value. In Chapter I, Section 7 I went over the notion of 'better than.' If one state of affairs is better than another, then it has more value than the other, and, given a choice between these two (and only these two), we ought to bring the better one into existence. Intrinsic value is called, by Moore, 'ought-to-be'. There is an opportunity to discuss the notion of ought-to-be in Chapter VII, but I think it appropriate to point out now that if something is better than something else, it has a claim for existence by virtue of what it is. The claim is a claim *on an agent*, to be sure. Thus Moore maintains, if an action in the power of an agent would bring the better world into existence *even if* no one would ever be in commerce with it, the agent has a duty to bring it into existence.

Moore believes his argument to be conceptually clear. He does not, of course, think he has, by means of the argument, *proved* Sidgwick's intuition to be false. But he does think he has shown that Sidgwick's intuition is not self-evident. He has shown, he believes, that it is not irrational—in fact that it is rational—to bring beauty into existence even if no one will be able, ever, to experience it.

CRITICAL BIBLIOGRAPHY: CHAPTER IV

In *Bloomsbury's Prophet* Tom Regan quotes a letter from Moore to Desmond MacCarthy dated August 14, 1898: "I have arrived at a perfectly staggering doctrine," Moore says. "An existent is nothing but a proposition: Nothing *is* but concepts" (p. 106). Moore was at the time working out the details of his "Second Dissertation," which was submitted later that same year for the Prize Fellowship at Trinity. It bore the same title—*The Metaphysical Basis of Ethics*—as his "First Dissertation" despite the fact that the earlier effort had failed to win the competition. In this second effort, as in the first, Moore was searching for a release from idealism and the theory of the internal relations of ideas. He would break out of the confines of what he took to be the mentalistic or psychological approach to truth—and hence to metaphysics— by means of this stunning discovery. "I am pleased to believe," he went on to say, "that this is the most Platonistic system of modern times; though it is also not so far from Kant, as you might think at first."

It was of course far from a system as yet. But Moore extracted from it the essay on "The Nature of Judgment" that forms the key to the ontology underlying *Principia Ethica*, as Sylvester points out in this chapter. In his Schilpp volume autobiography, Moore recaptures the significance of his new insight by recalling Bradley's contention that "truth and falsehood depend on the relation of our ideas to reality." Bradley understood this claim as requiring that the meaning of an idea consists in a part of its content "cut off, fixed by the mind, and considered apart from the existence" of the idea in question. Moore continues:

> It seemed to me, if I remember right, that the meaning of an idea was not anything 'cut off' from it, but something wholly independent of mind. I tried to argue for this position, and this was the beginning, I think, of certain tendencies in me which have led some people to call me a "Realist," and was also the beginning of a breakaway from belief in Bradley's philosophy, of which, up until then, both Russell and I had, following McTaggart, been enthusiastic admirers. I remember McTaggart once saying of an occasion when he met Bradley at Oxford that, when Bradley came in, he felt "as if a Platonic Idea had walked into the room." [Schilpp, p. 22]

Russell and Moore were revolting against Bradley's idealist and Hegelian tendencies, of course, not his Platonism.

Of this same period in their revolt against Bradley, Russell says this:

> I think that the first published account of the new philosophy was Moore's article in *Mind* on "The Nature of Judgement." Although neither he nor I would now adhere to all the doctrines of this article, I, and I think he, would still agree with its negative part—i.e. with the doctrine that fact is in general independent of experience. Although we were in agreement, I think that we differed as to what most interested us in our new philosophy. I think that Moore was most concerned with the refutation of idealism, while I was most interested in the refutation of monism. [*My Philosophical Development*, New York: Simon & Schuster, 1959, p. 54]

In any case, among Moore's readers at the time, Russell was to be almost alone in taking Moore's new Realism seriously. ⸖

Moore himself notes that James Ward, one of the dissertation's internal examiners, thought he showed all too much enthusiasm for "picking holes in accepted views" and that he was altogether "too skeptical." We have already quoted Sidgwick's judgment that Moore's acumen was "in excess of his insight," and Regan adds that Bernard Bosanquet, who had been brought in as an outside examiner, held that Moore's claims appeared to him to "lie beyond the limits of paradox permitted in philosophy" (Regan, p. 101). An assessment of Moore's theory of existents was confirmed in even less flattering terms in subsequent years by Gilbert Ryle, who is quoted by Regan from *Moore: Essays in Retrospect* (p. 99): "Moore here seems to have gone temporarily crazy."

But if Moore had "gone temporarily crazy," so of course had Russell. He wrote to Moore in September 1898, congratulating him on the dissertation and suggesting the unsettling effect that it was bound to have on the idealist establishment: "I fear Caird's hair will stand on end when he learns that an existent is a proposition" (quoted from *Bloomsbury's Prophet*, p. 106; Edward Caird, 1835–1908, a leading Hegelian idealist, was successor to Benjamin Jowett as master of Balliol College, Oxford).

Russell had his own reasons for being delighted with Moore's discovery of the independent reality of truth, for so conceived the truth of logic could be freed from the taint of subjectivism and psychologism—not to mention the reductive monism implied by the doctrine of internal relations—with which it had been infected since Kant. As Russell saw the matter, Moore's discovery that "an existent is a proposition" paved the way to the independence of logic, not only from psychology, but from the prevailing idealist neo-Kantian ontology as well; thenceforth it would be logic that set the parameters of ontology and the foundations of knowledge, not the other way round. For Russell, Moore's staggering conclusion helped open the path to a conception of the relationship of logic to mathematics that he was already exploring in the work of Gottlob Frege, the German logician and mathematician whose work Russell would introduce to an English-speaking audience for the first time in *The Principles of Mathematics* (Cambridge: Cambridge University Press, 1903).

Moore's autobiography in the Schilpp volume should be consulted for Moore's disclaimer of the extent to which he actually influenced Russell's subsequent development. Although Moore admits to the close relationship between their ideas at several points, he also says, "I do not know that Russell has ever owed to me anything except mistakes" (p. 15). This judgment of Moore's, if excessively modest, is nevertheless given some confirmation by that fact that the story of Russell's developments in logic is often told without any reference to Moore at all. As an example of this, see Martha and William Kneale, *The Development of Logic* (Oxford: Clarendon Press, 1984).

Perhaps because so much commentary and criticism of Moore's ethics is preoccupied with the matter of the naturalistic fallacy arguments, little attention is paid to Moore's insistence, in "The Nature of Judgment" and perhaps in *Principia Ethica* as well, that truth is a property directly possessed by true propositions. As Moore saw the matter, truth and falsity are not determined by anything like success or failure in achieving a correspondence between something in the mind and something real in the outside world; between internal ideas and external things. As a property, truth, like good, is both logically and ontologically independent of the mind, a doctrine that Moore does not begin to question until at least 1910 or 1911, as the essays in *Some Main Problems of Philosophy* show.

It is Moore's insistence—in "The Nature of Judgment"— upon the total independence of truth from whatever *we* may think it to be, that Sylvester wants us to see in the present chapter. This total independence, he points out, is stressed by means of the distinction that Moore makes between the psychological idea and the logical idea (or concept) to which it is supposed to be related. (Compare the similar notion in

Russell's *Principles of Mathematics*, pp. 44 and 47.) The argument is simply that Bradley's notion of universal meaning, which Moore takes to be equivalent to Kant's "*gemeinsamer Begriff*," cannot be reached by abstraction from *our* ideas or what Kant had called our *Vorstellungen*; thus Moore says "it is our object to protest against this description of a concept as an 'abstraction' from ideas" ("The Nature of Judgment," p. 177 [Regan, p. 61]).

As Sylvester reads "The Nature of Judgment," Moore was already laying the groundwork for the theory of ethics that he would work out in *Principia Ethica*. Concepts, if they are not to be abstractions that depend for their existence upon our minds, and are to have their truth and meaning in total independence of whatever we may think or experience, must *be* timeless in themselves. Like Platonic ideas they must *transcend* existence in time, but nevertheless be capable of entering into time in the framework of true propositions and judgments. That is, they must, when they enter into time, *be* what makes certain propositions about the world *objectively true*. It is in this sense that concepts can be said to have being without the *necessity* of having their being in existence.

As Moore wrote to Desmond MacCarthy, the view of truth expressed in the "Second Dissertation" is indeed Platonistic and also closer to Kant than "you might think at first." But it is far easier to see the connection with Plato than with Kant, for Moore's main arguments were all directed against Kant's— and Bradley's—views of the nature of synthetic a priori judgments. What Moore attacks, however, is not the notion of synthetic a priori judgment *as such*, but the account that idealism—*à la* Kant—gives in order to explain and justify it. Moore himself wants to make synthetic judgments that are *close* to being a priori—at least as close as acquaintance, intuition, and self-evidence can come to being a priori—but he wants to drop the psychological account of them that is implicit in Kantian and neo-Kantian idealism. He wants to shake completely free of the idea that truth is in any way dependent upon the internal powers of the mind or upon categories of the mind that impinge on experience. As Sylvester showed in

Chapter III, Moore worked out his own version of intuition in *Principia* by borrowing from Sidgwick's quasi-empiricist account of judgment rather than any Kantian account of the a priori forms of intuition. The staggering conclusion reached in the "Second Dissertation" merely anticipates that of *Principia Ethica*; like "existence" and "truth" itself, "good" names a concept that is entirely independent of the mind, both logically and ontologically.

In his own dissertation and in the Preface to the present book, Sylvester credits Gustav Bergmann and Herbert Hochberg with opening up access to Moore's ontology by showing the linkage between "The Nature of Judgment" and *Principia Ethica*. The seminal essays of Bergmann and Hochberg are conveniently collected in Klemke's anthology *Studies in the Philosophy of G. E. Moore*, which we have listed in the General Bibliography at the end of Chapter I. See also, in Klemke, the attempted refutation of Hochberg's thesis by John O. Nelson, "Mr. Hochberg on Moore: Some Corrections" (pp. 128–40), and Hochberg's reply, "Some Reflections on Mr. Nelson's Corrections" (pp. 141–54). In view of the emphasis that Sylvester places on the ontological foundations of Moore's ethics, and on the work of Bergmann and Hochberg in opening up the matter on the basis of "The Nature of Judgment," it is significant—oddly so—that Regan's *Bloomsbury's Prophet*, which contains a chapter largely devoted to that essay, includes no mention of Bergmann or Hochberg or, indeed, of the ontological implications linking that essay with *Principia Ethica*. It seems equally significant that Rohatyn's account of Moore's ethics, which skims lightly over the question of Moore's ontology altogether, makes no mention of "The Nature of Judgment" at all, though Hochberg's "Moore's Ontology and Non-natural Properties" appears in Rohatyn's bibliography. It would seem that neither Regan nor Rohatyn felt any need to deal with the ontological theory underlying *Principia*, for each in his own way has other fish to fry. Regan wants to show Moore off as a (somewhat local) social and literary prophet, and Rohatyn wants to display him as a (somewhat reluctant) naturalist. Whether these ends fully justify neglect of Moore's ontology, however, remains in question.

In the chapters that follow this one, Sylvester goes on to develop Hochberg's insight as to the connection between Moore's non-natural properties and the concept of good in a way very different from any that Hochberg suggests or may have intended. As it turns out, Hochberg was to become far more interested in the development of Russell's move in the direction of logical atomism than he was in Moore's development after *Principia*. See his *Thought, Fact, and Reference: The Origins and Ontology of Logical Atomism* (Minneapolis: University of Minnesota Press, 1978), which contains an excellent discussion of the early links between Moore and Russell during the period of their escape from idealism.

Although he neglects the application of Moore's ontology to the problems of ethics, David O'Connor devotes two chapters to abstract entities in *The Metaphysics of G. E. Moore* (Dordrecht, Netherlands: D. Reidel, 1982). O'Connor is well aware of the importance of these concepts in Moore's epistemology, especially with regard to their survival in modified form in Moore's common sense realism. But it is to be regretted that he insists upon missing the point of Moore's distinction between real and existent entities by speaking of their hypostatization by Moore (pp. 154–56).

Judgments in Particular Contexts

1. *The Problem*

Whenever we make actual aesthetic or moral judgments, we do so in some actual contexts in which we may be said to 'live through' the judgments we make. In this chapter I want to examine Moore's treatment of what it means to 'live through' such judgments. Hence I am not primarily concerned with theoretical or philosophical judgments as such, though the nature of such judgments provides the background against which practical judgments are made. I am interested in examining Moore's account of what is involved in actually judging that something is beautiful, or that some action is right, or that a particular motive is evil or a particular person is saintly.

I approach Moore's thought concerning judgments such as these from two vantage points. One point of view can be called philosophical, and it is from this point of view that I give an analysis of the elements that Moore takes to be involved in the experience of making judgments. The second vantage point that I use can be characterized as an experiential perspective. From this perspective I hope to elucidate the experience of the one who makes the judgment under investigation.

Judgments with practical ethical implications are judgments that involve reasoning and calculation. I am not primarily concerned with questions of either self-evidence or intuition here, but with the complexity of the judgment process. Aesthetic judgments likewise involve a complexity that, in symmetry with ethical judgments, cannot be exhausted by reference to the self-evidence of the terms involved, nor can they be explained simply by reference to intuition. So it may be helpful to begin with a look at such judgments.

2. *The* Guernica *Is Beautiful*

For a person to make the judgment [of Picasso's well-known painting] that the *Guernica* is beautiful, it is required that the person find value in the painting and have an appropriate emotional response to the value experienced. We have seen, from the discussion of beauty in Chapter I, that a person who judges that X is beautiful may be mistaken. In any given experience of a painting the person who views the painting may believe that there is value in it whether there is or not. Moreover, the person experiencing the painting may notice the value, but may have an inappropriate emotional response to that value. In either case, a mistake has been made.

Within the experience the viewer says "it's beautiful" because the viewer is involved both cognitively and emotively *with the object*. No actual truthful judgment that something is beautiful, Moore contends, can be made without the presence of this appropriate emotional response.

Philosophical analysis of the experience of beauty suggests the definition of 'beauty,' which Moore gives as *that of which the admiring contemplation is good in itself*. As we have seen, this means that an object is good and is an element in a wider context, which is *also* good. When someone notices that the *Guernica* is beautiful, he *both* notices that the *Guernica* is good *and* has an appropriate emotional response to the value he sees in the painting. Consequently, the whole organic unity—the viewer knowing and feeling the value in the painting—is good.

Moore does not claim that *in* the experience, when the viewer judges the *Guernica* to be beautiful, the viewer has *both* the painting and his own emotional state as objects for judgment. What he claims is that *unless* the viewer has an emotional response appropriate to the value in the painting, a judgment that it is beautiful cannot be *correctly* made. From the experiential point of view, the viewer sees, feels, and reports—"it's beautiful." If the experience is properly grounded, the report is true. In the experience the painting's value is known and felt as beautiful.

3. *The Experience of Being Obliged*

Suppose a person is working in an organization with a number of colleagues, some of whom are in the process of being evaluated for promotion or dismissal. Suppose, in one case, a colleague whom the person knows to be of quality is in danger of being dismissed. If the person in question speaks in behalf of the colleague in jeopardy, the termination will probably not occur. In such a situation the person may *feel* a duty, an obligation, to present the required evidence. It is from the felt givenness of such situations that intuitionist theories of obligation no doubt find their starting point. Moore does not dispute the psychological immediacy of such feelings, but he does deny that the question of obligation is to be understood and grounded at the level of psychological givenness.

In the case above, the person who feels the pull of obligation must discover whether he *is* obliged, and Moore has outlined the issues involved in that discovery. The agent must assess the likely consequences of, say, (1) speaking to the proper authority, (2) writing to the proper authority, (3) waiting until asked for evidence—three possible actions open to the person, and all well within his power to effect. We have seen that if it turns out that (1) is the action that will bring more intrinsic value into existence, then (1) is the duty of the person. If, however, the particular organization is structured such that the volunteering of evidence has most often counted against the person being evaluated (whether the evidence offered is true or false), then (1) seems an unlikely alternative. Thus if the agent sees that (3) is the action most likely to succeed (if the authorities do *in fact* request the information), then *even though* there is a stronger felt pull for (1) or (2), it will be the agent's actual obligation to do (3). I am obliged to speak with the proper authority only if I have reflected upon the likely consequences of alternative actions and have found that they are wanting.

Practical ethical judgments require that a moral agent be in an experiential context where some action or other is called for. To choose an action in a moral context is not *merely* a cognitive question. The moral requiredness of the situation prompts the individual *in* the context to seek the *right* action to do. One is in a moral situation when the question "What ought I to do?" is relevantly raised. The question of obligation involves the agent in making the world *be* a certain way [altering the world] as a consequence of something that the agent actually does.

Practical ethical judgments always demand the assessment of the context in which an agent finds himself. The agent must know how to effect changes in the world. He must have information about the social environment, the political environment, and the physical environment. He should have practical experience and wisdom. But he must be able at the very start to understand that he experiences himself in a situation in which "What ought I to do?" defines the context for choice.

4. *Ideal Rules and Rules of Duty*

Before we move on to the moral context in more detail, I want to point out that Moore speaks of a sense of *ought* which does not fit what I have been saying about obligation. There should be no particular problem with this *ought* since it is not one which is relevant to choices which men make in the world. In an essay written (probably) around 1920, "The Nature of Moral Philosophy,"[1] Moore distinguishes between two types of moral rules, called rules of duty and ideal rules. Choices that agents effect are understood under the notion of duty and the rules that duty requires. We have seen in Chapter III that, strictly speaking, no absolute rules can be suggested guaranteeing that the best possible outcome will be promoted by simply following the rule. Rules are not right or wrong—or our duty. Actions are right or wrong. *One* rule must be reserved, however, which is that we must do the action that will bring about the best possible consequences.

The concept of ideal rules is definitive of a state of being different from the condition that calls for duty. Ideal rules may be helpful in indicating what sort of *person* one ought to be. There are those who take rules such as "thou shalt love the Lord thy god" or "thou shalt not lust in thy heart" as ideal rules. A person who, as a matter of fact, has lusted upon a given occasion would have failed to observe the ideal rule and would not, as a consequence, be the type of person he hoped to be. Thus we can understand the lament of a person who complains about himself, saying, "I ought not to have had those feelings." But it is also clear that no one is in a position to offer helpful advice. There is, or was, no context for choice. The feeling in question overcame him; it could not be controlled. He did not, in any reachable sense, choose it.

The distinction between rules of duty and ideal rules is important for Moore. Let me quote Moore on the point. He compares several types of rules, among them [the "first"] a passage from the New Testament (Luke 6.27) that gives this rule: "Love your enemies, do good to them which hate you." Moore observes:

> Of these four rules, the three may be rules of duty, because they refer to things which are plainly, as a rule, at least, in the power of your will; but the first, if "love" be understood in its natural sense as referring to your feelings, is plainly only an "ideal" rule, since such feelings are obviously not directly under our own control, in the same way in which such actions as doing good to, blessing or praying for a person are so. . . . To do good to your enemies may, then, really be your duty; but it cannot, in the strict sense, be your duty not to have evil feelings towards them: all that can possibly be true is that it would be your duty if you were able.[2]

Moore deals with the notion of ideal rules, then, by pointing out that they are not, strictly speaking, in our power to obey or disobey. They are rules aimed at curbing our emotions, feelings, desires, fears, and hopes. Ideal rules are intended to cover the kinds of things that come to us unbidden and over which we can exercise little or no control.

Moore's point is that actions that are in the power of the agent to effect are to be measured for their moral content in terms of his definition of 'duty'. I think Moore felt that ideal rules, since they were drawn as not in our power to effect, could not conflict with duty. But there is a sense in which ideal rules and rules of duty can conflict, for if ideal rules have to do with the kinds of persons we ought to be, then one can imagine a possible conflict.

A person may wish to be the sort who never steals. He may find himself in a situation where the theft of a document, against the express wishes of its owner, may clearly be productive of the best possible consequences. Let's go so far as to say that the theft will be productive of the best possible world. Let's also say that theft is not one of the most basic prescriptions in his society. By the rule of duty the agent seems enjoined to take the document. Yet if he does so he cannot be the kind of person who never steals the property of another. The two kinds of rules seem to be in conflict. But I am not persuaded that the apparent conflict is important enough to upset the distinction, for the rule of duty is formulated in such a way that it can be said to override any ideal rule. [For reasons that are given below, however, it may not always do so. See also the bibliographic note on moral dilemmas.]

5. *Can We Ever Know What Our Duty Is?*

In a general sense, yes, of course we can know what our duty is in Moore's view. Our duty is to maximize the good. In *Ethics*, Moore systematically develops the position. The general answer, however, is very difficult to make real on any particular occasion. It is in the context of choosing this action or that one where the application of the general rule is to help, if it can help. So can we ever know, in any actual situation, what our duty is? Moore's answer to that question is no.

In order to *prove* that any action is a duty one would face certain insuperable difficulties. One would need far too vast an amount of causal information. One would be required to trace the consequences of the action into the unlimited future. There simply would never be enough current information or sufficient sophistication with respect to the influences that events have upon one another, to be able to be completely sure of any such tracing. Unless the information is made available, no precise assessment can be made of the value of the organic unity that represents the actual consequences of an actual choice. But even if it could be made, the possible consequences of possible alternative actions with their value(s) would also have to be assessed. "Accordingly," Moore writes, "it follows that we never have any reason to suppose that an action is our duty: we can never be sure that any action will produce the greatest value possible."[3] What is true about duty is true as well about any term defined as duty, such as right, morally permissible, obligation, or the expedient.

The most that practical ethics can hope to discover, according to *Principia Ethica*, is "which among a few alternatives possible under certain circumstances, will, on the whole, produce the best results."[4] But even this task, confesses Moore, is fraught with difficulties. One problem lies in the inadequacy of causal knowledge. We just cannot project whatever knowledge we have far enough into the future. For convenience' sake we may postulate that the salient effects of an action must dissipate in the foreseeable future. Yet as Moore himself points out, to so postulate is merely to confess utter ignorance of the future. Such a confession is of no worth for the sake of moral justification. The upshot of Moore's discussion of knowing our duty is that we can *at best* come up with some generalizations about classes of actions that tend to produce acceptable results. The possible discovery of actions that are *generally* better than alternatives, in given situations, cannot produce *certain* knowledge.[5]

Once again we see that philosophers who have classified Moore as an intuitionist with respect to duty or obligation are quite mistaken. I suspect that one source of their error lies in confusing the separable issues I pointed to at the beginning of this section. Do we know what our duty is? Yes. It is self-evident, Moore says, that we should maximize intrinsic value through our actions. That is Moore's view of the general question, the nature of duty or obligation. But in any particular choice context we can *never* know for certain what our duty may be.

6. *Rules Commonly Recognized: Their Utility and Morality*

Practical ethics has, as a matter of fact, classified certain actions as contrary to duty, as crimes or sins. Actions so classified in societies in the world are (generally) actions that threaten the fabric of the society in question. There are rules existing, Moore observes, in "any known state of society, [such that] a general observance of them *would* be good as a means. The conditions upon which their utility depends, namely the tendency to preserve and propagate life and the desire for property, seem to be so universal and so strong, that it would be impossible to remove them; and this being so, we can say that, under any conditions which could be given, the general observance of these rules would be good as a means."[6] Clearly Moore holds that such rules—though in a sense internal to each particular society as such—are nevertheless capable of being demonstrated to be *generally* productive of better results than if they are not observed.

If an agent is faced with a moral dilemma in which he may have to do something that will break a well-founded rule in the community, the agent must keep this generally productive feature of society's rules in mind. Let us grant that the agent believes he sees clearly that breaking the rule will bring better results than obeying the societal precept. Is the agent justified in assuming that the case in question represents an exception to the general rule? Moore says no. He argues that a given rule that is generally useful ought *always* to be followed. Moore's reason is stated in terms of probabilities. It's not that in this instance the rule must be proved to be useful, but rather that in other particular cases the usefulness of the rule has been demonstrated. In fact, there can be no certain grounds to hold that in *this* case the rule will not be useful. "In short, though we may be sure that there are cases where the rule should be broken, we can never know which those cases are, and ought, therefore, never to break it."[7]

There is, Moore thinks, an additional reason for the observance of well-established rules in society. The rule is obeyed by many people. If someone breaks the rule because of a purported extraordinary circumstance that the person takes to justify an exception, there is no way to impress upon others the unusual and exceptional character of the particular case. The de facto example set for others, then, is the breaking of the rule. Insofar as the breaking of the rule encourages others to disregard the rule, the rule's utility is clearly threatened. The wise course of action, then, is not to appear to disrespect the rule. Thus Moore: "The individual can therefore be confidently recommended *always* to conform to rules which are both generally useful and generally practiced."[8]

If a person sees that the theft of the [hypothetical] document, mentioned above, is very likely to bring about valuable consequences in his society, and yet knows that there is a strongly established rule, useful and nearly always practiced, against theft, the agent must obey the rule. Does this represent an action contrary to duty? It appears that Moore does not think so. We must remember that, in the first place, we can never really know that a particular action actually is our duty. In the case in question, we may genuinely *feel* that the theft is the exception, but we know, also, that the way it *feels* is not to the point. The second reason is that in breaking a well-established rule, one weakens one element in a strong society. The rule stands, with other societal rules, as part of the constitutive elements of the society. The rules are, according to Moore, the necessary grounds for bringing value into the social world.

7. Ethics: *Ignorance of Duty*

Although Moore's 1912 *Ethics* is correctly viewed as a systematic development of the problems encountered in Chapter 5 of *Principia Ethica* ("Ethics in Relation to Conduct"), a reader will note that Moore's concerns with respect to knowing the rules of duty expressed in the 1903 book are *not* extensively discussed in the *Ethics*. The *Ethics* sets forth what I call an ontology of right. In working this out, Moore takes up the fact of our relative ignorance of matters of fact in ways that allow him to avoid having to deal *directly* with the issues he raised in *Principia*, although he clearly is doing so indirectly. Moore does not mention, for example, the question of the overriding authority of well-established rules in society in the later book, but his analysis of the limits of our causal knowledge of the world leaves such well-established rules securely in place.

In the *Ethics*, Moore holds that the test of right or wrong is determined by the actual consequences of voluntary actions chosen by an agent. An action that in fact brings as much intrinsic value into existence as any alternative action open to the agent is right. The definition is familiar and represents no change from the *Principia Ethica* doctrine. In the 1912 text Moore suggests possible objections to the view in order to argue convincingly for it. One substantial objection is, of course, the one that concerns us in this chapter. If the Moore view is true, we can never know for certain that some action is really our duty. One objection in *Ethics* suggests that we give up the criterion of *actual* consequences and substitute in its place the notion of consequences that were antecedently probable, "or which the agent had reason to expect, or which it was *possible* for him to *foresee*. . . . An action is *always* right, whatever its *actual* consequences may be, provided the agent had reason to expect that they would be the best possible; and *always* wrong, if he had reason to expect they would not."[9] But Moore does not accept this suggestion. For one thing, it makes the criterion a subjective criterion, dependent upon what an agent *thinks* or has *reasons* for, *independent of the truth of the ideas or reasons*.

Moore does, however, recognize that the objection is substantial; and, in order to deal with it, he distinguishes different types of judgments we may make. We make judgments of right and wrong, and such judgments are connected to intrinsic value. They are judgments grounded objectively. We may also morally praise or morally blame a person or an action. A morally praiseworthy action brings value to be. So we may now grant that an agent could not be certain that an action he chose brought into being consequences that actually were better than any others possible to bring about. But if his action was chosen after reflection indicating that the act he chose was likely to bring about value in the world, and more value than anything else he could have done in the circumstances, then in doing the action he has done "the best he could have." If later events prove that his action was severely lacking in value production because of factors he could not foresee, and the action is quite wrong, he does not deserve blame. The moral judgments—praise and blame—are available for use in consort with judgments of right and wrong and help with confronting ignorance of the future.

8. *Motives and Moral Judgments*

Moore says in *Ethics* that, in our moral judgments, we do (and we ought to) take account of motives for action. Judgments about motives, however, are not judgments of right and wrong. They are subject to moral judgments of a different type; they are the objects of praise and blame. If an agent commits an act that has bad consequences, but the motive in performing the action was pure (or properly reflective and careful), we will want to have an appropriate judgment to assess the motive. The judgment, whatever it is, will not influence our analysis of the rightness or wrongness of the action. Judgments of motives, then, call for a separate analysis.

Moore holds that there are three distinguishable kinds of judgments that tend to become confused with judgments of right and wrong and are especially relevant to a consideration of motives. First, some may believe that certain motives are intrinsically good or intrinsically bad. Moore does not, for such a view is inconsistent with the consequentialist view he is espousing in *Ethics*. He holds instead that motives are subject to praise or blame, but he does not deal with the issue at any length. It appears to me that Moore thinks of motives as more like virtues than they are like things or events. It is things and events that are receptive to good's ingression. A motive, like a virtue, can be a means to intrinsic value's existence. But even if there were a sense in which a motive could be said to have intrinsic value, that sense would not conflict with an individual's acting from it and yet producing bad results. The motive, therefore, cannot make an action right or wrong.

Second, one might believe that good motives have a tendency to produce right conduct. The view is eminently plausible. Motives, then, could be said to be similar to well-founded rules in society *and* to the habit of virtue. Generally, when one acts from a pure motive the consequences of the action turn out well. We sometimes inquire of a person who has performed an action that has had tragic consequences why he did what he did. If we learn that his motive was acceptable and the tragic consequences were unforeseeable, we are not astounded. The world is that way. We tend to approve of the motive because we understand that, in general, the consequences of acting according to such a motive are good. There is no problem, then, in seeing that a judgment about motive differs from a judgment about right and wrong action.

Third, as has been pointed out, it is possible to confuse judgments about motives with judgments assessing the praiseworthiness or blameworthiness of an action or a person. We often praise a person for acting from a pure motive. If the hiker in our previous example pulled the child from the river because he wanted to beat her, the motive would be wrong even though the action was right and therefore praiseworthy. The judgments are of two different sorts, yet they are related in important ways. Moore holds that in condemning a particular corrupt motive one may tend to prevent wrong actions in the future, while in praising pure motives one may tend to produce right actions. It is perhaps because they are so closely related that judgments about motives and judgments of actions are sometimes confused with one another.

Moore does not spend time in probing these three types of judgments in *Ethics*, and his discussion of them may appear to be somewhat muddled, but his only purpose in raising these issues at all is to show that motives play a role in moral choice that is quite independent of judgments of right and wrong. The task of the 1912 book is to develop Moore's own brand of utilitarianism, and it is clearly consistent with that purpose that the motive of an action must be distinguished from its consequences.

As I end this section on motive and alternative judgments made in moral contexts I want to quote Moore on his reflection concerning the scope of the theory. He confesses that the view he has presented may seem paradoxical in a case where the evidence is that an action is best but in fact it is not.

> And so in this case I do not see why we should not hold, that though we should be justified in saying that [an agent] *ought* to choose one course, yet it may not be really true that he ought. What certainly will be true is that he will deserve the strongest moral blame if he does not choose the course in question even though it may be wrong. And we are thus committed to the paradox that a man may deserve the strongest moral condemnation for choosing an action which actually is

right. But I do not see why we should not accept this paradox.[10]

Since the *Ethics* doctrine is one that grounds right and wrong
objectively and ontologically, ignorance of actual consequences
points up the paradox. But from the point of view of judgments
that are at our disposal to use in moral contexts, the actual sting
of the paradox is not of crucial importance—as Moore indicates.

9. *The Right Action and the Expedient Action*

An action that is a duty is an action that produces
the best possible states of affairs. It is a means to good. In both
Principia Ethica and *Ethics* Moore argues that 'duty' and 'the expedient' refer to the same state of the world. An action that is the
truly expedient action is one that produces the best possible states
of the world. An expedient action is also a means to good. There
is no ultimate distinction between an act that is a duty and an act
that is (truly) expedient.

In saying that there is no *ultimate* distinction between an action
that is a duty and an act that is expedient, Moore means only to
indicate that the terms 'duty' and 'expedient' will always apply to
the same action, although the terms will have different meanings.
Actions done from duty are actions that it is useful to praise or
blame. People have a greater tendency to omit actions that duty
requires. The difference has a psychological aspect to it and is of
importance in moral education. Expedient actions are very often
thought of as actions toward which persons are more naturally
inclined. Generally we do not have to cajole a person into doing
what he takes to be an expedient act.

There is no *ethical* difference between a dutiful action and an
expedient action. We ought to do our duty, of course. We ought
to do the expedient thing as well. It is in this sense, then, that one
may assert that the end justifies the means, says Moore. No means
is morally permissible that is not conducive to the proper end: the
maximization of value in the world. The expedient action will always be the truly dutiful action because, like the dutiful action, it
too is a means to what is good.

It is true, the complex concept duty is different from the complex concept expedient. An analysis of the two complexes will reveal different combinations of more simple concepts, some of the differences we have just noted. The meanings are different. But the important ethical fact is that if, upon a particular occasion, I know that Smith has done the expedient thing, I know that he has done what he ought to have done. I may suspect, also, that he was not reluctant to do it and that he might have balked if he had been told that the action was his duty. Thus according to Moore there may be no reason for me to praise Smith. Although this may seem to be an odd feature of Moore's position, it seems less so in the light of his concern for the way in which the moral character of persons is assessed.

10. *Moral Assessment of Persons*

Although Moore does not discuss judgments about the moral character of persons explicitly, the issues he does discuss may provide speculative possibilities. From what we have seen in the present chapter, the fact that a person performs an action that is consequentially wrong is hardly sufficient ground for holding the person to be bad or evil. An action that is wrong may be performed from a motive that is most acceptable and even from one that is completely praiseworthy. A person may also perform an action that is right and is his duty, *even while intending harm.*

It seems to be clear that if a person tended, in all or most of his actions, to do things that usually turned out to be right, we would feel moral approbation for the person and would judge his moral character accordingly. From Moore's vantage point our judgments are made about the person in the good-as-a-means context. In the same context we would judge the person who tended in his actions to produce bad or evil consequences with appropriate moral disapproval. We look to persons as agents—moral agents—and we judge their behavior in that sense. Thus the kind of moral being a person is may often be judged on the quality of the choices that person makes.

It is to be emphasized that Moore does not investigate the moral assessment of agents qua agents. Yet in the last chapter of *Princi-*

pia Ethica, where Moore talks about what things have intrinsic value and in what degree, he says: "By far the most valuable things, which we know or can imagine, are certain states of consciousness, which may be described as the pleasures of human intercourse and the enjoyment of beautiful objects."[11] I suggest here, and take up again in Chapter VIII, that the moral person has intrinsic value; and, much in the Kantian tradition, the fact of human choice in the creation of value in the world—the making of conditions in the world that are receptive to value—is definitive of morality. I think that the whole of Moore's writings on moral philosophy clearly presupposes that persons have intrinsic value because they are persons. But this has yet to be shown.

CRITICAL BIBLIOGRAPHY: CHAPTER V

In this chapter Sylvester begins to disclose certain features of Moore's ethics that link it more firmly with Bentham's and Mill's social utilitarianism than with Sidgwick's strongly intuitionist, and egoistic, utilitarianism. He does this, first, by bringing out the close relationship (or resemblance) between the processes of reaching aesthetic judgments on the one hand and moral judgments on the other. Without conflating good with beauty, as Sylvester shows, Moore nevertheless held that the actual process of reaching a value predicate is similar in both aesthetics and ethics. He does this, in the first section, by emphasizing Moore's insistence upon the difficulty encountered in reaching correct judgments of beauty or goodness in living through the experience of doing so. Sylvester returns to the lived-through experience and its importance for Moore's ethics again in the last chapter.

It is in this vein that Sylvester shows that the difficulty of seeing Picasso's *Guernica* as a beautiful painting is residual, if all that we have to go on is our own immediate, direct, and personal apprehension of the work. In a like vein, Sylvester suggests, we would have a residual difficulty in formulating a viable personal moral ideal if all that we had to go on consisted in our innermost feelings plus an odd apprehension or two of what things are good in the world.

However, in taking this line Sylvester wants the emphasis to fall less upon the *epistemological* similarity between aesthetic and moral judgments than upon their *phenomenological* similarity. He wants to show that Moore insists that noncognitive elements enter both, that the presence of emotive response is a characteristic of both. At the same time, however, Sylvester wants to contrast the situation faced in aesthetic response with the situation that calls for an ethical response. He wants to bring out Moore's point that there is a "requiredness" of response in situations calling for ethical judgments that is absent in aesthetic contexts; that the experience of beauty does not *demand* that we choose it as the experience of obligation does. Where beauty *invites* appreciation, duty *requires* action. One must *feel* that requirement; one must have a sense that the situation calls for a choice to be made and acted upon.

In taking this line Sylvester moves to a consideration of Moore's account of obligation or duty and shows how such matters of conduct involve the necessity of reference to far more contextual (empirical) *and* psychological elements than might be expected were Moore to be read simply as an intuitionist. By starting this chapter as he does, Sylvester is able to show how Moore can account for the emotive content of both ethical and aesthetic judgments without reducing his position to the psychologism or emotivism that critics such as Ayer, Frankena, and Stevenson thought should be the logical consequence of the naturalistic fallacy argument.

Among Moore's critics, only John Hill (see the General Bibliography at the end of Chapter I) seems to have seen the validity of the point that Sylvester makes in this chapter, namely that the answer to the question of the *meaning* of 'good' does not get us, *or Moore himself*, very far in answering the remaining questions of what things and actions in the world *are* good. But Hill directs his criticism of Moore's interpreters at what he takes to be their mistake in thinking of Moore as conducting an exclusively metaethical investigation rather than as undertaking the sort of metamoral task that Hill sees as

Moore's purpose. (Hill apparently means by 'metamoral' simply a moral theory as opposed to a metaethical theory *about* morality. Hill's terminology is not in general use, but he seems to mean by 'metamoral' something like Frankena's normative ethics: an ethics that pays special attention to the establishment of its norms.) He thinks Moore's critics have assumed that once the meaning of 'good' has been established by Moore, the rest of ethics can be, as it were, deduced from it. He writes that for these critics: "Definition takes place at the outset as in geometry; the science of ethics follows from this original definition, and it is metaethical, logical, morally unbiassed [sic], hermetically sealed off from the moral problems to the solution of which it contributes" (p. 22).

Moreover, once Hill has made clear the grounds of his dissatisfaction with interpretations based upon such assumptions, he devotes the remainder of his dissertation mainly to showing how one critic after another stumbles over the same obstacle. In the end, therefore, it is not surprising that Hill's new interpretation of Moore's metamoral theory turns out to miss the main point that Sylvester wants to make in this chapter: The great difficulty and uncertainty about what things and what actions *are* good and, perhaps even more important, the practical ethical question of what actions are *right*, drive Moore farther and farther into an extremely conservative attitude toward, and acceptance of, conventional standards of moral behavior.

Sylvester's emphasis is to point out, as Moore himself does in Chapter 5 of *Principia* as well as in *Ethics*, that much more is involved in ethics than simply the apprehension of good. Sylvester wants to show, moreover, that the two books are closely linked; that although *Principia* has sometimes been taken to contain a doctrine of moral certitude that is absent from the *Ethics*, in fact there is little more difference between them than can be accounted for as matters of variant emphasis. We may be certain of good when we apprehend it, Moore maintains, but that sort of certainty is far from giving us transparent solutions to our moral dilemmas. While the emphasis in *Principia* is on the self-evidence of good in our apprehension of it, the emphasis in *Ethics* is on the difficulty of acting on our value apprehensions when they are made in actual contexts where, indeed, the practical difficulties of calculating maximal value abound.

Unlike most critics, and to a far greater extent than Hill, Sylvester pays attention to Moore's insistence upon contextualizing the questions of duty and obligation. He shows how Moore fleshes out these questions by the discussions of the possible conflicts that can arise between personal ideals and the rules of society. In this way he shows how the question of duty, like all practical moral questions, moves Moore's focus from principle to practice. And he shows how, as the focus moves, the clarity of the principle gives way to the confusions of practice. We know in principle that it is our duty to maximize good. But what *practices* will accomplish that end are far more difficult to discern. We can never be sure, Moore tells us, that we have hit upon the right course. Nor can we be sure that the conventionally accepted rules are the rights ones; the difficulty of discerning what course of action *is* right cuts both ways.

In this way, Sylvester brings out—as most critics have failed to do—that the allegedly conservative strain in Moore's ethics does not foreclose the possibility, as unlikely as it may seem, that an individual may encounter a valid obligation to act in a way that runs counter to the accepted norms of social behavior. Moreover, and in the same vein, Sylvester emphasizes the consequentialist implications of Moore's cautionary remarks about the risks to be run in failure to conform to the conventional rules of society. In the end, Sylvester shows, Moore's argument leads him to focus upon the moral agent, the person and his motives, as the locus of intrinsic value.

Little more can be said in a strictly bibliographical sense with regard to Sylvester's theme in this chapter save that the practical side of Moore's ethics is very nearly universally neglected. Perhaps because most critics have been mainly concerned with the theoretical rather than the practical side of Moore's position, they fail to acknowledge that Moore himself balances his doubts about our capacity to arrive independently at our very own clear and distinct personal choices by equally pervasive doubts about the grounds of conventional morality. The immediate certainty of our value apprehensions may be clouded with myriad doubts, and—even if we *are* able to see them clearly—they are likely to conflict with the well-established rules of the society in which we live. But as Moore himself points out, the validity of even well-established rules is in question.

The presumption in favor of living according to the well-established rules is great, Moore argues, but clearly he wants us to see that there is ample room for exceptions to be made. The failure to see how Moore tries to achieve some sort of balance here, and the assumption that Moore is straightforwardly conservative in practical ethics, result in criticism of Tom Regan's conception of Moore as "Bloomsbury's Prophet." For it seems possible to maintain that Moore somehow influenced or inspired the social renegades of Bloomsbury only if we can understand him as the proverbial prophet without honor—or at least understanding—in his own country.

Some, but not all, of the reviewers of Regan's book have criticized his arguments for neglecting the socially conservative strain in Moore's approach to ethics. Thus Thomas Baldwin, in what is the most substantial review of *Bloomsbury's Prophet* thus far (*Mind*, January 1988), chides Regan for treating *Principia* as an "Edwardian essay *On Liberty*" that expresses Moore's quasi-religious attitude toward the good (pp. 129, 132). And Avrum Stroll, in a far briefer compass (*Journal of the History of Philosophy*, 26,3 [July 1988]), suggests that it is simply a mistaken reading of *Principia* to think that the vagueness of conventional moral rules with respect to their application—discussed by Moore in Chapter 5—can be taken to justify the freedom of "individual human judgment to decide on the proper course of action in a given situation." Succinctly, Stroll says: "The evidence Regan introduces on behalf of these assertions is exiguous" (pp. 504–5).

These are serious charges indeed, but the more extensive discussion they deserve must be postponed until we have seen how Sylvester develops his own thesis concerning the moral role of the individual more fully in the chapters that follow. In the Critical Bibliography for Chapter VIII, in which Sylvester develops Moore's implicit conception of the moral individual, we need to return to the question mooted here; the question of Moore's residual moral conservatism.

Ontology and
Non-natural Qualities

1. *The Problem*

Granting that the notion of good is central to Moore's moral philosophy, it is essential that we be as clear as possible as to the sense in which the doctrine holds that good is the unique quality it is said to be. As we have seen, the general view is that good is *in* things; it is a property of the things it is in. But Moore tell us that it is not a natural property of them. Nor is it a subjective predicate projected onto the things it qualifies. Good is held to be objective and, in this sense, independent of any awareness of it as a property of the thing in question. It does not depend on our perception of it or upon our consciousness of its presence. Good is uniquely intrinsic to the thing that has it, and it is objectively real. But these assertions are far from being self-explanatory. Moore must offer an account of what these assertions concerning good and its status in the world mean; but, as many critics have noted, the account given in *Principia* is less than complete or satisfactory. In order to fill in that account we need to examine some of Moore's earlier essays as well as the *Ethics* and other later work.

One such helpful essay, "The Conception of Intrinsic Value," for example, was written well after the publication of *Principia Ethica*. It was written three or four years later than *Ethics* as well, probably in 1916. As I have said in the Introduction, this essay may be seen to stand to *Ethics*, and the practical ethical theory stated in that book, as the first four chapters in *Principia Ethica* stand to the chapter entitled "Ethics in Relation to Conduct," which is the chapter given over to practical ethics in *Principia*. The essay was obviously written to shed light upon the concept good

131

as exemplified in things in existence; it is a study of value-in-things. In the essay Moore's remarks have explicit ontological implications for good's coming to be exemplified in the world.

Moore's ontology of value is the central topic of the present chapter. Hence I count heavily on Moore's views in this late essay. But I also make use of much earlier work as well: the first four chapters of *Principia Ethica* and some of the early essays that I have already introduced, such as "The Nature of Judgment" (1899) and "Identity" (1901).

2. *The Concept: Intrinsic Value*

Intrinsic value is a property of things. Moore says of it, in "The Conception of Intrinsic Value," "(1) it does depend *only* on the intrinsic nature of what possess it . . . and (2) that, though this is so, it is yet not itself an intrinsic property."[1] The quotation requires investigation.

Good's existence depends upon the way a thing or event is actually constituted. A thing that is good is composed of certain properties that account for its being the [good] thing it is. It is those precise properties that are required if good is to be exemplified in the thing or to be the thing's property. Moore's characterization is stated as follows: "*To say that a kind of value is 'intrinsic' means that the question whether a thing possesses it, and in what degree it possesses it, depends solely on the intrinsic nature of the thing in question.*"[2] Intrinsic value is a property of the thing, but not an *intrinsic* property. The properties that are intrinsic to the thing are those Moore calls *natural* properties. Properties that depend upon the intrinsic properties of the thing are called *non-natural* properties of the thing. Good, or value, depends solely on the intrinsic properties of things that are good. Thus good is intrinsic to that thing. Yet even though good is intrinsic to the thing that has it, and is a property of the thing that has it, it is not an intrinsic property.

Much more must be said about Moore's distinction between natural and non-natural properties, for it has been a central bone of contention between Moore and a host of his critics. But the central point is just this: A natural property is intrinsically part of a thing in such a way that the thing could not be what it is without the property. A non-natural property is simply a property that is dependent on what the intrinsic properties of the thing are, though it is not itself an intrinsic property. Thus intrinsic value may be a property of a thing that has it, though it is not an intrinsic property of that thing.

3. *Non-natural Properties*

In *Principia Ethica* Moore argued that good, as a property of natural things, is not itself a natural property. "The Conception of Intrinsic Value" took the matter further. In 1903 Moore held that natural properties give to the natural thing the substance that it has as a natural thing. Natural properties were held to constitute the thing. Good, a non-natural notion and a property, is not constitutive of the thing in this way.

Moore suggests a criterion in terms of which one may distinguish natural properties from non-natural properties. We are to notice, he urges, that natural properties exist in time, by themselves. Non-natural properties, as such, do not exist in time.

The doctrine claims that things that are good are natural objects. Natural objects are constituted by natural properties. Natural properties exist in time all by themselves. Natural properties are seen to be *parts* of the natural objects they constitute. He claims that if they are [conceptually] peeled away, or removed from the natural objects they constitute, one by one, there will be nothing left when the final natural property has been taken from the erstwhile thing; no object left at all, not even a bare substance.[3]

Let me repeat Moore's view, for there must be no doubt about the position *Principia Ethica* takes on the question of natural and non-natural properties. Natural properties are, as I have said, the substantive (substance-making) properties that constitute a thing. They produce the very existing complex that is the natural thing. Good, being a non-natural property, is not one of the substance-making properties. Good has nothing to contribute to the constitution of the object of which it is correctly predicated. Again, good, as a non-natural property, does not exist as such (of itself) in time. The constitutive elements of the natural object, the natural properties, do exist in time.

4. *Existence in Time: C. D. Broad's Refutation*

A criticism of Moore's criterion of existence in time for natural properties argues that, as usually understood, the criterion cannot do the job assigned to it by Moore. C. D. Broad points out, in the Schilpp volume, that every property one can mention, for example, of a penny—the hardness, the brownness, the roundness—is in the same boat with goodness.[4] None of them can be said to exist in time. Yet Moore counts hardness, brownness, and roundness as natural properties. Moore of course agrees that Broad is correct. It is necessary to look at the distinction, and the criterion, once again to see why Moore does not think that Broad's criticism vitiates his way of distinguishing natural from non-natural properties.

In the chapter of *Principia Ethica* entitled "Metaphysical Ethics" Moore offers the criterion "existence in time." The chapter has two main tasks. One task is to refute the errant views in ethics that are metaphysical in conception. The second task is to show that metaphysics has a positive dimension, that it has provided a necessary service to philosophers. Metaphysics has insisted on the reality of certain kinds of entities, entities that do not exist, yet have being nonetheless. Such entities are of cardinal importance for moral philosophy. Moore writes:

> It is not *goodness*, but things or qualities which are good, which can exist in time—can have duration, and begin and cease to exist—can be objects of perception. But the most prominent members of this class [non-natural entities] are perhaps numbers. It is quite certain that . . . two itself does not exist and never can. Two and two *are* four. But that does not mean that either two or four exists, yet it certainly means *something*. Two *is* somehow, although it does not exist.[5]

I have already discussed Moore's view of the being of certain entities that do not exist in time. They are, in Moore's vocabulary, concepts. Chapter IV showed that good, for example, is a concept among other concepts. In the 1899 "Judgment," truth and existence were also mentioned as unanalyzable concepts along with good. Moore's view is that no concepts, qua concepts, exist in time. Broad shows that this is what Moore himself has firmly maintained and argues that Moore is simply wrong in proposing the criterion of existence in time as a way of distinguishing natural from non-natural properties so long as he also holds good to be a non-natural property. According to Broad's argument, Moore cannot hold that good can both exist in time and be a non-natural property. But does Moore actually hold that good *does* exist in time?

It is relevant to recall that Moore lays down a stipulation about properties that exist in time. Refer back to the quotation above. It reads, in part, "can have duration, and begin and cease to exist— can be objects of perception." Taking the comment about perception to be part of Moore's meaning for the notion of existence in time, it seems clear that Moore wants the criterion to apply in the realm of experience in which sense perception is operative. Natural objects are constituted by properties that can be the proper objects of sense perception. Brown is perceived as a property of a penny by an appropriate sense receptor. Hard is perceived as a property of a penny also by an appropriate sense faculty. Natural properties are discovered by sense perception.

Pencil$_a$ is hard, yellow, and so on; pencil$_b$ is hard, blue, and so on. Pencil$_a$ and pencil$_b$ are on the table. One may say, correctly, there are two pencils on the table, one yellow and the other blue. The term 'two' points to an objective fact; so does the term 'blue.' Blue is found by exercise of the organ of vision. How is two found? We see two pencils. We can touch two pencils. Yet strictly speaking we 'see' a yellow and a blue, and we 'feel' a hard thing here and a hard thing there. But we do not, in the same sense, see or feel that there are two pencils. We *judge* that there are two pencils. The concept two is not found by means of sense perception in the same way that blue and hard are. That, I take it, is Moore's point, or—more accurately—part of Moore's point. Like good, numbers are non-natural; neither number nor good is an object of sense perception or exists in a span of temporal duration, though both may be exemplified in objects of sense perception that do exist in time.

In Chapter II, I went on at some length about grasping the quality good in an act of direct acquaintance. A similar process is evident here. The judgment that there are two pencils on the table is true, is self-evident to direct acquaintance. The judgment that the pencil on the right of the table is blue is true, is likewise self-evident to direct acquaintance. The number judgment judges the existence of a non-natural property of an event, whereas the judgment of hardness or color judges the existence of a natural property of a thing.

We must understand that Moore's distinction between natural and non-natural properties is a metaphysical one, in the sense that it is not meant to be empirically verifiable. For Moore, metaphysics is an enterprise that keeps us alert to the being of entities whose mode of being is not to be a proper object of perception. Broad does not seem to see that Moore's version of metaphysical realism places good in the same category as number; in other words, as *beings that are capable of qualifying* objects of perception without themselves *being* objects of perception.

But even if we accept Moore's distinction between natural and non-natural properties as a priori or analytic or both, it may still be that he is confused about the natural properties' capacity for existence in time. Broad's point may still not have been met. For in what possible sense can even *natural* properties exist in time, *all by themselves*? It seems that this question remains even if we accept Moore's stipulations concerning the distinction between natural and non-natural properties that his metaphysics requires. Or does it? Perhaps the answer lies in a further feature of the metaphysics that Moore accepted in 1903.

By 1942, when Moore answers the critics in the "Reply" (in the Schilpp volume), he had long since moved away from the views he held at the turn of the century. When Moore was at work writing *Principia Ethica* he held a view about the world that supports the notion that natural properties do exist in time *by themselves* in the sense that good does not. This doctrine is explained in what follows, but I will say here that Moore's view clearly espouses a metaphysical thesis—if we count Plato and Aristotle as metaphysicians—and it is a thesis that Broad does not countenance. Moore held, in 1901, that simple particulars exist, and exist temporally. Natural properties are simple particulars. Good, on the other hand, is not a simple particular and has no simple particular instances.

5. *Moore's Metaphysics and Mixed Ontology*

The fundamental distinction between natural and non-natural properties is grounded in an interesting mixed ontology that Moore held at the time he was working out his *Principia* views. I mean by "mixed ontology" a position that combines a Platonic and an Aristotelian element on the relationship between universals and particulars. Before I continue my discussion I wish to acknowledge my debt to the work of Herbert Hochberg and Gustave Bergmann. Both have studied Moore's early views and have published illuminating analyses of the early ontology. I count heavily on their insights in the present chapter.[6]

Moore's ontology requires the following entities to be acknowledged. (1) *Universals*: Moore's commitment to the being of universals has been pointed out in almost every chapter. The early essays, *Principia Ethica*, and the 1910–1911 lectures are all agreed that universals have being but do not exist. Moore refers to universals as concepts and as objects of thought. The point is that universals are regarded as intelligible objects having a status in reality that is independent of space and time. (2) *Simple particulars*: Simple particulars may be said to "fall under" the universal that accounts for their intelligibility. For example, this $blue_1$, this $blue_2$, this $blue_3$ . . . this $blue_n$, all fall under the universal blue; "it seems certain that this red and that red do exist, but very doubtful that Red itself does" Moore says in "Identity." Simple particulars, then, *exist*. They have reality in space and time.

Moore puts the matter this way: "It seems impossible to deny that universals do differ from particulars, since different things are true of them: as, for instance, *that particulars certainly exist*, while it is at least doubtful that universals do"[7] Simple particulars ground existing things since they constitute (3) *composite particulars*. Composite particulars are what I have called *things*, common ordinary things of experience—dogs, stones, trees, houses, rivers. I continue to call composite particulars things. I use the term "event" to name collections of things—the battle of Waterloo, a child floating on an inner tube on a river, a sunset in the White Mountains. Things are natural entities and are composed of natural properties. Natural properties are grounded in simple particulars.

I also make use of two terms suggested by Herbert Hochberg to refer to different ontological bindings, or ties. (4) *Contain*: A composite particular *contains* the simple particulars that constitute it. This penny—a composite particular—contains this brown, this round, this hard; it is constituted by these simple particulars. Things, then, contain the natural properties that make them what they are. The second of the bindings is (5) *exemplification*: Certain complex particulars and certain events exemplify certain universals. The following two propositions are two examples of exemplification: (*a*) The act of pulling the child to safety is good, and (*b*) There are two pencils on the table. Universals that are non-natural concepts have exemplification instances in the existing world. Universals of this sort are exemplified in the natural world in things and events.

I want to explicitly re-present *Principia Ethica*'s thesis using the terminology suggested above. There is an immense number of different kinds of things in the universe. Things we come into contact with in everyday existence are things that exist in the natural world. Existing things are constituted by properties that are natural. Natural properties are ontologically grounded in simple particulars. The natural sciences, including psychology, study natural properties and the relations among natural properties.

Most of the choices that people are required to make in the world involve an understanding of what will happen as a consequence of doing one action as opposed to another. One learns what actions are wiser than others by paying attention to funded experience. It is in the context of the natural causal system that moral decisions are to be made. So since the natural sciences study the natural causal system it is a wise and practical person who pays attention to the information that the sciences uncover. To have any insight into what one ought to do one must have a sound opinion as to how much good one can cause to come into [exemplification] existence.

Bringing good into existence is a causal question that involves our moral choices. Certain natural states of existence (causally) allow more good to become exemplified in existence than others. Moreover, we need to recognize that Moore's warnings with respect to the naturalistic fallacy clearly have no bearing upon the question of what we ought to do when it is posed in this way. We ought to create those natural states or conditions that will allow the most possible good to be exemplified in the world and—in this sense—to come into existence.

Moore's practical ethical theory is grounded in his conception of simple particulars. Everything that exists is constituted by simple particulars existing in time. Indeed, everything that exists, exists in time. Things exist in time because everything that exists contains simple particulars that exist in time. Let me say it another way: The intrinsic nature of every composite particular is the sum of the simple particulars along with their relations, which are contained in it. So it should now be clear why Moore held that good, although intrinsic to a composite particular and therefore a legitimate property of the composite particular, cannot be an intrinsic property of the composite particular. Good is not *contained* in the composite. Good is *exemplified* in the composite particular.

Contrary to Broad, Moore was not inconsistent in *Principia Ethica* when he invoked the criterion of existence in time for natural properties. Simple particulars, the ground of natural properties, exist in time. There are no simple particular instances of non-natural properties, no simple particular this good or that good, no simple particular this two or that two. Non-natural properties appear in the world through exemplifications in natural entities. Broad was right, of course, that brownness, roundness, and hardness are not in time, and *Principia* agreed. Universals have being. None of them exists; though existents may exemplify them, none contains them.

6. *Causal Laws: Exemplification as Ingression: The Notion of 'Depends Upon'*

If a composite particular, or an event, is constituted so that value becomes exemplified in it, it is *necessary* that value be there. If a sunset that exists now is good, then any sunset that is exactly like it will also be good. [Supervenience again.] Moore spells this view out in "The Conception of Intrinsic Value," and the thesis is the same in *Principia Ethica*. Yet the sunset's exemplifying good does not depend upon current causal laws. It is still a natural causal question as to whether a sunset just like this one will ever come to be again. In order for good to ingress into the world it requires a natural occasion that permits good to qualify a thing or an event. This is true quite independently of the particular causal laws that happen to describe the natural order at any period in the natural history of the universe.

Good has no power. Good cannot force itself into existence. It has no efficacy. Humans have efficacy. Humans act. No simple particular goods can be contained in things or events. So in order for value to become exemplified, good must wait, so to speak, for the natural world to become constituted in such a way as to be receptive to value ingression. When a sunset exactly like this beautiful one is produced by the causal conditions that account for such sunsets, then value falls into the sunset, as it were.

It is important that Moore's point be clear. Suppose a sunset we are experiencing is good. It follows from the view that $sunset_2$, exactly like this one, must be good. But does it follow that $sunset_3$, which we learn is good, must also be like this one? No, it does not. $Sunset_3$ may be good but have no shades of purple, as this one does. All that we know is that $sunset_n$, if it is exactly like $sunset_3$, must be intrinsically good. Moore says this, in "The Conception of Intrinsic Value": "If a thing is good (in my sense), then that it is so *follows* from the fact that it possesses certain natural intrinsic properties, which are such that from the fact that it is good it does not follow conversely that it has those properties."[8]

Good, then, depends upon the natural causal conditions for the opportunity to "fall into," or to "ingress," or to "become exemplified" in existence. I have used these three ways of speaking to indicate the way that value relates to existence, but I hope it is clear that the three ways of speaking are intended as support for a single theory of how value relates to existence and not three different theories.

There are, however, more theories than one to account for what I have been calling value's ingression into the world. I contrast the ingression theory with two alternative ways of dealing with the question, using a somewhat contrived example. Consider a complex particular that is square, hard, blue, and good. Suppose each of the properties mentioned is a natural property. There are simple particulars: this blue, this square, this hard, and this good. The four simple particulars combine into the complex particular, this blue thing. Causal laws may be found that describe the conditions under which the blue thing comes into existence. Under this view, the simple particular *good* is seen as one of the co-participants in the constitution of the blue thing. It would be, then, a natural property; it would be on an ontological par with the other simple particulars. All four simple particulars would ground natural properties. But this would not of course be Moore's view.

I refer the reader to the discussion of beauty in Chapter I, where a similar view was examined. In it, Austin Duncan-Jones's analysis of Moore's definition of 'beauty' posited the existence of a large number of so-called pulchrific qualities. These pulchrific qualities joined with other qualities to create an object that was beautiful. I argued that the view was mistaken, but pointed out that the ontological alternative was interesting even though it contradicted Moore's explicit statement, that there was only *one* unanalyzable predicate of value—good. It should be clear that Duncan-Jones's alternative, unless carefully reworked, comes close to making pulchrific qualities what I have referred to here as simple particulars. If that is what the analysis comes to, beauty [pulchritude] exists in time and passes the criterion for a natural property. Value, then, would turn out to be a natural property.

A second alternative analysis suggests that good is an *emergent* quality. This view would hold that this hard, this square, and this blue combine into a composite particular, this blue thing. On the occasion of combination, value emerges as a real but dependent quality of the blue thing. The blue is a simple particular in this case, but good would not be. Good would be an *emergent* reality. Good would not be a simple part of the composite, but a quality of it. In the Schilpp volume Broad suggests to Moore that it is the natural characteristics of the good thing that cause good to emerge, and he calls them good-making characteristics. But Moore does not at all warm to the suggestion, and the reason is not hard to imagine. Moore finds it necessary to ground value. Thus if good is analyzed as an emergent characteristic, its ground lies in other qualities. Its reality is "borrowed." Good would be real, real as emergent, but it would be, in Moore's sense, definable. It would be analyzable into the set of properties from which it emerges, and Moore rejects the reductionism implicit in this alternative.

Moore is committed to the view that we know good to be independently real. Good comes before the intellect as a simple meaning. It has being, then, as other intelligibles do. It is an object of thought, a concept. As an emergent quality, good's ground would lie in other things and events and thus in other meanings. Good would be, at best, a second-order meaning. The alternative of emergent realism will not satisfy Moore's insistence upon the ontological irreducibility of value to natural facts.

Materially there may be no significant difference between the notion of ingression and the notion of emergence. It is true that, upon the occasion of this blue, this hard, and this square combining into the complex particular, this blue thing, an ontological ground is prepared for good to become existent. The blue thing is good—it has the property good. Good is real and good is objective; it is really good because the natural properties are as they are. The natural properties are, under either analysis, constitutively prior to the existence of good. The natural properties are necessary conditions for good's coming into existence; they might even be said to be logically as well as ontologically prior on either account.

But there is an ontological difference between the two views. Moore holds that good is real *on its own*. It is as irreducible as are the natural properties. The natural properties are constitutively and logically prior (in the sense mentioned), but when good *ingresses* it is as an independent characteristic or property. The natural characteristics of the thing do not make it good; they merely provide the existential context in which good is exemplified.

7. *The Lawlike Character of Value Ingression*

I want to suggest a way of looking at Moore's conception of value ingression that may help to clarify his insistence upon the ontological independence of value, his resistance to naturalism, and at the same time his acceptance of the moral relevance of natural conditions. On Moore's account value does not enter into any situation arbitrarily, but it does so in very regular or lawlike fashion. Moore never uses such a term, but I think it may help to make it clear that the connection between these natural conditions that permit the ingression of value and value itself is one of determinate regularity—hence lawlike.

The point I want to emphasize is the one that Moore makes central to "The Conception of Intrinsic Value." Value's ingression into the world of existence is related to causal regularities in determinate ways. A painter comes to learn how to mix pigments and how to apply the oils to the canvas. The painter learns the rules of perspective. Knowing these matters, and a great deal more as well, the painter is able to create an object that has value. The more of a craftsman and artist the person is, the more value he is able to cause to come into existence. In Moore's view the craftsman–artist causes the artifact to accept value; he makes value's ingression possible. A composite particular painting must exemplify value when the painting has been created as value-requiring. For these reasons we can say that value ingresses into the painting in lawlike fashion.

The same order of lawlike necessity governs practical ethical choice. The moral agent is required to choose an action that will bring those natural conditions into existence that exemplify more value than any other action available to him. The moral agent deals with the natural causal nexus. Whatever choice of action the agent comes to, the consequences of his choice will call for value's ingression, in some degree or other, or will discourage it.

It is to be noted that the lawlike character of value ingression (value law) does not depend upon any particular set of causal laws. I have pointed to this feature of Moore's doctrine on other occasions. The regularities we experience in the world today could very well change. A painter may not be able to mix pigments 100 years from today to produce what can be produced today. There may even be places in the universe where creatures like ourselves could find no reliable value-inviting regularities. Value ingression occurs only in those natural conditions that are receptive to its entry. Value looks only to the conditions that call for it.

We human beings are able to understand the world's natural causal sequences, processes, and contexts. Because we do, it is possible for us to be creative artists. It is also possible for us to be moral. We can choose to make the natural order become configured so as to accept aesthetic and moral predicates. The claim that value ingression obeys a law peculiar to it and does so independently of particular causal laws is clearly articulated by Moore:

> When I say that if a given thing possesses a certain degree of intrinsic value, anything precisely similar to it *would* necessarily *have* possessed that value in the same degree, I mean that it *would* have done so, even if it had existed in a Universe in which the causal laws were quite different from what they are in this one.[9]

In "The Conception of Intrinsic Value" Moore recognizes the strength of his claim. He acknowledges that he is dealing with a kind of necessity that is close to logical necessity but not quite the same. The quotation above is completed as follows:

> it is *impossible* for any precisely similar thing to possess a different value, in precisely such a sense that, in which it is, I think, generally admitted that it is *not* impossible that causal laws should have been different from what they are—a sense of impossibility, therefore, which certainly does not depend merely on causal laws.

I have chosen to refer to value ingression, then, in such a way as to capture Moore's feeling for its special ontological and nomological characteristics.

8. *A Shift in View?*

In the 1942 "Reply" (in the Schilpp volume) Moore has additional things to say on some of the points we have gone over. He appears to have shifted his views from *Principia* to some extent, but whatever shift there may be in 1942, the basic requirements for value law do not change. An example is his position with respect to the role of consciousness and feeling in relation to value judgment. In response to the criticism of H. A. Paton, to the effect that Moore's ethics tends to eliminate a role for the emotions in arriving at moral conclusions, Moore says: "no state of affairs can be good, unless its existence entails that somebody is having some *experience*." [10] The reply seems to indicate a modification of the 1903 view as we have explicated it and to introduce an element of subjectivity that we have not accounted for. An examination of the *Ethics* may support the "Reply," however, and show that Moore's position remained unchanged with respect to the consciousness of value.

In the summary paragraph closing the 1912 book Moore says that nothing can be an intrinsic good "unless it contains *both* some feeling and *also* some other form of consciousness." [11]

Principia Ethica is read by many—and Paton may be among them—to imply that good can come into existence independent of any form of consciousness. I think *Principia* does present that thesis and I have argued so throughout the book. However, if that is the case, the quotation from *Ethics* would indicate a change in Moore's position, a shift that occurred in 1912, just nine years after *Principia*'s publication, and not in 1942—nearly forty years later. The issue may be somewhat cloudy, but the situation is not nearly as confused as it may seem.

Matters clear up considerably, for example, if we take certain passages in the final chapter of *Principia* as presaging the view of practical ethics developed in the *Ethics*. Moore says there, for example, "By far the most valuable things, which we know or can imagine, are certain states of consciousness, which may be roughly described as the pleasures of human intercourse and the enjoyment of beautiful objects." [12] Of course, Moore does not say that the *only* valuable things are things we can experience and feel. The chapter is concerned to answer the question, "What things are good, and in what degree?" and Moore deals with what humans can be said to experience. Even in *Ethics* the universe of discourse is confined to what humans experience and has thus an epistemically limited scope.

But for the purposes of understanding value and its ingression into an existing world it is not necessary to date, or even argue for, a purported shift in view. As I have shown, Moore believes that there is a system of value law, or a logic, which governs intrinsic value's existence–instances in lawlike fashion. It is a consequence of this logic that when conditions are sufficient for value exemplification, value *must* become exemplified. The theory, as stipulated in "The Conception of Intrinsic Value" and grounded in the early essays and *Principia*, is general. If it turns out, in a particular instance, that one of the necessary natural grounds for value's ingression is an act of human awareness, the general theory is satisfied. But if human experience, cognitive or affective, is not one of the natural conditions required, the general theory is satisfied as well. Needless to say, it is an *epistemic* necessity that in order for good to be *known* to ingress in any instance, an act of human awareness is called for.

I want now to offer some comments on the apparent shift in Moore's view. I want to indicate why I think Moore may have modified the view from the initial statement in *Principia*, although the grounding ontology does not change. In a letter to *Mind* in 1962, A. C. Ewing wrote that Moore swung back to the *Principia Ethica* position from his 1942 "Reply." [13] If so, this should not be a surprise since the basic ontology remains intact, whether or not human experience be taken as a requirement of value's ingression or exemplification.

In *Principia Ethica* Moore maintains a distinction between the ontological grounds and the epistemological requirements of the value theory. The doctrine of self-evidence, especially the criterion of intuition's fallibility, is an indication of this distinction. Take, as an example, the assertion "This is a chair." One cannot prove this to a skeptic, Moore holds. And we face a similar situation with respect to value claims. An action may be good, but one cannot prove this either. Both propositions—this is a chair, this action is good—are synthetic statements. Chairs exist independent of any human experience of them. If a chair is good, good is an objective property of the chair. Since chairs exist independent of acts of awareness, good chairs do, and thus good's exemplification (in this instance) does as well. *Knowledge* of either the chair's existence or its goodness, however, cannot exist independent of all consciousness.

In *Ethics* the analysis is given over to practical ethical theory. The notions investigated, such as right, duty, obligation, are grounded in human awareness, at least insofar as all these matters involve conscious choices and acts of decision. The problems, the issues, the objections and considerations arise within the practical context. So in this context, the distinction between the ontological ground and the epistemological conditions is not explored by Moore. The question is not of any systematic relevance for the practical ethical *contexts* with which the *Ethics* is concerned.

As I remarked earlier, "The Conception of Intrinsic Value" does the job for *Ethics* that the first four chapters of *Principia Ethica* do for Chapter 5 in the 1903 text. It struggles with the ontological questions involved, especially as concerns the exemplification of good in particular instances. Moore is concerned with intrinsic value as value exemplified, as well as with showing how it is that things that have intrinsic value come into possession of it. He is not concerned with how we know such things, and he does not raise the epistemological questions that concern Paton in the Schilpp volume. The essay does not say, or imply, that human awareness or human experience is a necessary element in the sets of conditions required for value exemplification. It fits the *Ethics* context, it fits the *Principia Ethica* context, and it is consistent with them. No gap is articulated since the epistemological question is moot. The first four chapters of *Principia Ethica* deal with good, qua concept. The epistemological question, although not explicitly raised, must be dealt with in Chapter 5—and it is; hence it is there that the gap is made explicit.

A clear instance of the closure of the gap comes about in the 1932 essay, "Is Goodness a Quality?" In that piece Moore says that "intrinsically good" means *precisely* the same as "worth having for its own sake." He had used the expression "worth having for its own sake" in *Principia* as well, but he did not go on to say what he says in "Is Goodness a Quality?" In 1903 he says that the expression is used by people when they have in mind what he means by the simple notion good. But in 1932 he concludes that since "intrinsic good" and "worth having for its own sake" mean the same, it follows that "nothing but an experience can be 'had' in the sense in which an experience is 'had.'"[14] I think it is clear that a thing, if it is good in Moore's *Principia* sense of good, is worth having for its own sake. I think it is true that if a thing is worth having for its own sake, then it must exemplify good in the *Principia* sense of good. But from the conjunction of these two statements it does not seem to me, nor does Moore imply, that it follows that everything that *is* good must be experienced *as* good.

The thesis of "Is Goodness a Quality?" does not state, nor does it imply, that human experience creates goodness. It does not imply that goodness is in any sense subjective. It does not suggest that it is the experience that *causes* value to become exemplified. It claims at most that a crucial, and necessary, condition for acknowledging value ingression is that an experience be had. The view implies, strictly, that no *object* of an awareness could have value independent of the awareness—by itself. Since experience "had" is one of the necessary conditions, it follows that value is always, and only, exemplified in a complex event, and not merely in some composite thing. In certain ways the analysis in the 1932 essay reminds one of Moore's analysis of beauty in *Principia Ethica*.

The point I am concerned to emphasize here is that good "looks for" certain specific ontological conditions to prevail. Whatever the conditions are, good must wait until they are created. When they are, good enters the situation. The conditions receptive to value ingressions appear to be somewhat wider in the context of *Principia* than they are in the 1932 essay.

Finally, in response to Paton in the "Reply" doctrine (1942), Moore takes a less restricted position than the 1932 view, thus returning at least part way to the *Principia* conditions. In the "Reply" Moore seemed to think that value can become exemplified when there is either (1) an experience worth having for its own sake, or (2) a complex event in which a constituent element is someone-having-an-experience. There is no restriction on condition (2). It could be (a) an experience worth having for its own sake, or (b) an experience neutral with respect to value, or (c) an experience itself unworthy of being had for its own sake. The principle of organic unities teaches that (b) and (c) could very well be parts of wider contexts that were intrinsically good. In the "Reply" Moore has no occasion to consider such possibilities, but we take the next section as a chance to do so.

9. *The Principle of Organic Unities*

In Chapter III, Section 7 the method of isolation was paired with the principle of organic unities in a discussion of value ingression in the world of experience and our human experience of coming to know value in the world. I have mentioned the fact that there is a gap between the two in the sense that if we are able to isolate conceptually a possible state of existence in order to judge it to have intrinsic value, any intuition we have that [epistemically] confirms value may be mistaken. Self-evidence may bring psychological certitude, but it can never guarantee epistemic certitude. Still the method of isolation is the only way we have for making careful judgments of value. It is the epistemic counterpart to the principle of organic unities.

Let us consider an event where $thing_1$, which is good, and $thing_2$, which is neutral with respect to value, are joined together into a unity. The principle of organic relations tells us that we cannot deduce the value of the unity by knowing the value of each of the parts and then summing. The unity of the two creates a discrete thing with its own integrity, and its value is to be assessed by a judgment of it in its integrity.

Moore explicitly warns the reader to examine the complex event *itself* so that he may come to grasp "*exactly what it is* which we declare to be good." What we declare to be good will be, *nearly always*, organic unities of real complexities. "It is *this* whole, which we know to be good, and not another thing."[15] The core of the principle can be found in the very first chapter of *Principia* and is stated clearly, "the value of such a whole bears no regular proportion to the sum of the parts."[16] In *Ethics* the principle is again affirmed "that the *amount by which the value of a whole exceeds one of its factors is not necessarily equal to that of the remaining factor.*"[17]

The specific application of value law can be discovered, not by knowing the value of the elements involved in a complex situation, but by being able to grasp the entire complex itself. The natural conditions that constitute the whole are those that will either call for value or be unreceptive to value. The principle of organic unities emphasizes the integrity of each unity. It is the unity of conditions in each situation, event, or thing that grounds the ingression of value. But these are grounds only; they are but the necessary and not the sufficient [constitutive] conditions of value. In a constitutive sense they do not make, they do not cause, they do not produce value. Good, however, does depend upon the natural world for its exemplification in existence in just the ways I have tried to make clear in this chapter.

CRITICAL BIBLIOGRAPHY: CHAPTER VI

It is easier to explain than to justify the general neglect of the ontology upon which Moore bases his ethics. There is, in the first place, evidence that Moore—like Russell—came eventually to abandon much of the Platonistic ontology that grounds *Principia Ethica*. By the publication of *Ethics* in 1912, the ontological foundations that Moore had laid out in *Principia* were scarcely in evidence despite the fact that he devoted at least three chapters (3, 4, and 7) to issues that bear directly upon those foundations. Already Moore was more concerned with the explication and defense of the epistemological implications of the anti-naturalistic position he had adopted—and for which he was already internationally famous—than he was with such underlying doctrines as the independent reality of concepts and the ontological basis for the distinction between natural and non-natural properties that were central to *Principia*.

The fact is, or at least seems to be, that Moore himself was no longer much interested in defending the extreme realism of *Principia* with its extraordinary Platonistic doctrine of the timelessness of good. And yet the *Ethics*, as Sylvester shows, is clearly incomprehensible without it. Whether Moore was consciously downplaying the role of his ontology in *Ethics* or not, however, it is clear that the philosophical world he lived in was fully prepared to do so.

In this fact lies a second reason for the subsequent and general neglect of the ontology in which Moore's ethics is grounded. It was the attack on what were perceived as the *logical* and *semantic* errors of ethical naturalism—thought to have been exposed by the naturalistic fallacy arguments—that made *Principia* famous, not its ontology. Indeed, with the rapid rise of logical positivism in the decade following World War I, metaphysical inquiry, hence ontology, not only fell into discard in mainstream British philosophy, but was positively discredited. By 1936, in Chapter 4 of *Language, Truth and Logic*, A. J. Ayer was ready to exclude from the subject-matter of philosophy not just metaphysics and ontology but ethics as well, consigning metaphysics and ontology to oblivion and ethics to the social sciences instead, using a mutation of the naturalistic fallacy argument as justification.

That Moore's argument survived at all in this context meant that it was no longer understood as Moore himself had formulated it in *Principia*. It no longer depended on the crucial—and explicitly *ontological*—distinction between natural and non-natural properties. For once the respectability of all ontological distinctions is called into question, Moore's distinction emerges as a matter of semantics. Moreover, even such a verbal distinction seems all but worthless. Thus Mary Warnock writes that Moore's meticulous attention to matters of definition is eccentric, saying: "There is a certain amount of confusion here and elsewhere in the discussion, about whether we are supposed to be discussing a word or some object denoted by a word, such as a property; but this confusion is not very important" (*Ethics Since* 1900 [London: Oxford University Press, 1960], p. 24). Among the anthologies of Moore criticism only Klemke's *Studies* includes anything substantial in the way of attention to Moore's ontology in *Principia*. And even there it is only because of the essays of Gustave Bergmann and Herbert Hochberg, which we have already mentioned and Sylvester refers to in this chapter, that the issue comes up at all. Perhaps even more surprisingly, the essays in the Schilpp volume contain so little discussion of ontological matters that the term is not even indexed. (Under metaphysics and related terms the bulk of the indexed references are to the colloquy between Moore and Paton, which Sylvester discusses below in his final chapter.) There are exceptions to this general neglect, but the most recent studies are not among them.

Not surprisingly, Richard Soghoian's artful ploy of treating David Hume's *Treatise* as a response to Moore's refutation of ethical naturalism altogether dodges the question of the ontology that Moore supplies for his non-natural properties. (*The Ethics of G. E. Moore and David Hume: The Treatise as a Response to Moore's Refutation of Ethical Naturalism* [Washington, D.C.: University Press of America, 1979]. Soghoian's reference is of course to Hume's *A Treatise of Human Nature*, ed. L. A. Selby-Bigge [Oxford: Clarendon Press, 1960], originally published in 1739.)

Dennis Rohatyn, since he wants to argue in defense of ethical naturalism against Moore in *The Reluctant Naturalist*, finds it similarly convenient to pass rather lightly over Moore's ontology. The use he makes of it is, moreover, somewhat perverse. Rohatyn wants us to accept that Moore showed the alleged dichotomy between fact and value to be a false one, but that he did so at the cost of contradicting himself by erasing (in *Principia*, Chapter 6) the very distinction he set up (in Chapter 1) between natural and non-natural properties. (See Rohatyn, *The Reluctant Naturalist*, Chapter 6, "Intermezzo: Ontology and Value.") To support this claim Rohatyn makes use of Robert Hartman's earlier "axiomatization" of Moore's ethics to argue that "we need not be deterred by Moore's antique way of comparing (or contrasting) the ontological status of 'good' with that of natural objects" (p. 43). Hartman's "breathtaking" (Rohatyn's term) account of Moore's ethics is in *The Structure of Value* (Carbondale: Southern Illinois University Press, 1967).

Rohatyn rejects Hartman's account, not because of its total neglect of Moore's ontology, but because of the semantic force of Moore's own open question argument when directed at Hartman's (assumed) definition of 'good.' In this move

Rohatyn agrees with John Hill that "Hartman's extraordinary conclusions are the result of an entirely false preconception of scientific philosophy" (Rohatyn, p. 52). He goes on to point out, however, that Hill agrees with Hartman in rejecting the generically Platonistic character of Moore's ontology (Hill, p. 31).

That Hill *does* reject Moore's Platonistic ontology, however, is based upon grounds very different from Hartman's logical positivism, which abandons metaphysics as well as ontology altogether. Hill's objection is to the Platonist cast of Moore's ontology as sufficient ground for rejecting the sort of Aristotelian moral realism that Hill favors. He regards Moore's version of ontological realism as empty of anything but formal significance. "Good," he says, "is undoubtedly a principle, but it is formal and vacuous: Moore's principles have the same function within ethics as the principles of logic have within that science" (Hill, p. 31).

Rohatyn correctly sees that the only way to defend Moore against Hill's charge of vacuousness is to "defend Platonism (or some near relative) as the correct interpretation of the status of (axio)logical laws." But he goes on to add: "This is an additional burden, not to mention a gratuitous imposition on Moore's text" (Rohatyn, p. 52). It is of course precisely because Sylvester does *not* accept the alleged burden as a gratuitous imposition on Moore's text that he devotes this chapter to an excavation of the ontology of Moore's *Principia*.

The issue, as Hill explains, is indeed a central one for the contemporary doctrines of moral realism that arise, in part at least, from Moore's influence. The classic source for the linkage between Moore and the moral realists is given by R. M. Hare in connection with the introduction of the doctrine of supervenience in *The Language of Morals* (Oxford: Clarendon Press, 1952). See also Hare's *Freedom and Reason* (Oxford: Clarendon Press, 1963); and his *Moral Thinking* (Oxford: Oxford University Press, 1981).

The doctrine of supervenience is defined by Simon Blackburn simply as "the requirement that moral judgments supervene, or are consequential upon natural facts," in his

Spreading the Word (Oxford: Clarendon Press, 1984), p. 220. In this sense, as Sylvester shows in this chapter when discussing the way the ingression of good depends upon natural properties according to value law, that if the doctrine is present in Moore's *Principia* at all, it is clearly grounded in Moore's *ontological* distinction between natural and non-natural properties. However, as Blackburn points out, not all subscribers to the doctrine of supervenience—Hare himself being a leading instance—subscribe to Moore's ontological non-descriptivist and non-prescriptivist way of making the distinction. Thus Hare, in *Freedom and Reason*, combines a descriptivist analysis of value terms (such as 'good') with a prescriptivist analysis of their use. Accordingly, Blackburn suggests that Hare departs from the original meaning of supervenience altogether in favor of the alternative of a universalizability criterion, defined as "the requirement that moral judgments are somehow dependent only upon universal facts; facts specified without reference to particular individuals or groups " (Blackburn, p. 220).

What this suggests, however, is that supervenience is a notion capable of a variety of interpretations and groundings, some of them not *at all* ontological, and many quite independent of the arguments for moral realism that have their roots in Moore's *Principia*. As Blackburn puts the matter in *Spreading the Word*: "Supervenience claims are very popular in philosophy, because they promise some of the advantages of reduction [of value to fact] without the cost of defending [the actual reductions of] necessity claims. But the promise is slightly hollow: supervenience is usually quite uninteresting in itself. What is interesting is why it holds" (p. 186). Various versions, all different from Moore's, of why it holds have been given in John Mackie, *Ethics: Inventing Right and Wrong* (Baltimore: Penguin, 1977); Jaegwon Kim, "Supervenience and Nomological Incommensurables," *American Philosophical Quarterly*, 15 (1978); and J. Dancy, "On Moral Properties," *Mind*, 90 (1981).

An excellent introduction to the variety of ways in which supervenience has been interpreted and applied in ethics and aesthetics is to be found in "Spindel Conference 1983: Supervenience," *Southern Journal of Philosophy*, 22, Supplement (1984). There is a selection of essays and an extensive bibliography linking supervenience with moral realism in "Spindel Conference 1986: Moral Realism," *Southern Journal of Philosophy*, 24, Supplement (1986).

In a collection of essays honoring of the fiftieth anniversary of the publication of A. J. Ayer's *Language, Truth and Logic*, Graham Macdonald's "The Possibility of the Disunity of Science" contains an extremely deflationary definition of supervenience: "that magical solution which allows us to commit a variety of linguistic sins without ontological guilt. Its exact definition need not detain us apart from the characterization which says that a set of properties A supervenes on a set of properties B if any change in the set A must be accompanied by a change in the set B" (*Fact, Science and Morality: Essays on A. J. Ayer's 'Language, Truth and Logic,'* eds. Graham Macdonald and Crispin Wright [Oxford: Blackwell, 1986], p. 243). Although Macdonald's essay is the only one that focuses on supervenience, several valuable essays (by Simon Blackburn, Hartry Field, and Michael Williams, among others) bear upon issues raised by Moore's ethics and the naturalistic fallacy argument.

VII

Fact and Value: The Logic of Moral Discourse

1. *The Problem*

The doctrine known as the naturalistic fallacy brings Moore's name to mind more surely than any other for which he could claim authorship. Its notoriety, however, depends on a variety of applications quite independent of Moore's own use of it in *Principia Ethica*. In his own work the use of the fallacy as an instrument of criticism remains embedded in the context of the 1903 text, and only there.

It may seem odd that there is no mention of this distinctive doctrine in *Ethics* or in the crucial essay "The Concept of Intrinsic Value." It is not cited in "The Nature of Moral Philosophy" (1920). No one raises questions about it in the Schilpp volume, so Moore does not refer to it in "The Reply to My Critics." William Frankena, long associated with discussions of the naturalistic fallacy, has a long critical essay in the Schilpp volume on the relationship between the allegedly simple concepts good and obligation. Moore has a detailed reply, and though Frankena mentions the fallacy in passing—in a remark about his own paper on the subject—Moore does not react. Their exchange is important, however, and I comment upon it at the end of this chapter.

The central problem that I deal with in this chapter includes two separate but related issues that I call the irreducibility thesis and the is-ought thesis. Both issues involve what has been called the logic of moral discourse; that is, the setting forth of conceptual boundaries in such a way that the evidence one brings forth for a moral judgment is adequate for the acceptance of the judgment. I want to show that Moore depends heavily upon the irreducibility thesis in the formulation of the naturalistic fallacy. I point out that

157

as Moore applies the fallacy in the context of his own work, the major emphasis falls upon the notion of irreducibility. I argue that Moore has almost nothing to say about the is-ought thesis as that thesis has been conventionally understood; he simply does not connect the argument from statements of fact to normative claims with the naturalistic argument. Although it may well be the case that arguments from *is* to *ought* are fallacious, Moore does not make this claim in the context of his formulation of the naturalistic fallacy.

2. *Moore's Formulation of the Naturalistic Fallacy*

The doctrine of the naturalistic fallacy is set forth in Chapter 1 of *Principia Ethica*. It is reformulated in each of the three following chapters as needed; that is, as required for the purposes of these three polemical chapters. In each he holds that it is mistake to define 'good' as identical with allegedly more basic characteristics. The initial statement of the fallacy seems clearly formed:

> It may be true that all things which are good are *also* something else, just as it is true that all things that are yellow produce a certain kind of vibration in the light. And it is a fact that Ethics aims at discovering what are those other properties belonging to all those things which are good. But far too many philosophers have thought that when they named those other properties they were actually defining good; that, those properties, in fact, were simply not other, but absolutely the same with goodness. This view I propose to call the 'naturalistic fallacy' and of it I shall now endeavor to dispose.[1]

In Chapter VI of the present text we saw that Moore requires a natural nexus for good to become exemplified in the world. In *Ethics*, he claims that some important characteristics are common to absolutely all intrinsic goods. The naturalistic fallacy is framed as a warning: Do not confuse the natural grounds for value ingression with the value that is exemplified.

The initial formulation of the fallacy (above) appears in the text shortly after an argument purporting to demonstrate that good is known as a simple object of thought. The claim is well known. We studied it in Chapters I and IV. Good means good. Good is a simple object of thought, a concept that is incapable of definition. Good cannot be defined because in defining one demonstrates "what are the parts which invariably compose a certain whole, and in this sense 'good' has no definition because it [good] is simple and has no parts."[2] The commission of the fallacy has most often involved treating good, which is simple in the above sense, as if it were complex. The doctrine also warns against substituting one simple concept for another simple concept; for example, pleasure is simple in the sense discriminated, but must not be thought to be the same as good.

Moore fashions—he says discovers—the naturalistic fallacy with a specific purpose in mind. I suspect that he does not refer to the fallacy in later writings because it has served its purpose as a tool forged for specific use in *Principia Ethica*, but the point is not of major importance. What is important for our purpose is seeing the scope of the fallacy in the *Principia* context.

Moore holds that the first question in ethics is 'What is good?' for until this question is settled we can broach the two other general questions—'What things are good and in what degree?' and 'What ought we to do?'—only at the cost of confusion. Chapters 2 through 4 in *Principia* contain Moore's attempts to refute naturalistic ethics, hedonism, and metaphysical ethics, respectively. He purports to show that the reason most rival doctrines fail is that they have committed the fallacy and are not even aware of the error involved.

Perhaps the most interesting discussion in application of the fallacy and its scope comes when Moore confesses that he *cannot* use it to refute the hedonism of Sidgwick. Moore says, "of all the hedonist writers, Prof. Sidgwick alone has clearly recognized that by 'good' we do mean something unanalyzable, and has alone been led thereby to emphasize that, if Hedonism be true, its claim to be so must be rested on its self-evidence—that we must maintain 'Pleasure is the sole good' to be a mere *intuition*."[3] A simple charge that the naturalistic fallacy has been committed, according to Moore, cannot be brought against Sidgwick's argument. But he goes on to show, as we have seen, how another and more subtle form of error has been committed, and he uses it to dispose of Sidgwick's position.

After the three polemical chapters the fallacy is mentioned three more times in *Principia*. On page 120 Moore claims that the fallacy is committed in aesthetics whenever 'beauty' is defined in naturalistic terms alone. Again, page 176, Aristotle is charged with its commission in his discussion of good and the virtues. But the third instance, page 173, is by far the most interesting, for it is there, in a single sentence, that Moore reveals most tellingly and concisely what he believes the naturalistic fallacy to entail. He puts it this way: "Almost all ethical writers have committed the naturalistic fallacy—they have failed to perceive that the notion of intrinsic value is simple and unique."

3. *The Irreducibility Thesis*

I think all commentators agree that an essential premise of the naturalistic fallacy argument is the irreducibility of good. But not all these commentators have realized the ontological status that Moore ascribes to good as a conceptual entity. Moore's doctrine of the logical idea (used in thought), the theory of concepts articulated in "The Nature of Judgment" (1898) and its companion piece "Identity" (1900), which we discussed in detail in Chapter IV, should have fully prepared us for the importance of distinguishing simple concepts from complex concepts. Simple objects of thought, qua concepts, are; they have being. They have ontological status in being as universals, but they do not exist. Simple concepts cannot be reduced, nor can they be further analyzed. Each simple concept is discrete and should not be confused with any other simple concept, though this is apparently what happens when good and pleasure are identified by some advocates of hedonism.

It is possible, of course, to experience a similar confusion when, in daily life, one has difficulty in saying whether a particular patch of color is dark green or dark blue. But one could *never* confuse the *concept* blue with the *concept* green, both of which concepts are simple and irreducible. Moreover, this is just what Moore holds the concepts of good and pleasure to be, discrete concepts that are simple and irreducible and that should not be confused with each other.

Simple irreducible concepts are the foundations of Moore's position in *Principia*. At the conceptual level, then, complex concepts are nothing but combinations of less complex concepts, and those less complex concepts are combinations of simple concepts. Thus the irreducibility thesis does not forbid the analysis of complex concepts. Indeed, it grounds the program of analysis. In *Principia Ethica* and in *Ethics* the practical ethical concepts of duty, right, obligation, and so on are treated as complex and are analyzed. As we have seen, some concepts used to analyze a complex may be simple, such as good, while others may be complex, such as choice. Moore holds that in principle one could reduce all complex concepts into ultimate simples.

Good is a simple object of thought. It cannot be more ultimately analyzed, a point that Moore makes in this way:

> we may, when we define horse, mean something more important (than merely showing how Englishmen use the word 'horse'). We may mean that a certain object, which all of us know, is composed in a certain manner: that is, that it has four legs, a head, a heart, a liver, etc., all of them arranged in a definite relation to one another. It is in this sense that I deny good to be definable.[4]

It is also true, and must be kept in mind, that there is another equally essential feature to the doctrine of the naturalistic fallacy. Moore has told us that good is simple, and he has told us that good is unique. Good's uniqueness is tied to the fact that it is a non-natural property when it is exemplified in things and events. It is when one confuses good with a natural property, such as pleasure, or with a complex of natural characteristics, such as life according to nature (p. 41), that the *naturalistic* fallacy is committed. "Its being made with respect to 'good' marks it as something specific."[5]

Part of the uniqueness of good may be understood better by saying that *it* must not be confused with anything that *exists*. Moore attributes the naturalistic fallacy to metaphysicians that blur the boundary between existence and being when it comes to value judgment. He says in the chapter (4) devoted to the criticism of metaphysical ethics, "since 'good' is a predicate which neither does nor can exist they [the metaphysicians] are bound to suppose either that "to be good" means to be related to some particular thing which does exist 'in reality' [Kant]; or else that it means merely 'to belong to the real world.'"[6]

One could say that good, as non-natural, cannot be reduced to natural characteristics, but this alone is not enough to make the point that Moore insists upon. There are other non-natural objects of thought and other simple concepts. What is unique about the simple concept good—its value creating capacity for ingression into, or exemplification in, naturally existing things—is what distinguishes good as a simple concept. I mention this for I want to be sure that the reader understands that the naturalistic fallacy, grounded on the irreducibility thesis, is specifically called *naturalistic* because of the *uniqueness* of good, and not just because of good's status as a simple object of thought.

4. *William Frankena's Critique of Irreducibility*

William Frankena's influential study, which he calls simply "The Naturalistic Fallacy," encompasses both the irreducibility thesis and the is–ought thesis. As we have done, he too holds that the heart of *Principia*'s claim lies in the irreducibility of good. But Frankena, in his analysis, suggests that the fallacy is broader than Moore takes it to be and renames it. Frankena calls it the definist fallacy. The definist fallacy occurs, argues Frankena, whenever one confuses or identifies one property with another. So in this argument it is not relevant to the process of definition whether the properties are simple or complex. Frankena believes that Moore himself holds this form; that is, the definist form, of the fallacy. Frankena says:

This formulation of the definist fallacy explains or reflects the motto of *Principia Ethica*, borrowed from Bishop Butler:

"Everything is what it is, and not another thing." It follows from the motto that goodness is what it is and not another thing. It follows that views which try to identify it with something else are making a mistake of an elementary sort.[7]

The definist fallacy understood in terms of the Butler maxim makes good, like anything else, to be simply what it is and not something else. The definist fallacy strips from good (and from anything else that may be held to be simple) the importance of the notion of simplicity as a relevant factor in the process of analysis. Frankena claims, "to be effective at all, [the borrowed motto] must be understood to mean, 'Every term means what it means, and is not what is meant by any other term.'"[8] The critique is then completed by Frankena with the remark, "The point is that goodness is what it is, even if it is definable."[9]

5. Application of the Butler Maxim

The Butler epigraph stands opposite the title page of *Principia Ethica*, and it stands alone. It is clearly thought by Moore to be the motto for the work. Frankena is not the only philosopher who remarks about the maxim in terms relevant to Moore's insistence upon the indefinability of good. R. M. Hare in *The Language of Morals* makes a similar observation:

It has sometimes been alleged against Moore's refutation of naturalism that it proves too much—that if it were valid for 'good' it would be valid for any word whatever that is claimed to be definable in terms of other words. Certain phrases of Moore's lay him open to this objection, especially his quotation of Butler's slogan 'Everything is what it is, and not another thing.'[10]

It may be that Hare has followed Frankena's lead in thinking of the Butler motto in terms that make light of the distinction between irreducibility and indefinability. He does not say. The point is that neither of them indicates why he thinks Moore applies the Butler epigram to irreducibility. I raise the question since Moore himself quotes the maxim again in the body of the work and tells us there why he uses it and what we are to glean from its use.

In Section 2 of the present chapter I briefly outlined Moore's use for the fallacy. I said that after Moore disposes of rival moral theories early on in *Principia*, he drops all reference to the naturalistic fallacy. In the final two chapters of *Principia Ethica* Moore turns to speak to (1) 'What things are good and to what degree?' and (2) 'What ought we to do?' In the last chapter (6), Moore deals also with the question, 'What things are good?'

What things are good in themselves? Moore tells us how to find out what things have intrinsic value. We grasp them in thought. He writes: "it is necessary to consider what things are such that, if they existed *by themselves*, in absolute isolation, we should yet judge their existence to be good; and in order to decide on the relative *degree* of value of different things, we must similarly consider what comparative value seems to attach to the isolated existence of each." [11]

Compare two possible situations. Situation D: A child is in an inflated inner tube and floating on a river; she approaches a turbulent waterfall; she is caught up in the current, is swept over the falls, and is dashed upon the granite rocks below the falls. Situation S: A child is in an inflated inner tube and floating on a river; she approaches a turbulent waterfall; before being caught by the current and dragged to the falls, she is pulled to the banks of the river. The method of isolation suggests that by conceptual isolation of D and S one can judge that S has value (is good) and that D lacks value. Now, unless the mind is capable of such judgments, Moore's analysis of practical ethics and its concepts is in jeopardy.

The method of isolation requires that when one judges things or events to have value, and when they are composed of a great many elements, one must keep the thing or event steadily before the mind. To float in an inner tube on a cooling river in the heat of the summer is by itself an event that may have great value. It is when it becomes part of a more ominous whole that another judgment, encompassing the part, may (and does) yield a far different value assessment. Moore tells us, for example, that the enjoyment of beautiful objects is one of the most valuable things we can know or imagine. [12] But part of what has great value may be worthless. Material elements contained as parts of an aesthetic experience, for example, may lack any value in themselves, yet they may be necessary conditions for the value of the whole.

> The chief thing necessary to be considered *is exactly what it is* that we declare to be good when we declare the appreciation of beauty in Art and Nature is so. . . . But if we admit it, we should remember Butler's maxim that Everything is what it is and not another thing. I have tried to show, and I think that it is too evident to be disputed, that such an experience is an organic unity, a complex whole.[13]

The principle of organic unities, which we discussed in Chapter VI, Section 9, is the ontological counterpart to the method of isolation. The principle tells us that the value of a whole depends upon the constitution of the whole. The value in the whole cannot be grasped by noting the value of the parts and taking the sum of those parts. Moore directs explicit criticism to idealist philosophers who deny the existence of the material world as relevant to perfection. He argues that they violate the principle of organic unities. "It must be admitted on pain of self-contradiction—on pain of holding that things are not what they are, but something else—that a world from which material qualities were wholly banished would be a world which lacked many, if not all, of those things, which we know most certainly to be great goods."[14]

The Butler maxim is explicitly quoted and strategically aimed at the analysis of the ontological and epistemological conditions that ground the existence of value—and our discovery of it—in the existing universe. What things are good in themselves? Those things are good in themselves that are receptive to value ingression and in which it is exemplified. By reflective conceptual analysis—an act of conceptual isolation—we are able to judge of situations with respect to value. Situation S, the child pulled to shore, is good. The contemplative appreciation of a production of "King Lear" is good.

One must conclude that the Butler maxim is not intended by Moore to help clarify or underscore the naturalistic fallacy. Frankena is mistaken in applying it to the fallacy in order to reduce the naturalistic fallacy's import to the more trivial level of the definist fallacy. The issue of good's status as a simple conceptual entity, significantly different from other simples and complexes, is not directly touched by Frankena's arguments.

The Butler maxim, it is fair to say, has nothing to do with the issue 'What is good?' On the other hand, it *does* have importance for understanding 'What *things* are good?' Both (*a*) the principle of organic unities and (*b*) the method of isolation are of crucial import for grasping Moore's practical ethical theory. The Butler maxim is an affirmation of the central importance of these two principles, so one can fully appreciate why Moore chose the epigram to stand as the frontispiece for *Principia Ethica*.

6. *The Naturalistic Fallacy: Concepts and the Open Question*

Once we have the ontological doctrine that undergirds *Principia Ethica* in mind, certain objections to Moore's formulation of the naturalistic fallacy doctrine can be readily dismissed. However, if the ontology that grounds the theory of judgment fails, whatever truth remains in the teachings of the doctrine, if any, will have to be grounded anew. Moore is working from the view that (*a*) simple and complex concepts have being; they *are* (This view continues to be held by Moore at least through the 1910-1911 lectures, *Some Main Problems of Philosophy*); and (*b*) complex concepts are to be analyzed into their constituent elements. Concepts are objective and independent of any acts of consciousness through which we may come into contact with them.

Consider the following objection: In *Ethics* (and in *Principia*, for that matter) Moore argues that 'duty' and 'the expedient' are alternate ways of referring to the same reality; namely, the best possible consequences of an action capable of being chosen by an agent. Why can't good and pleasure be understood in the same way? Duty and the expedient are concepts like good and pleasure. Why can't 'good' and 'pleasure' refer to one and the same reality, each in its own way?

The objection misses the point of simplicity. Concepts are not private notions; they are not merely subjective. Concepts are, as we have said, logical ideas; they do not refer to anything other than themselves. Concepts are, in a very clear sense, meanings for Moore. Good and pleasure are two such simple meanings. In contrast, duty and the expedient are not simples. They are complex concepts. They are a gathering of more simple notions; which is to say, they are analyzable.

Let me put the second objection in terms of actual experience. One might say, reflecting upon a particular rendition of Bach's *B Minor Mass*, "It gave me great pleasure." Another might say of the same performance, "It was good." Isn't it plausible to hold that the two terms, 'good' and 'pleasure,' refer to the same experience, the one term pointing to the subjective pole of the experience, the other indicating the objective pole? We might then say that the two terms comprehend the same "thing," but each does it in its own way and with its own emphasis. Given any experience of value, then, there would be various alternative ways to cite what Moore calls good. It would make little difference, on this view, which set of terms one actually uses to commend the experience in question, 'good' or 'pleasure.'

Moore's answer to objections of this sort is to lean back on the theory of meaning implicit in his doctrine of concepts. He holds that the objector who says that 'good' and 'pleasure' are merely two labels for the same reality is actually offering a *definition* of good. The open question argument is the device to counter this maneuver. On page 15 of *Principia Ethica* it is sketched in this way: "Whatever definition be offered, it may always be asked with significance, of the complex so defined, whether it itself is good." [15]

When one says, "it gave me great pleasure," the question may be posed, "but is that good?" In other words, "is it good that the experience gave you great pleasure?" is an intelligible question, according to Moore, and it seems that he is correct. If the question is a synthetic one, and the question does not appear conceptually absurd or patently redundant, then one may be assured that there is more than one meaning before the intellect. The meaning of good and the meaning of pleasure are two distinct meanings. So if pleasure refers to the experience of hearing the B Minor Mass, it refers to its bringing its own discrete sense, which is not the same sense as good; though 'good' may refer to the same experience, it brings its own and different sense with it. There is just no way in which the one sense can define the other.

The point to be taken from the discussion is the one I have been insisting upon all along. The cornerstone of the naturalistic fallacy, the irreducibility of the simple concept good, lies in the theory of concepts that Moore held during the early years. For our purposes the early years include his work from the publication of "Judgment" in 1899 through the publication of *Ethics* in 1912.

7. Concepts of Different Logical Types: Facts and Values

I began discussion of the irreducibility thesis by pointing out that it is an essential feature of the naturalistic fallacy doctrine that good is irreducible. At the end of Section 3 I said that good's uniqueness was another essential feature. Moore says, "to confuse two natural objects, one with another, defining one by means of the other . . . is a mistake, and a fallacy," but he is not inclined to call such a fallacy naturalistic. The naturalistic fallacy occurs only when one jumps the boundary between good and natural objects or properties.[16]

Moore emphasizes a difference in both logical and ontological types. The difference he is most concerned with is marked by calling good a *non-natural* property of things in which it is found. The difference between natural and non-natural properties is grounded ontologically. The difference may be shown to consist in two different modes of predication. [The matter is discussed above in Chapter VI.]

One traditional way of stating the difference in logical types has been to separate statements pointing to natural characteristics of things or events—we call them factual statements—from statements pointing to non-natural or value-making characteristics, which we call value statements. Another way is to distinguish between descriptive and normative statements, but neither of these two ways of drawing the logical boundary is helpful in grasping Moore's moral theory, for both fail to reflect accurately the ontology that Moore supplies to undergird the theory. (I give a more adequate presentation of this point in the next section.)

As imprecise as the distinction between fact and value is for appreciating Moore's views, the distinction between the is and the ought, although it is often employed by Moore's critics, is even less satisfactory. This is especially true as we try to keep clear about the terms of the naturalistic fallacy. Since Moore never mentions the fallacy in the context of practical ethics where predicates such as obligation, right, and duty are analyzed, no one should be surprised to learn that the naturalistic fallacy in Moore's hands does not deal with the is–ought thesis.

I do not wish to be misunderstood. Moore thinks it is a mistake, and indeed even a fallacy, to draw an ought-to-do conclusion from a mere statement of fact when no value premise (explicit or implicit) is supplied. In fact, I quote from three of his little-known essays, all published the same year as *Principia*, or thereabouts.

In each instance, note that the naturalistic fallacy is not mentioned as the error in question. The first quotation comes from Moore's review of Brentano: "The great merit of this view over all except Sidgwick's is its recognition that all truths of the form 'this is good in itself' are logically independent of any truths about what exists."[17]

Second: In another review, this of McTaggart's *Ethics* published in 1903—the same year as the Brentano review, the publication of *Principia Ethica*, and "The Refutation of Idealism"—Moore discovers an alleged error in McTaggart's work and points up the fallacy. It is a fallacy, we are told, to make "a direct inference from 'is' to 'ought.'"[18] I presume that if Moore thought, in 1903, that the is–ought fallacy is the same as the naturalistic fallacy, he would have said as much in the review, though we cannot be sure.

Third: In a slightly earlier essay, first delivered as a lecture before the London School of Ethics and Social Philosophy on the topic of the nature of religion and published in 1901 under the title "The Value of Religion," Moore says:

An appeal to faith, then—to intuition—is the sole ground for asserting the truth of religion. That truth, if it be true, is coordinate with the facts of daily life and cannot be inferred from them, as they can be inferred from one another. And so far it would seem that religious belief stands in the same position as our moral beliefs. These moral judgments too, it may be said, are independent of beliefs about the world; their truth also can never be inferred from that of daily facts.[19]

Moore claims that there is a logical independence between moral or value or ought beliefs and existence, or is or daily life beliefs. But he does not in 1901 use the expression 'naturalistic fallacy' to cite false inferences that rest upon the denial of that independence. Of course, "The Value of Religion" was published two years before *Principia*, and Moore may not have worked out his coinage of the naturalistic fallacy that early. The point to be taken is the awareness Moore has of the logical difference between statements mentioning only natural conditions in the world and statements dealing with value, whether the value be in religion, in ethics itself, or in value theory. The systematic distinctions come about when Moore attends directly to the study of ethics.

The logical independence of value, mentioned in the Brentano review and in "The Value of Religion," is reviewed in Chapter IV. There it is pointed out that whether the concept 'existence' is or is not part of a complex of concepts—that is, a proposition—has no logical bearing on the proposition's *truth* in the case of ethical judgments. This is a consequence of the view of the nature of judgment that Moore held in 1903, and it strengthens the claim of the logical independence of facts and values.

8. *The Is–Ought Thesis*

In arguing for the centrality of the irreducibility thesis in Moore's ethics, I noted that William Frankena's celebrated essay on the naturalistic fallacy construes the doctrine as applying to the is–ought relation, and that this is an application broader than what can be clearly warranted by reference to *Principia Ethica* itself. In order to show that Frankena misconstrues Moore's conception of the fact–value distinction, I use Frankena's formulation of the ways in which the distinction can be made as a foil for setting forth Moore's thought on the matter. I want this known, however: I am not claiming Frankena thinks that the ways he discusses are actually stressed by Moore. Frankena may think Moore is saddled with them, but I am not concerned to show that he does. Frankena does, however, attribute them to the intuitionists, and I plan on showing that Moore does not belong in any such camp.

Frankena identifies three ways that an intuitionist might state the fact–value bifurcation:

(1) Ethical propositions are not deducible from non-ethical ones.
(2) Ethical characteristics are not definable in terms of non-ethical ones.
(3) Ethical characteristics are different in kind from non-ethical ones.

Frankena claims that the intuitionist bifurcation *actually* is captured by (3). He says that (3) entails (2) and (2) entails (1).[20] I study the three statements in the light of Moore's own views.

I want to be clear on one matter at the outset where there is a chance for immediate conceptual confusion. We must not gloss the meaning of the term 'ethical' in Moore's usage. It is left undiscussed in the quotation from Frankena's essay, and Moore may have inadvertently promoted a possible confusion. His own use of the term 'ethics,' as we have seen, covers two different questions, which, he says in the Preface, generate different inquiries. "These two questions may be expressed, the first in the form: What kinds of things ought to exist for their own sakes? the second in the form: What kinds of actions ought we to perform?"[21]

The first sort of question requires us to look for intrinsic value (good) in things. Before we can do that, we must be clear about the proper analysis of the term 'good.' The naturalistic fallacy is a tool devised to help us in that task. The second question, What ought we to do? involves us in the analysis of right, duty, and obligation. Since the is–ought controversy (or thesis) involves terms of this sort, I point out that the word 'ethical' is used to cover the practical ethical concepts (or terms).

I consider three different types of statements that are distinguished implicitly in Moore's moral theory. They are:

V-statements, which indicate value judgments.
E-statements, which indicate ethical judgments.
N-statements, which indicate judgments of natural conditions.

I next consider two examples of N-statements and one each of V-statements and E-statements:

P4: Situation D consists of a child, an inflated inner tube, a river, a waterfall, the banks of the river, granite rocks below the falls, such that: The child floating in the inner tube on the river is carried past the banks of the river to the brink of the waterfall, is carried over the falls, and is dashed on the rocks below.

P3: Situation S consists of a child, an inflated inner tube, a river, a waterfall, the banks of the river, granite rocks below the falls, such that: The child floating in the inner tube on the river is pulled to the banks of the river before being carried to the brink of the falls.

P2: I ought to bring S into existence.

P1: S is good.

P4 and P3 are N-statements. P2 is an E-statement. P1 is a V-statement. Moore's practical ethical theory—sometimes called ideal utilitarianism, although not by Moore himself—entails the following:

If I see that P3 is an outcome that is in my power to effect, P3 *itself* does not contain enough evidence required to deduce P2. That is, if the agent is aware of P3 as an outcome that is in his power to effect, and if P1 is true, then the agent is in a position to notice that P1 is true. So, if one is aware of P3, and P1 is true, one can intuit the truth of P1. But if P3 is understood and P1 is intuited as true (and P1 *is* true), P2 still cannot be deduced from the conjunction of P3 and P1. P2 is justified only if P3 is better than

P4 and any other possible outcome of any action open to, and in the power of, an agent to effect.

Keeping P3, P2, and P1 in mind, let us turn to the three Frankena statements we began with at the outset of this section. I show how Moore's trifurcation fits with the intuitionist bifurcation offered by Frankena:

F(1): Ethical propositions are not deducible from non-ethical ones.
Under Moore's analysis, (*a*) P2 cannot be deduced from P3.
E-statements cannot be deduced from N-statements. (*b*) P2 cannot be deduced from P1. E-statements cannot be deduced from V-statements.
F(2): Ethical characteristics are not definable in terms of non-ethical ones.
Under Moore's analysis, (*c*) P2 cannot be defined in terms of P3.
E-statements cannot be defined in terms of N-statements. (*d*) P2 cannot be defined in terms of P1. E-statements cannot be defined in terms of V-statements.

I must add a word of elaboration that is relevant to an important issue taken up in more detail in Section 10 below. As we know, good is also known as intrinsic value; furthermore, Moore refers to good also as ought to be. I draw attention to the fact that it is a thing that has value that ought to be, or a thing that has value that is a thing of intrinsic value. So P1 (S is good) could be restated as P1* (S ought to be). It is the situation S that ought to be, yet it does not follow that anyone ought to make it come into existence merely because it ought to be.

F(3) Ethical characteristics are different in kind from non-ethical ones.
Under Moore's analysis, (*e*) P2 is different in kind from P3.
E-statements are different in kind from N-statements. (*f*) P2 is different in kind from P1. E-statements are different in kind from V-statements.

From *Principia Ethica* through *Ethics*, and indeed in all Moore's writings in moral theory, the view I have been stating has remained constant. E-statements are analyzed such that they include reference to V-statements that necessarily involve N-conditions. Put slightly differently, N-statements describe N-conditions, such that if a V-statement is true of them, an E-statement *may* also be true of them [but not unless the V-statement includes a truth to the effect that nothing better could be done]. But because the terms of reference of the traditional is–ought thesis bypass the essential linkages [V-statements] between natural conditions and obligation, the terms of reference are not at all helpful in indicating the kinds of evidence and information required to justify moral choice in Moore's ideal utilitarianism.

9. *Natural Conditions, Value Judgments, and Ethical Judgments*

In Chapter VI, Sections 7 and 8, I spent a good deal of time probing the relationship between natural properties and value ingression into the world. I distinguished between contingent causal regularities and value law. I wanted to show that Moore held that good becomes exemplified in existence whenever the natural conditions are suitably arranged so as to call for it. Moore argued that if a natural complex (a thing or an event) has intrinsic value upon an occasion, then any natural complex exactly like that thing must have value, and in the same degree. [Moore's supervenience] N-conditions are the necessary conditions for good's existence.

The naturalistic fallacy warned that although N-conditions are necessary conditions, good cannot simply be identified with these conditions. Natural properties, admitted to be necessary for good's existence, are not sufficient for an explanation of value's being in the world. Good is as fully real a property of the things that are good as any property of the things in question. What is important to grasp about Moore's views, insofar as the fact–value dichotomy is concerned, is that value is as objective a part of the existing world as any of the natural properties. Moral agents find value *in* things and are enjoined to help make more value come into existence as a matter of duty.

Moore has consistently held that in order to do what is right one must have as much knowledge of the way the world works as is possible. One must know about the physical "laws" as well as the "laws" of society. If one is on the banks of the river when the child floats past on the inner tube, one perfectly well understands the possibilities, D or S. One perfectly well "knows" what action is called for.

It should be no surprise, then, that Moore does not equate the naturalistic fallacy analysis to the standard is–ought controversy, for it has no grounds for application in his theory. The logic of his theory is not faithfully represented by the standard is–ought distinction or the usual fact–value dichotomy. I have argued that his is a three-level logic of discourse: E-statements, V-statements, and N-statements.

10. *Ought to Be and Ought to Do*

"Whenever (anyone) thinks of 'intrinsic value' or 'intrinsic worth,' or says that a thing 'ought to exist,' he has before his mind the unique object—the unique property of things—which I mean by 'good.'" [22] Moore makes it clear, here and elsewhere, that several terms point to the simple object of thought that he calls good in *Principia* and intrinsic value in *Ethics*.

I mention this again so that no one will misunderstand my contention that Moore does not apply the naturalistic fallacy doctrine to the is–ought controversy. It has been pointed out to me that when Moore charges John Stuart Mill with commission of the fallacy, he seems to say it violates the ban on deriving an ought from an is. Moore says:

The fact is that 'desirable' does not mean 'able to be desired' as 'visible' means 'able to be seen.' The desirable means simply what *ought* to be desired, or *deserves* to be desired, just as the detestable means not what can but ought to be detested and the damnable what deserves to be damned. [23]

The error Mill makes has to do with the meaning of value; it does not refer to an issue of practical ethical importance, in the above context. In Section 40 of *Principia Ethica* Moore is intent upon refuting the notion that good can be reduced to desire or to pleasure.

There remains an issue generated out of the stipulation that 'ought to be' and 'ought to exist' are mere alternative ways of signaling good. I am once again indebted to William Frankena's work for help in setting the problem. This time I deal with his critical essay in the Schilpp volume, where he scrutinizes Moore's attempt to generate normative content [an ought to do] out of the predicate of value. The argument can be put as follows: If good is simple, then statements of the form "X is good" neither include nor are identical with statements of obligation. If this is so, then statements of the form "X is good" are not normative. If "X is good" is not normative, the idea that "act P is that act which will bring about the most good in the world" has no normative aspect to it. Therefore, Frankena concludes, there is no reason to say that one ought to do act P.

Frankena's arguments hit at the distinction between V-statements and E-statements. It's not that he contests the distinction itself, I should say. Rather it's that he claims that if there isn't an explicit obligatory content to V-statements on Moore's account, then it is impossible to discover obligation in E-statements. I understand his argument to claim that on Moore's view one must give a V-statement as (one of) the justifying reason(s) for an E-statement. Accordingly, unless the V-statement has some normative content, no obligatoriness can be found in the E-statement. Because good is simple, it cannot have a normative aspect. Therefore, E-statements are at best mere factual statements.[24]

Moore replies that good does have normative content, as simple; that good's simplicity and good's normative nature are compatible. In attempted refutation of Frankena's view, Moore breaks down Frankena's arguments into five steps and claims that the step between (2) and (3) is faulty. I reproduce the first three steps so that we can work with the issues:

From the statement:

(1) Good is simple, it follows that
(2) Statements of the form "X is good" neither include nor
are identical with any statement about obligation, but from
(2) it follows that
(3) Statements of the form "X is good" are not normative.[25]

As I have indicated, Moore allows (2) to stand, but holds that
statements of the form "X is good" have normative content and
therefore (3) does not follow from (2) as is claimed. His reply to
Frankena is lengthy. I shall not attempt to summarize all of the
points; but I will say that a famous argument he offers is of interest. He says that there is a sense of 'includes or is identical with' in
which the statement "X is good" does not include and is not identical with any statement about obligation. And yet upon certain
occasions it follows from the very nature of anything that is good
that there *is* something normative about the thing. The argument
is an analogy from 'this is a cube' and 'this has twelve edges'; such
that 'this is a cube' does not include and is not identical with 'this
has twelve edges,' yet "It follows from the very nature of a cube
that anything which is a cube has twelve edges."[26] [See bibliographical notes for Chapter VI.]

I ask the reader to keep firmly in mind Moore's basic view
about the nature of good. It is a simple concept that may be exemplified in the existing world. Keep in mind, especially, that it appears as a property of things in the world. "It is not goodness, but
only things or qualities which are good, which can exist in time—
can have duration, and begin and cease to exist—can be objects of
perception."[27] Things are good, and when a thing appears as
good, we can and do say it ought to be. If it is possible within
some context of choice to make something exist, and we know
(from experience) that *that* sort of thing is good, then, when we
think we ought to bring it into existence, the quality of that sort of
thing that appeals to us to make it exist is called good.

Suppose good qualifies the situation S, the child being pulled to
safety. One may judge that S is good or, alternatively, that S ought
to be. In either case the *situation* ought to be. In judging that S
ought to be, one is not making a *further* and different judgment

that it is someone's duty to bring S into existence. The question is, does the notion *ought to be* or *ought to exist for its own sake* "seem to mean that someone has a duty to bring whatever has the quality into existence"?[28] Frankena says it does, but Moore says that unless a good deal more information is supplied, the judgment that a duty is required cannot yet be made.

Good, all by itself—qua concept—is a simple meaning. All by itself, it is not a thing of intrinsic value. It is not an existing thing at all, nor is it intrinsic to anything; it simply is. When good is exemplified in something, the *thing* has intrinsic value, *it* ought to be, and *it* ought to exist for its own sake.

Moore holds that the failure to keep this distinction clearly in mind is a source of much confusion in the ethics of hedonism and utilitarianism.

In order to see this point we might contrast Moore's doctrine of ideal utilitarianism with the simplistic hedonism of pleasure utilitarianism. Here is a criticism of the latter along the lines of Frankena's argument:

From the statement (1) that pleasure is simple, it follows that statements of the form (2) 'X is pleasant' neither include nor are identical with any statement about duty or obligation. Thus from (2) it follows that statements of the form "X is pleasant" are not normative.

A pleasure utilitarian may well hold that pleasure has a normative aspect to it. He may well claim that pleasure either *does* or *ought to* move us to action. He may claim that if one has a choice between an action that will bring a significant amount of pleasure into the world and another that will bring less pleasure, we *will* or *ought to* choose the one that maximizes pleasure. But the point is that the fact that pleasure is a simple meaning, or is a simple concept in Moore's sense, is quite independent of the fact that pleasure either *does* or *ought to* move one to action. I suppose one might say it's the nature of man—human nature—that reacts to pleasure in the way that the pleasure utilitarian thinks.

It is not happenstance that Moore models his own theory after the utilitarian model. The first two chapters of *Ethics* carefully build a pleasure utilitarian theory, which is critically developed in the remaining chapters. It is refined to Moore's own requirements.

The final touch is the removal of pleasure as the operative goal for action and the substitution of states of affairs that are intrinsically good. In Moore's version of utilitarianism, good is substituted for pleasure. What remains, of course, is *the pull*, as it were, that intrinsically valuable consequences have on moral choice, similar to the pull that pleasurable states of sensorium have on animal choice. That is, intrinsic value calls for choice to actualize it as it appears qua value to a person with moral awareness. Frankena seems to recognize the parallel, I think, for he says: "If goodness is either simple or a quality, it can be connected with obligation only synthetically. The most that can be said of it is that it is a characteristic whose presence *makes* things such that they ought to be brought into existence—as pleasantness is sometimes said to be." [29]

There are two points to be made in bringing the present chapter to a close. First, with respect to Moore's ultimate reason for thinking we ought to bring into existence that which ought to exist for its own sake (under stipulated conditions), in *Ethics* Moore gives us the reason. *It is self-evident* that our duty is to maximize the good. [30]

Second, 'obligation' is a defined term. It is not simple; it is analyzable. The practical ethical notions are analyzed such that agents are required to choose to do those actions that will promote the best possible consequences. Good is (merely) the quality that, when exemplified in things, makes the things in question to be ones that ought to be. It is in the nature of the moral being where the ought to be and the ought to do are synthesized. It is the task of Chapter VIII to lay out the notion of the self and the moral context.

CRITICAL BIBLIOGRAPHY: CHAPTER VII

It is indeed the case, as Sylvester says, that the naturalistic fallacy doctrine "calls Moore's name to mind more surely than any other for which he could claim authorship." But it is also apparent that its notoriety depends to a very great extent upon the version of the doctrine that William

Frankena is responsible for and Sylvester discusses in this chapter. It is an irony that does not escape Sylvester that it is *Frankena*'s and not *Moore*'s doctrine that is so widely discussed in the literature as to justify use of the term 'notoriety'; nor does he fail to notice that it is doubly ironic that in the literature so little attention is paid to the grounds upon which Moore bases his doctrine. It is in fact Sylvester's recognition of the latter irony that prompts his criticism of Frankena's interpretation of Moore.

What Sylvester distinguishes as two theses that have often been linked to the naturalistic fallacy argument, the irreducibility claim and the is–ought thesis, are both customarily traced back to Hume. (See Soghoian's discussion, pp. 73-78; also A. N. Prior's clear showing of earlier sources for Hume's is–ought dichotomy in *Logic and the Basis of Ethics* [Oxford: Clarendon Press, 1949].) The first thesis is traced to Hume's epistemological claim that moral distinctions rest upon simple impressions and not upon complex ideas; the second is traced to what is often called the is–ought paragraph, which concludes Hume's discussion of moral distinctions not derived from reason in *A Treatise of Human Nature*. Because that paragraph is so often referred to in the literature and so rarely quoted it may be useful to quote it here:

In every system of morality, which I have hitherto met with, I have always remark'd, that the author proceeds for some time in the ordinary way of reasoning . . . when of a sudden I am surpris'd to find, that instead of the usual copulation of propositions, *is*, and *is not*, I meet with no proposition that is not connected with an *ought* or an *ought not*. This change is imperceptible; but is, however, of the last consequence. For as this *ought*, or *ought not*, expresses some new relation or affirmation, 'tis necessary that it should be observ'd and explain'd . . . how this new relation can be a deduction from others which are entirely different from it. [*A Treatise of Human Nature*, ed. L. A. Selby-Bigge (Oxford: Clarendon Press, 1960), pp. 469–70]

Frankena, in the essay cited by Sylvester, interprets the paragraph this way: "Hume's point is that ethical conclusions cannot be drawn validly from premises which are non-ethical." This essay, "The Naturalistic Fallacy" is reprinted in *Readings in Ethical Theory*, eds. Wilfred Sellars and John Hospers [New York: Appleton-Century-Crofts, 1952], an anthology that is quoted here and reprinted in Klemke's anthology, pp.30–43.)

In view of Frankena's conflation of Hume's view, as interpreted above, with Moore's, it is not surprising that he reads Moore's argument erroneously in terms of what he calls the definist form of the naturalistic fallacy. Frankena's reading arises partly from a failure to see the centrality of good's simplicity (as expressed in the irreducibility thesis), and partly from a failure to appreciate Moore's use of Butler's epigram ("everything is what it is and not another thing") as making an ontological point. Sylvester sees Frankena's failures here as confirming the importance of Moore's admonition against confusing the question 'what *things* are good?' with the question 'what *is* good?' In effect, Sylvester simply denies that Frankena's definist version of the is–ought thesis has captured the essence of Moore's naturalistic fallacy argument.

Sylvester shows that, in Moore's terms, the meaning of 'X is good' entails that 'X ought to be' but does not entail any proposition about an agent, A, such that 'A ought to do something to bring about X.' By his failure to see the possibility of a necessary (but non-analytic) connection between ought to be and ought to do, Frankena, according to Sylvester, fails to grasp Moore's point that the normative force of good in duty and obligation rests (or supervenes) upon a particular kind of complex fact. (It would be a situation in which X is good, *and* is an element in a complex that would be the most good achievable by A, *and* is in a context of choice in which all this is recognized by the agent.) By his frequent use of the context in which the child's life is threatened by the waterfall that is just ahead as she drifts downstream, Sylvester emphasizes the complexity of situations upon which good supervenes, or—to use Sylvester's phraseology—into which good ingresses and is exemplified. In such contexts of choice there is no reasonable doubt about what one ought to do. As Sylvester puts it, the moral agent in the context of moral choice provides the synthesis of the ought to be and the ought to do. Just how this is done is addressed in Sylvester's final chapter.

It is a feature of Moore's conception of the *simplicity* of good that good, by itself, carries no obligation to action whatsoever. It is this same absence of normative force, which Hume finds missing in simple impressions, that drives him to propose that duty and obligation rest upon the appropriate blend of reason and the passions. (See David Hume, *An Enquiry Concerning the Principles of Morals*, reprinted from the edition of 1777 [La Salle, Ill.: Open Court, 1938], esp. pp. 109–13.) However, in Moore, Hume's passions are severely muted in favor of rational deliberation. What Hume misses, according to Moore's analysis, is that the *supervenience of good*, its ingression into the complex situation, is what a rational person can discover to be self-evident. As Sylvester has shown, intuition for Moore has nothing at all to do with anything like Hume's moral sentiments of benevolence or justice.

Two essays in the Ambrose and Lazerowitz anthology are virtual *desiderata* for the investigation of Moore's use of the naturalistic fallacy argument: C. D. Broad's "G. E. Moore's Latest Published Views in Ethics" (1961); and Casimir Lewy's "G. E. Moore on the Naturalistic Fallacy" (1964). Both take up the discussion in the context of Moore's continuing interest in clarifying his views subsequent to the publication of the Schilpp volume in 1942. Of the two, Lewy's essay is more relevant to the issue of the naturalistic fallacy, for he recounts Moore's own criticism of the way the argument is stated in *Principia*.

According to Lewy, Moore prepared—but did not complete—a draft of a revised preface to the edition of *Principia* that was published in 1922. In this draft Moore clearly anticipated many of the later criticisms and interpretations that the work would receive. Not least among them is the mistake his readers might make in understanding his use of the word "fallacy" in *Principia*, where it is properly applied to confusions of

one thing with another, rather than in its customary use to refer to mistakes in deductive inference (p. 297). In short, Lewy
shows that Moore never intended his naturalistic fallacy argument to apply (in Humean fashion) to the deductive inference
of "ought" from "is." As Lewy puts it, the kind of interpretation and use of the naturalistic fallacy argument that Sylvester
criticizes in this chapter was "fully anticipated by [Moore]
many years earlier."

Both Regan and Rohatyn have contributed useful discussions
of the naturalistic fallacy argument in *Principia*, though it is
striking that neither challenges Frankena's interpretation of it.
Both cite Lewy's essay, which provides ample basis for such a
challenge—as Sylvester recognized—but neither Regan nor
Rohatyn sees fit to take it up. Regan, in fact, ignores Frankena's thesis altogether even though he accords full recognition
to Lewy's essay (pp. 204–5). Though Rohatyn gives far more
attention to Moore's arguments for the naturalistic fallacy—he
discovers no less than twelve distinct versions—his object is
simply to show that Moore was himself confused about the
anti-naturalistic conclusions to which all twelve were supposed
to lead. Accordingly, he cites Frankena merely to state his con-
ditional agreement with him that Moore's entire approach "is
as useless as an English butcher in a world without sheep"
(Rohatyn, p. 68; Frankena, in Klemke, p. 38). Be that as it
may, it is nevertheless a feature of Rohatyn's book that he supplies an extensive and useful bibliography of books and articles
dealing with all sides of the naturalistic fallacy controversy
(pp. 131–40).

In one of the few critical treatments of Frankena's reading of
Moore's naturalistic fallacy arguments, Morton White takes
exception to Frankena's neglect of Moore's ontology. But his
treatment differs sharply from Sylvester's in that White wants
to reject *both* Moore's Platonistic ontology as backing for the
fallacy *and* Frankena's definist grounds (see Chapter 10, "The
Naturalistic Fallacy and the Nature of Goodness," in White's
Toward Reunion in Philosophy [Cambridge: Harvard University Press, 1956]). White wants to reconcile Moore's analytic
view of ethics with the pragmatic view he defends elsewhere in

the book, a project he regards as primarily one of epistemology. Hence White's consideration of Moore's theory of obligation takes a very different tack from Sylvester's.

In another context Morton White contributes an anecdote concerning Moore that might be construed as squaring better with Sylvester's account of the moral agent than his own. Here is the anecdote:

When I was staying with the Moores in the Spring of 1951, Mrs. Moore came into the room after dinner to announce that Bertrand Russell was about to speak on the B.B.C. Long silence. "Moore," she asked (she called him "Moore" when she didn't call him "Bill"). "Moore, don't you think we ought to listen to Russell? I feel an obligation to listen to him. Don't you?" And then there was another awfully long pause as Moore puffed on his pipe. One felt that Moore was tuning in on him*self* to see whether *he* felt that obligation. After the pause he reported with utter seriousness: "Dear, *I* don't feel any obligation to listen to Russell tonight." ["Memories of Moore," in the Klemke anthology, p. 296]

It is perhaps worth noting that by the date of this incident Russell had long since abandoned ethical cognitivism, which he once shared with Moore, in favor of the non-cognitivist and emotivist position that he shared with Ayer and Stevenson. (See Russell's *Religion and Science* [New York: Holt, Rinehart & Winston, 1935], pp. 236 ff.) White also shared this view in his "Value and Obligation in Dewey and Lewis" (*Philosophical Review*, 58 [1949], pp. 321–29). White *may* have thought he and Moore were in agreement that obligation is something felt and not known, but that agreement is not clear from the anecdote.

Although, as we pointed out above, Tom Regan does not examine Frankena's treatment of the naturalistic fallacy extensively in *Bloomsbury's Prophet*, he does so in an earlier essay, *Moore's Use of Butler's Maxim* (*Journal of Value Inquiry*, 16 [1982], pp. 153–60).

VIII

Choice, Consciousness, and Freedom: The Moral Self

1. *The Problem*

There are a number of issues in moral philosophy that Moore never explicitly discusses but are nonetheless important to consider. Some mention of these is made in the *Ethics*, and I have touched upon a few of them already. Such issues as the role of motive and the analysis of moral praise and blame are acknowledged by Moore as important for moral philosophy, but he chooses not to study them as such. Moore views his work as prefatory to the consideration of all such matters, reckoning on the issues he does attend to as fundamental. The fact that Moore does not present us with a comprehensive moral philosophy reflects his intent, and we should not approach his work as if it were otherwise than it is.

Moore makes his limited intentions clear in *Principia Ethica* when he says: "I have endeavored to write a 'Prolegomena to any future ethics that can possibly pretend to be scientific.'"[1] Again in the *Ethics* he sets forth a well-bounded program for the work; it will argue a general theory of practical ethics. As I have noted, *Ethics* presented a utilitarian doctrine, criticized, honed, and shaped into a general doctrine worthy of serious consideration as a practical ethical theory. But Moore also acknowledges that a reader who takes the book seriously will want to engage in more study of the issues. On pages 156–57 in the *Ethics* Moore instructs the person "who wishes to form an important judgment as to what the fundamental problems of Ethics really are" to read more in the discipline. He even provides a list of eight texts for the

185

reader to start with; Plato, Kant, Aristotle, Spencer, and others are mentioned, including some of his contemporaries.

One such issue that Moore does not deal with directly in either *Principia* or the *Ethics* has to do with a notion of the moral self. In this chapter I attempt a sketch of the moral self as far as I can derive such a notion from working over some of the things Moore writes about choice, free will, and the context for moral choice. Most of the material to which I refer will already be familiar, but I also deal with some lesser known articles. Certain views are attributed to Moore in full knowledge of the fact that if he holds them at all, he holds them only implicitly, for they do not find explicit expression in his work. Yet I claim these views lie well within the spirit, if not the letter, of what he has written.

2. *Ambiguity in the Notion of Duty*

In order for a person to make a moral choice, the power to effect choice must be available to him. Moore begins the moral theory developed in the *Ethics* on this note. Right and duty have to do with voluntary choice—and I have something to say about Moore's account of voluntary actions below—but here I want to make a distinction that is implicit in Moore's writings. In doing so, for the moment I put aside the question of the analysis of what is right, concentrating attention on duty.

I make a distinction between (*a*) ontological duty and (*b*) moral duty. Duty (*a*) stipulates that, in any given choice situation for any actual (or potential) agent, there is an act (or acts) that will, if chosen by the agent, produce the best possible consequences. Duty (*a*) stipulates that the agent can perform the action (or one of the actions) in question, *if he is conscious of, or thinks of*, the action (or actions) in question. Duty (*a*) does *not* stipulate that the actual (or potential) agent will (or must) be conscious of, or think of, the action (or actions) in question. Duty (*a*) I call ontological duty.

Duty (*b*) stipulates that there is an act (or acts) that we have reason to expect the actual (or potential) agent to have consciously entertained. Duty (*b*) does not stipulate that the agent entertain the action that is *the* one (or one of *the* ones) that will bring about what are ultimately the best consequences. Of the actions that the actual (or potential) agent might have entertained, and that we have reason to expect he might have entertained, the action (or actions) that would have brought, or probably would have brought, to existence the best possible consequences he is conscious of, or thinks of, *is* the moral obligation; that is, duty (*b*).

Moore has suggested something like this distinction in *Principia Ethica*. Here is the textual statement:

> We must, therefore, distinguish a possible action from an action of which it is possible to think. By the former we mean an action which no known cause would prevent, *provided* the idea of it occurred to us: and that one among such actions, which will produce the greatest total good, is what we mean by duty. Ethics certainly cannot hope to discover what kind of action is always our duty in this sense. It may, however, hope to decide which among one or two such actions is the best: and those which it has chosen to consider are, as a matter of fact, the most important of those with regard to which men deliberate whether they shall or shall not do them. A decision with regard to them may therefore be easily confounded with a decision with regard to which is the best possible. But it is to be noted that even though we limit ourselves to considering which is the better among alternatives likely to be thought of, the fact that these alternatives might be thought of is not included in what we mean by calling them possible alternatives.[2]

I find that Moore here presents three distinguishable categories for the reader's consideration: (A) a possible action, (B) an action of which it is possible to think, or likely to be thought of, and (A$_1$) one or two of the (A)s. The (A$_1$)s are cited in *Principia* in order to indicate the contrast between practical ethics and the hopeless enterprise of discovering exact moral duty in *Principia's* strictly defined sense. What ethics *can* discover, Moore tells us, are some very firm moral generalizations of great reliability. (One should consult *Principia Ethica*—pp. 150, passim—for the scope of the argument in its complete manifestation. I have gone over some of the salient features of Moore's view of moral laws in Chapter III.)

For the purposes of the discussion in this chapter, I maintain that (A) corresponds to (*a*) ontological duty, and (B) corresponds to (*b*) moral duty, at least in the sense that among the actions we are likely to think of are our moral duties. Being such an action is a necessary, though not a sufficient, condition for being a moral duty. I am not concerned with category (A₁) except as it is a sub-category of (A) and is comprehended under it.

Still the quotation is by no means crystal clear. As I read it Moore tells me that faced with the necessity of choosing to do one thing or another, moral deliberation is to be practical. That is, one is to seek the better alternative among those alternatives of which one is in fact likely to be aware. It is clear that this kind of duty, duty (*b*), needs the conceptual backdrop of duty (*a*) to gain its force. Duty (*a*) is characterized as the action that will bring more good into the world than any other action in the power of the agent to effect. It is this meaning that gives content to duty (*b*). Obviously, alert moral agents will have as their goal the doing of those acts that really *are* their duties; that is, just those acts among all the alternatives that maximize intrinsic value. The goal of practical ethics, then, is to bring actions done under the aspect of duty (*b*) closer to and, if possible, identical with, duty (*a*). As before, the fundamental role of ontology in morals for Moore is evident.

3. *Voluntary Actions: Right (a) and Right (b)*

In order for an action to be right or wrong, the action in question must be voluntary. The theory says "that a voluntary action is right whenever and only when its total consequences are *as* good, intrinsically, as any that would have followed for any action which the agent *could have* done instead."[3]

What about involuntary actions? I mean by involuntary, in the present context, something that was done by a person but was not chosen by the person qua *agent*, such as the blinking of an eye, ducking in order to avoid a thrown missile, the twitching of a muscle, a sneeze. An example of a context where something involuntary occurs, where the occurrence has important consequences, appears in the following: A prearranged signal for the charge of a platoon of soldiers is the nod of the platoon leader's head. The platoon leader happens to sneeze. The sneeze causes the head to move in a vigorous nodding fashion. The platoon charges. The battle is engaged and won, and years of peace follow. The state of affairs consequent to and attributable to the nod is the best possible. A nod, occurrent at time $_t$, represents an action it was possible to think of at time $_t$; and thus (B), an action it is possible to think of. The consequences are the best possible, yet the platoon leader did not think of nodding at time $_t$. Nevertheless, the consequences of the nod show it to be (*a*) ontologically right.

But Moore does *not* think of the nod as right. It was not, as we have seen, voluntary. So it is tempting to suggest, though Moore would not, that actions that are morally right (*b*) differ from ontologically right actions (*a*) in that right actions (*a*) can be involuntary and right actions (*b*) cannot. My only hesitation has to do with whether a bit of involuntary behavior can in any sense be called an action. It would seem that this question is one of terminology and not of fact. The nod, an integral element in the sneeze, served as a signal because of the prearranged nature of the battle context. It, qua nod, was an action it was possible to think of at time $_t$, although it was *not* thought of at that time as a possible act.

Moore has no hesitation in seeing certain constrained actions as right (*a*). A person, the platoon leader, could be "forced" to nod his head. And if the enforced activity occurred at time $_t$, the best consequences would have ensued. Yet Moore would not call the forced nod right (*b*). It was not chosen, in the required sense.

For a choice to be voluntary, it might seem that there must be conscious deliberation involved. Sneezes, twitches, jerks, accidental stumbles, are not deliberate activities. Some may wish to argue that the nod of the head under the threat of death *does* involve consciousness and deliberation. But the deliberation is over the threat to life or health, not about the advisability of a charge in battle. At any rate, Moore denies that deliberation in the context of constraint counts as blameworthy in any case [*Ethics*, p. 133].

There may be borderline cases that tempt the stretching of the notion of deliberation. After several hours of strained waiting for the correct moment to send the troops into battle, the platoon leader may relax his attention during a conversation with a superior. The superior may put a whispered question that the platoon leader, after thought, may answer with a pronounced nod—yes! The platoon leader deliberates and chooses to nod as an answer to the question. The charge occurs. But again, although deliberation and choice occur, the context for the right battle signal is missing. The platoon leader did not deliberately signal the troops, although he deliberately answered his superior. The action was not voluntary in the proper setting.

The point I wish to establish is that the morally right action, right (*b*), occurs only when deliberation is *already* consciously grasped *as* moral deliberation. If a person, for example, deliberated with the utmost seriousness about the purchase of a new automobile, if he worked out the questions of budget, the make of the car, fuel consumption, problems of safety, the gamut of practical and technical questions involved as direct and indirect consequences of the purchase, but never wondered about the best possible consequences from the point of view of maximizing intrinsic value, it seems mistaken to classify the choice in the sense of right (*b*) or wrong (*b*) action. To make such a judgment it would seem to be a necessary condition that a conscious intention to maximize value be present in the context of the deliberation preceding the action.

4. *The Moral Context*

Imagine a young boy who enjoys throwing stones into a lake near his home. He is perfecting the art of stone-skipping. He has a sense of real accomplishment when a skip sequence appears to be successful. The art requires deliberation, coordination, strength, and skill. He does not perform the activity, as it were, involuntarily or under constraint. People have thrown stones involuntarily, under psychic compulsion. Some may have thrown stones under constraint, at the command of a bully acquaintance. The actions involved in the stone-throwing are voluntary and deliberate, as we have seen. It is a very ordinary leisure-time activity.

Imagine that the young man can join a group of local people digging an irrigation ditch on the other side of the lake. Let us suppose, also, that the value that will come about as a consequence of the ditch's being operative is greater than the total amount of value that will come about from the boy's tossing stones, or anything else he might do; that is, the action of helping to dig the irrigation ditch at a particular time is right (*a*). Does it make sense to claim that it is right (*b*)?

Grant that the boy had knowledge of the digging planned for the day he threw the stones. He heard his teacher announce it at school in hopes that several students might join the project. His mother has also brought it to his attention indicating that it would be a nice thing if he helped. So it stands as a live option, one well within the boy's power to do. Moore distinguishes between willed and voluntary actions, including willed actions in the class of voluntary actions as a special class.[4] The boy has willed to throw the stones, so the action is both voluntary and willed.

We might also notice that the boy threw the stones with his right arm, as he always does. Yet he did not will to throw the stones, this particular day, with his right arm. He did so, as we say, by habit. If he had overexerted himself in early spring, throwing a baseball, had severely sore muscles in the right arm, and so deliberated about the wisdom of testing the arm this morning by throwing stones, the choice to use the arm despite the soreness would represent not a habitual action, but a *willed* one. I mention this because the notion of right (*b*), the question at hand, Moore connects with actions that are voluntary *and* willed. It is a necessary but, once again, not a sufficient condition that morally right actions must be willed.

Our example has accepted the fact that the right (*a*) thing to do is for the boy to join the irrigation crew. The boy has the option as one of the possible actions he was likely to be aware of. The boy wills to skip stones. And so, according to the distinctions in *Ethics*, and given the strictures laid down in the example, the lad seems to have chosen the morally wrong—wrong (*b*)—action.

Suppose the contextual facts are altered such that the digging occurs on schedule and represents the right action (*a*), as before, but the boy was never informed by teacher or parent, and hence never had occasion to bring the possibility of joining the crew to mind. He willed to skip stones without a choice context, which included the conscious option of helping to dig an irrigation ditch. His choice, then, misses out on duty (*a*), although he cannot reasonably be faulted under the circumstances. To that extent he is morally blameless, for although his choice was a willed action, it has no moral content. And yet it is, in Moore's perspective, an action that is ontologically wrong, wrong in the sense of the ideal utilitarianism that he embraces.

The problem we actually face in moral choice is not as easily summed up as the example suggests. One may of course accept the assertion that digging the irrigation ditch will in fact bring more value into existence than exercising one's body by skipping stones. For Moore there is *no* epistemic certitude that in *any* choice context we will choose the ultimately best, or ontologically best, alternative. As we saw in our earlier discussions, Moore accepts that our causal knowledge is usually far from complete enough for us to make with certitude our moral predictions as to ideal utility. And yet the distinction between the ontologically right and the morally right *is* a coherent one and still may be shown to have a useful function in moral contexts.

5. *What Ought (b) to Be Done—Morally?*

In *Principia Ethica* Moore was explicitly concerned about the relationship between human ignorance in causal matters and the moral choices that nevertheless must be made in the face of that ignorance. Despite our inability to predict the ultimate moral consequences of our actions, Moore argued, we can be perfectly clear about at least one important matter. We make our moral choices in social contexts. Hence whatever our moral choices may be, we must take *moral* account of the fundamental rules of the society in which those choices are made. An undermining of the well-founded and constitutive rules of the society—those that are generally observed and useful—leads to the destruction of the necessary conditions for moral choice. If the causal conditions we depend upon to show us what actions will bring value into existence are no longer reliable, we will be incapable of rational deliberation. Thus we may judge any violation of the well-founded rules of society as blameworthy actions. That we may even be morally *obligated* to do this follows quite simply from the distinction between what is ultimately, or ontologically, right on the one hand and what is morally right, and a duty, on the other. It follows because we may simply be unable to recognize that some action that is plainly socially destructive and immoral in the immediate instance may, in the end, work out for the social benefit of all concerned.

I want to comment on what may seem odd in what I have just said. The notion of right (*a*), the *ontologically* right, stands as the *ultimate* moral criterion. But the *morally* right, right (*b*), may consist in a well-founded rule, useful and generally observed, that stands as a guide to citizens in society. When such a rule is obeyed by people, *usually* (almost always) the best consequences follow. But it seems true that in some highly unusual cases, breaking the well-established rule would ultimately bring more value into existence than observation of the rule. The rule-breaking action in such a case, whatever it is, would then represent the ontologically right, or (*a*), choice.

But it is not the right (b), or moral, choice. As we have seen in Chapter V, there are two compelling reasons why the agent is not morally allowed to assume that the case facing him is unusual. (1) An epistemological reason: One cannot know for certain that this case is one of the exceptions to the rule, even if one can be psychologically certain that there are some exceptions as instances that will occur. (2) A pedagogical reason: Those who notice the agent's breaking of the rule will be struck, *not* by the fact of the alleged exception (which may justify breaking the rule), but by the fact that it is a *breaking* of the rule. It will tend to promote disrespect for the rule. Hence it will tend to diminish the very efficacy of the rule that grounds persons living together in society. Once we can no longer count upon the rule, our ability to understand the ways in which we can bring more good to be is diminished. This means we will have even more difficulty in working out what the right (*a*) may be, and thus the likelihood of our doing what is morally right, right (*b*), diminishes.

Suppose, for example, we had learned that the boy who chose to skip stones disobeyed his mother's explicit command. He was asked to mow the lawn before going about his own activities. He chose to disregard the parental requirement and broke a well-founded rule in the society: Obey your parents! Suppose further that at the lake's edge he met a person who had recently left the state mental hospital (in town) unsupervised. The boy was able to keep the individual amused and pleased by his prowess in skipping stones. By his actions the young man was able to keep the unfortunate's interest until he was located by the hospital and returned to proper supervision. Moore's theory allows for a series of possible judgments in assessing the situation.

Judgment (1): The act of disobedience is wrong (*b*). Obeying parents (and, in general, proper authority under well-defined conditions) is a well-founded, generally obeyed, and useful rule in any society. It is most probable, on any specific occasion, that value will be maximized by obeying the rule. Its efficacy must be guarded. Judgment (2): The act of skipping stones to amuse the escapee from the hospital was right (*a*), let us say. And it may also seem to be right (*b*). But this does not mean that the act of skipping stones is both right (*b*) and wrong (*b*). What is wrong (*b*) consists in *not* mowing the lawn and instead going to the lake. The action is an explicit, deliberate disobeying of the request of his mother. The action of skipping stones at the lake is not the action judged to be wrong (*b*). The example has the boy skipping stones in order to amuse someone else. It is the consequences of *this* choice, the act of throwing *to amuse*, that is right (*a*) and apparently right (*b*) as well.

According to Moore, the boy is blameworthy for disobeying the parents. The blameworthiness holds even if the lad is hailed as a hero for having kept the escapee benignly engaged until found and placed in protective custody. The act of disobeying is wrong (*b*), though its consequences would allow us to say it is ontologically right. Moore recognizes the apparent paradox: "that a man may really deserve the strongest moral condemnation for choosing an action, which actually is right."[5] The quotation may seem more significant than the example calls for, perhaps, but the point is that the distinction between ontological right, right (*a*), and morally right, right (*b*), is a distinction that makes the apparent paradox intelligible.

6. *What Ought I to Do?*

When is an issue a moral one? There are times when one may wonder, quite explicitly, "What ought I to do?" and thus raise what is patently a moral question. But there are times when a non-moral question comes to mind in the disguise of a moral one; we may ask ourselves, "Ought I to order lobster this evening?" yet mean merely to ask ourselves, "Should I order lobster this evening?" According to Moore's ontology of right there may be many occasions when we do something that is right (*a*), though we are oblivious of the *moral* aspect of the action in question. And it may be supposed that there are at least as many times when we do something that is wrong (*a*), while remaining oblivious of the ultimate consequences of what we do. A decision to order lobster instead of donating the price of the dinner to UNICEF is most likely to be wrong (*a*). But choosing to regard the context of a dinner evening out as a moral choice context in which the lobster option is pitted against UNICEF would surely be the mark of a moral zealot.

I want to return to the example of the stone-skipping boy for a moment, but I want to alter its content. The boy has no chores assigned, no other requests from his parents, no general commitments pressing (homework, music lesson). Suppose he wonders what to do with his time. His thoughts follow his interest, and he decides to go stone-skipping. Granted, he could have joined the irrigation crew. His teacher had mentioned it in passing one day in class. He could have gone to the recreation department's Saturday morning class in woodworking. His uncle had sent him a flyer announcing the class a week ago. Let us even stipulate that either of the two alternatives would be better than the stone-skipping. The alternatives could have occurred to him, but they did not. From the previous discussion it appears that the stone-skipping boy has done what is wrong (*b*). But I do not think it is Moore's intent to have us think that the boy *is* wrong (*b*); although there can be no doubt that he is wrong (*a*).

If the boy had pondered his choices and had thought that learning woodworking would be better for him, that he would become a more value-producing citizen if he took the course, then to reject the course of action on the day in question (whether or not the alternative actually occurred to him at the moment of choice) would have been wrong (*b*). The boy does not think of the irrigation possibility or the woodworking possibility as *moral* alternatives. They start, for him, as competing interest possibilities, but he has more interest in stone-skipping.

I suggest that Moore's intent in laying down the type of utilitarianism he does is to indicate that when the agent is or has been aware of the choice context as defined by, or appropriate to, the question 'What ought I to do?' the matter of morality is raised. The ontological backdrop remains what it always is, or was: From the choice (a willed and voluntary choice), does more good come into existence or not? If so, the action is right (*a*); if not, the action is wrong (*a*). When the question 'What ought I to do?' is part of the deliberation, then the choice is between actions that are right (*b*) or wrong (*b*). If the question 'What ought I to do?' is not part of the deliberation context, the action chosen is neither right (*b*) nor wrong (*b*), even though it will be right (*a*) or wrong (*a*). Morally right or wrong actions are grounded in the ontological sense of right but are not equivalent to it. An action, that is to say, can really be morally right and yet be wrong from the perspective that is able to take into account its ultimate ontological consequences.

7. *The Person: Experience of Beauty and Experience of Right*

Sometimes, driving through the mountains, one is suddenly struck by the beauty of a particular view in a way that had never been experienced as such before. There are times, also, when a painting, which one has often experienced as beautiful, seems ordinary—that is, the experience is not one in which beauty is found. Moore's analysis of beauty is useful in interpreting the facts mentioned above. Moore defines 'beauty,' as we have seen, as "That of which the admiring contemplation is good in itself."[6] I showed that for the definition to hold there must be (1) an object, qualified by value, which is (*a*) grasped *conceptually* and (*b*) *felt*, with an appropriate emotion. I suggest a crude schema to display the experience's form, as follows:

$$[(A\text{--}\!\to O_v) \cdot (E_a\leftarrow\!\text{--}\!\to O_v)]$$

Verbally transcribed: (An awareness of an object qualified by value) *and* (an appropriate emotion *called forth from* and *directed at* the object qualified by value). What Moore wanted to clarify was that, in the experience, shown between the brackets, there is a cognitive act that is the awareness of the object's value. It is shown in the parentheses on the left side, before the dot. There is also an appropriate emotion directed to or called for by the object's value. It is shown in the parentheses on the right of the dot. A point to remember is that the cognitive act extends to the object that has value and not to the emotion felt. I do not mean that the person cannot know that he is also feeling in a certain way. Moore's view is that if the object is seen to have value, but there is no emotional response at all, then one does not experience beauty. There will not be an authentic aesthetic experience. When an appropriate emotion is felt, the entire experience—both sides of the expression within the brackets—is valuable.

In order to be able to discuss a definition of 'beauty' Moore seems committed to the view that one is able to reflect upon experiences that one calls beautiful so that one can grasp the elements involved. Such a reflective experience, I suggest, can be schematically understood as follows:

$$A^r\text{--}\!\to[(A\text{--}\!\to O_v) \cdot (E_a\leftarrow\!\text{--}\!\to O_v)]$$

The schema merely adds the reflective act. One is aware of the awareness of a valuable object and the having of an appropriate emotion in response to the value in the object. In the reflective act, however, the explicit noticing of the appropriate emotion is a requirement. I presume that I should add one crucial element in the schema since I should show that the whole experience has intrinsic value, as below:

$$A^r \dashrightarrow [(A \dashrightarrow O_v) \cdot (E_a \longleftrightarrow O_v)]_v$$

I want to emphasize that Moore holds the view that the mind is capable of reflective acts of the sort schematized. He writes: "Admirable mental qualities do, if our previous conclusions are correct, consist very largely in an emotional contemplation of beautiful objects; and hence the appreciation of them will consist *essentially* in the contemplation of such contemplation."[7]

I am going to hazard a similar schema for moral choice also. I want alternative actions designated: K^1—stone-skipping, K^2—ditch-digging, K^3—woodworking class. The schema appears as follows:

$$A^r \dashrightarrow [\{[(K^1 \supset C^1{}_v{}^1) \lor (K^2 \supset C^2{}_v{}^2) \lor (K^3 \supset C^3{}_v{}^3)] \cdot C^3{}_v{}^{3*}\} \supset_c K^3]$$

Verbally transcribed: Awareness of three possible actions, K^1, K^2, K^3 in the moral context; each one of which is likely to produce three different consequences of specific value, v^1, v^2, v^3. The horseshoe indicates the causal connection. The v indicates any one of the three are possible actions to be chosen. The starred expression ($*$) indicates the set of consequences that is the most valuable. The horseshoe with the c inside ($\supset_c$) indicates that the action K^3 is *morally* required.

I emphasize that the Ks represent possible actions in the sense Moore discriminated in the quotation that appears in Chapter VII, Section 2 above. I want it understood that the choice of an action is morally required when an agent has understood his choice context to be governed by the question 'What ought I to do?'

Moral choice, then, demands awareness of the fact that actions have consequences that are value-laden; and, depending upon the action one chooses, more (or less) value is likely to come into existence. It requires, as a matter of ontology, that one set of consequences provide a complex of natural conditions that provide greater ingression of value than other sets. It follows, then, that one *ought* to choose the action that will bring about the most valuable consequences. Moral behavior and choice necessitate reflective thought in their own existential contexts.

In terms of the formal schema I suggest a difference between aesthetic experience and moral experience. An experience of beauty is indicated by the expressions inside the brackets. There is no element of choice; no necessity of a willing to do anything. One does not, for example, *choose* an appropriate emotion. One notices the object that is intrinsically valuable and one has an emotion—one feels in a certain way. Insofar as moral choice is concerned, the fact that one notices that a valuable set of consequences will probably follow from an action within one's power to effect indicates that one *must* choose the action in question. True, in the beauty schema the valuable object calls for an emotion on the part of the one having the experience. The emotion is directed toward the object; *it* is seen *as beautiful*. Yet even though there is a pull, there is no *action* called for. It is of consequence, however, that the pull of value appears both in practical ethics and in aesthetics.

8. *The Person Who Chooses*

Moore never explicitly discusses the concept of person. Persons would be a complex concept in Moore's view. There are many places in his writings where elements that may be said to constitute a moral self appear and that Moore could have worked into an explicit definition, had he been so inclined. In fact, in "The Value of Religion," when examining the nature of a personal God, Moore offers a beginning analysis of "person":

> There are two properties which must belong to a person, whatever else may belong to him besides. (1) A person must be endowed with that which we call a mind as distinct from our brains and our bodies; and (2) he must also have that positive quality whereby we distinguish ourselves from other people.[8]

For the purpose of developing a concept of the moral personality, analysis would add something more to this. For the person we are concerned with is capable of choosing in contexts we call moral; the distinction right (*b*) and wrong (*b*) points to issues the moral person must comprehend. In order to see what Moore must at least hold as an analysis of *person* I want to go over some of the things Moore says in both his moral, as well as his non-moral, writings.

Many choices are made in social contexts where the problem of moral action seems not at stake. A teacher's working out a seating chart for recording attendance in a large lecture course and grading an objective true–false examination for a large lecture class are examples of actions that are done and are not usually thought to be in a moral context. The task of an office manager assigning the day's work for the persons under his jurisdiction is another example. What is said about Moore's view of person holds for these non-moral situations as well, of course. There is nothing, therefore, specifically to be added to the analysis of the moral person as long as it is acknowledged from the start that the person sees the world of choice upon (many) occasion(s) from a moral point of view.

In some publications, not generally considered to be contributions to his moral philosophy, Moore has occasion to suggest views that have implications for a theory of person, or self. For example, in an essay published roughly at the time of *Ethics* Moore gives us reasons for thinking that "the I" is an entity "distinct from every one of my mental acts and from all of them together . . . which is conscious when I am conscious." He flirts with a Lockean position, the view that my body is that entity, but rejects it. He suggests a Humean analysis but is not satisfied with it either. He concludes: "Every mind would be, then, a mental entity of a new sort, and it would be "mental" in the sense that it was something, *not* the body, of which certain mental acts were the acts—that it was that which is conscious whenever anyone is conscious."[9] I have quoted Moore's conclusion from "The Subject Matter of Psychology." In it he presents a possible and, Moore thinks, a plausible view of the nature of the self. However, taken in isolation it does not shed much light on Moore's ethical thought; no conclusive picture emerges of the moral person.

In the 1910–1911 lectures Moore speaks of the existence of acts of awareness that are associated with material entities (bodies) in space and time. It is clear that in the lectures Moore believes mental acts really do exist, qua acts. The grounding of judgment in the 1898 theory of judgment seems to commit Moore to the existence of an entity that is the center of the various activities of judgment engaged in by any individual knower. The judgment view—that there is a subject-center for acts of cognition—is implicitly present in all that Moore writes in the period of his major publications in moral philosophy, 1909–1916. There exists a self, a person, at the center of the activities of consciousness, including (specifically) the activities of cognition and emotion (feeling), which are connected in intimate ways with the body. The acts of cognition, furthermore, although linked with the body, are not reducible to it and are, in this sense, independent. The self, or person, has an ability to initiate actions in the world. That ability is, as we shall see, to be understood in terms of the cognition of alternative possibilities open to the person from which the person has the power to select an alternative to actualize.

Moore seems to think of the self as primarily mental in character. He acknowledges the affective (bodily element) as important, however, such as in its function as defining 'beauty.' For unless the self has an intimate relationship with (its) body, beauty could not be known or appreciated. In Moore's ontology there are, in addition to selves—and I am referring to selves as the centers of activities of cognition and emotion—the following categories of entities: (*a*) objects of thought and (*b*) entities that exist in the world of experience. He holds that both (*a*) and (*b*) are independent of the self, and by the time of *Principia Ethica*'s publication he holds that (*a*) and (*b*) are not identical; that is, that (*b*) is not merely reducible to (*a*). [Concepts are entities that are independent of the world, and thus of the self. Entities that exist in the world are not reducible to objects of thought (see Chapter IV).]

The famous essay "The Refutation of Idealism"[10] emphasizes the independence of consciousness from the objects of consciousness, supporting the view I am suggesting. There Moore argues for the independence of objects of sensation from acts of sensing in a way similar to the argument in "The Nature of Judgment," where acts of cognition are shown to be independent of the objects of cognition. Blue-things are independent of our sensing them just as blue, the logical idea or concept, is independent of our awareness of it.

I do not wish to be misunderstood. I do not claim that an analysis of the moral self—the person—is identical with the analysis of consciousness, or yet of the analysis of thought. I do claim that one can transfer distinctions made in the analysis of cognition and sensation to the theoretical analysis of volition. I am convinced that Moore does not hold a doctrine of a compartmentalized mind. I think we may safely presume that reference to a presiding entity is not exhausted by the objects over which it presides.

In "The Refutation of Idealism" Moore confesses that it is not possible to become directly acquainted with consciousness in an empirical sense. However, in "The Subject Matter of Psychology" he concludes that it is plausible to think there *is* a mental entity of a unique sort. I have urged that such an entity be taken as indicative of the presence of a self; or rather that Moore's view in presenting the plausible hypothesis mentioned can be understood as a partial analysis of a self, a person.

In another essay, published shortly after 1912, Moore tries to work out some implications of his thought concerning sense experience. He thinks, as we know, that there is a distinction between the act of awareness of a sense presentation and the object as the source of the sense presentation. The distinction is similar to the one argued in "The Refutation." To make the distinction clearer and more telling, Moore adds an element on the side of the experience itself. He calls the added element "lived through." The suggestion is interesting and the notion provocative:

> When I observe that a given mental act or state of mind, an act of judgment or an emotion, has ceased to be lived through by me, I am, I think, always at the same time observing that the act or state in question, has ceased to exist; that it has ceased to be lived through by me. But in the case of presentation, while there are cases in which I do observe *both* that a given sensation ceased to be presented to me *and* that it has ceased to exist, there seem to be others which differ from them in respect of the fact that, though I do observe that a given sensation has ceased to be presented to me, I do *not* observe that it has ceased to exist.[11]

We have now a picture of an entity—an I—related to sensations, judgments made, and emotions felt, such that the entity (the self or person, I) *lives through* many of those experiences. Some of the experiences are not lived through, but co-exist in contrast to those that are lived through. All that now need be done is to see whether the entity referred to here can be connected in any likely way to a more explicit doctrine of a self that makes moral choices from among available alternatives. I think such a doctrine is clearly suggested in Moore's review of McTaggart's *Studies in Hegelian Cosmology*. The review appeared in 1902, a year before *Principia Ethica*. I quote the relevant passage:

> When we remember our past states we have to them some unique relations which we have to the present object–self, and when we think of our future self as remembering our present, it is again not mere thinking, since we are relating it as a subject to the present object–self which is actually perceived. Of course, we do speak of retaining our personal identity, without meaning that the future self will have memory of our present self at every moment; but we feel hesitation, even in so speaking, unless we think of it as *capable* of so remembering, as it was in this present life. And by this *capability* we do not mean a mere potentiality: we mean a real relation, which does exist between various periods of our present life.[12]

I think it very likely that Moore would have analyzed the person as a self, an I that is conscious of itself as an I; that is conscious of sense-presentations as independent of the I; that is conscious of concepts, as independent of the I; that is conscious of its past states as past *states of itself*, and that is conscious of itself as involved in its own future in a world independent of it but in which its choices *make* a difference. The self, the I, persists in time. The self lives through certain of its experiences, especially its choices.

9. *The Power to Choose*

The material we have been working over in this chapter suggests that we can distinguish three senses of possibility/impossibility. Let me state the three in the following manner: (1) Possibility/impossibility: I could have drawn four one-inch squares on this paper this morning. In this sense, one utters a clear and comprehensible statement in saying it is possible that I could have drawn . . . (2) Physical possibility/impossibility: I could not have drawn five million one-inch squares on this paper this morning. It is clear and comprehensible for one to claim it is a physical impossibility that accounts for the fact that I could not have drawn . . . (3) Logical possibility/impossibility: I could not have drawn one round square on this paper this morning. It is clear and comprehensible for one to claim, the reason that I could not have drawn one round square is that it is a logical impossibility.

Even if a person did not draw four squares on a page on a particular morning, he could have, had he so chosen. If the person thought about drawing the squares and decided not to do so, he has fulfilled the basic conditions for Moore's classification of his actions as voluntary and willed. The notion of a willed action is connected with the notion of "could have if (it) had been chosen." And *that* notion is grounded (has a real foundation) in the notion of the self. Moore says, "Our theory holds that, provided a man could have done something else, if he had chosen, that is sufficient to entitle us to say that his action is right or wrong."[13] In the context of the *Ethics* the right and wrong alluded to are to be seen as *ontologically* right and wrong—right (*a*) and wrong (*a*).

In response to the pressure of criticism in the Schilpp volume, Moore modified the *Ethics* view slightly toward the *moral* sense of right and wrong—right (*b*) and wrong (*b*). He says:

> A *necessary* condition for its being true that his action was morally wrong, is that he should have been *able to choose* some other action than the one he did. If he [the agent] *could not* have chosen any other action than the one he did choose, then his action could not have been called morally wrong.[14]

In Section 2 I distinguished between (A) a possible action and (B) an action of which it is possible to think, a distinction made by Moore in *Principia Ethica*. I indicated there that (B) actions (of which it is possible to think) are relevantly similar to morally right and morally wrong actions. It is this sense of right and wrong that is required for grasping Moore's account of the moral dimension of experience.

The point is that any analysis (such as the one suggested in the *Ethics*) concluding that a certain action is the only action that could have occurred and maintaining *also* that the action can be judged right or wrong, requires a view of right and wrong that is strictly ontological. To allow room for the specifically moral, which requires that an action be voluntary and willed—that is to say, as we know, chosen by an agent—Moore uses the hypothetical 'could have,' which he grounds in the capacity of an agent having the power of choice. It is this capacity for choice that is central to the notion of a moral person.

An example may serve to flesh out the notion. Consider the case of an academic who deliberates between staying at his present teaching post and moving to a new opportunity. Such a decision requires much deliberation. It involves assessments of consequences and of the comparative value that the differing alternatives and their consequences may bring. The deliberation requires a "living through" the ratification and the eventual choice, whatever the precise moment of making the choice. (The verbal commitment to the hiring officer? The signing of the written agreement? The written notification of resignation to the former institution? The sum of all the aforementioned moments?)

Once the academic has agreed to move from one institution to another (and makes the actual move), others may easily describe certain occurrences in the career that have followed the move. The descriptions are external. Certain students now study with the individual in question who could not have done so had the other alternative been selected. Certain programs are open for the person that were not present in the former setting. Opportunities to work and study abroad open up that would not have occurred otherwise. External observers note and link the actual consequences without noting, or feeling, the stress of deliberation. Living through the experiences involved in and consequent upon the decision is not a choice that is open to the experience of an external observer.

I want to recall the schema for moral choice that was proposed in Section 7 above and state it once again, this time omitting the A^r factor, the element of reflective choice:

$$\{[(K^1 \supset C^1{}_v{}^1) \lor (K^2 \supset C^2{}_v{}^2) \lor (K^3 \supset C^3{}_v{}^3)] \cdot C^3{}_v{}^{3*}\} \supset K^3$$

I show it without the reflective awareness because I want to indicate that, as a calculus, once $C^3_v{}^{3*}$ has been determined to be the one that will bring more value into existence, K^3 is (logically) *called for* by definition. Choice involves deliberation; it involves what Moore has called lived through by me. Choice requires an *active* reflection, A^r. An A^r is grounded in a thinking self *capable* of acting when called to action by a set of consequences that maximize value. [Starred * in the schema.] The choice of K^3 is morally called for, and logically must be *chosen*. And yet it may be rejected. To omit the A^r, and all that the reflection entails in the *moral* situation, is to omit the moral problem of *choice*.

10. *The Moral Self as a Causal System*

I suggested in Chapter VII, Section 7 that Moore's ethics requires, as parts of the world, both a natural causal system and an independent value causal system. The value system, which is ontologically independent, nevertheless depends upon the natural causal system for the occasion of its exemplification in actual existence. The two systems are conceptually distinguishable, but the universe that they together comprise is manifested as one in the everyday experience of moral agents.

What this latter point suggests is that a third system must be identified, which takes account of the natural system and the value system as they cooperatively constitute the world of experience. It has an efficacious autonomy independent of the other two systems. The third system is of course the moral self. This suggests that Moore borrows from the strength of the early Kantian influences on his thought in order to present us with a view of the moral agent as able to engage in actions that cause the world to be different from what it would have been had the agent chosen other than he did.

Moore does not come at the question of free will in the same terms as he does the matter of sense presentation. He does not explicitly invoke the notion of living through that I have attributed to him. He does, however, accept the principle of causality—the view that everything that happens has a cause—and finds that free will is compatible with it. He writes:

It is, therefore, quite certain (1) that we often *should* have *acted* differently, if we had chosen to; (2) that similarly we often should have *chosen* differently, *if* we had chosen so to choose; and (3) that it was almost always *possible* that we should have chosen differently, in the sense that no man could know for certain that we should *not* so choose. All these three things are fact, and all of them are quite consistent with the principle of causality.[15]

I suggest Moore believes the moral agent fits into the general causal nexus, autonomously, as a cooperating causal element with the natural and value causal systems. The moral agent reflects upon alternatives open to him: K^1, K^2, and K^3. He finds, in the deliberation process, that certain sets of consequences are likely to occur as a result of the actions chosen. In assessing the value in the alternative sets of consequences, as best the agent can, he might find that, for example, $C^3_{v}{}^3$ appears to be the most valuable. He believes he is obliged to do K^3. Yet he would much rather do K^1. He has to choose. He can do what he ought not to do. But only if he chooses. On the other hand, he can do what he ought to do. Again, only if he chooses.

Moore clearly supposes that, from the midst of deliberation and struggle with inclinations and lack of information, we can do what we ought to do—if we choose. He says:

The philosopher Kant laid down a well-known proposition to the effect that "ought" implies "can": that is to say, that it cannot be true that you "ought" to do a thing, unless it is true that you *could* do it, if you chose. And as regards one of the senses in which we commonly use the words "ought" and "duty," I think that the rule is plainly true. When we say absolutely of ourselves or others, "I ought to do so and so" or "you ought to," we imply, I think, very often that the thing in question is a thing which we *could* do, if we chose; though of course it may often be a thing that is very difficult to choose to do.[16]

Moore has proposed, in effect, an enriched view of the causal nexus. His view rests upon three functionally independent and autonomous elements. Each element has its own discriminable characteristics, which must be understood if we are to grasp the nature of the moral act. The three must be understood to be independent of one another in the sense that none of the three can be reduced to terms set by the others *alone*. The criteria for right and wrong, for obligation or duty, for morally permissible and impermissible actions, cannot be appreciated unless the interaction of these three systems is grasped.

It is clear that neither the natural system nor the value system either forces or causes the moral agent to do what he ought to do. The natural and value systems set the ground and provide the reason for the moral agent's moral choice. It is the moral agent *himself* who voluntarily wills to act in the way that he ought to act. There is therefore nothing *sinister* in suggesting that an agent may be morally *required* to do an action freely. The fact of *moral* choice entails free volition.

The Kantian cast of Moore's doctrine should not be at all surprising. As I have indicated elsewhere, Moore's first publication was an article sympathetic to Kant's doctrine of freedom. But there he criticized Kant for postulating two "selves": an empirical self and a noumenal self. The noumenal self was said to be free while the empirical self was bound in the regular causal system. Moore could discover no way, in Kant, to link the two selves. Without a link, freedom in the empirical world was a mystery. Kant, says Moore, left the problem virtually unsolved.[17] Moore, on his own, refuses a distinction between two selves. He argues that the self has cognitive powers and is capable of discovering alternatives for action. The self is directly acquainted with value in the world. The self can assess sets of likely consequences that flow from imagined alternatives for action. The self is free to choose; which is to say, the self *can actualize* one of the possibilities for action. The self can do what it ought. Moore writes in his "Reply":

For to say that x ought to do so and so is equivalent to saying that, if x had a rational will, he *would* do the thing in question—in at least one sense of the expression "rational will." That expression may be and is properly so used that to say a person has a rational will is to say that, so long as he has it, he *will* do what he *ought*. I should myself say that this is a case not merely of equivalence but of identity—that the notion of having a rational will (in this sense) can be defined in terms of "ought"; that is to say that so and so has a rational will just *means* that he makes the choices that he ought to make, or (in other words) which it is rational to make.[18]

This comes, of course, some forty years after *Principia Ethica*, and thirty after the *Ethics*. And yet the basic contour of Moore's thought remains the same. The criterion for making the right choice is of course Moore's own brand of utilitarianism, but the notion of choice, the requirements of obligation, and the concept of volition remain guided by the Kantian mode.

11. *Moral Choice and Bringing About Good*

In Chapter VII, I was concerned to argue that Moore's notion of good's simplicity was not undercut by William Frankena's worry about an *obligation* to bring good about. Frankena had wondered how it was that good had a normative aspect while being simple. I indicated there that, analogously to pleasure for orthodox utilitarians, simplicity was independent of the general rule that value is to be maximized in actions if those actions are to be right or obligatory. I want to go over the question again now that I have discussed the crucial role of the person and free choice.

Consider, first, a gourmet who has three possible delicacies to choose from in a given meal: D^1, D^2 and D^3. The gourmet asks himself which of the three he should select. When he wonders about such matters he takes as his rule, I should imagine: Select the item that, in the given meal-context, will cause the entire meal situation to be the most pleasurable. Why that principle? It's self-evident! (The orthodox pleasure utilitarian takes something very much like this for the general rule of moral action.) The pleasures likely to flow from the three possible items are P^1, P^2 and P^3. The gourmet, leaning upon his experience and assessing the present conditions, finds that P^2 is likely to be the most pleasurable; that is, P^{2*}. So the gourmet is "required" to choose ($\supset$)D^2. The schema is:

$$A^r \dashrightarrow [\{[(D^1 \supset P^1) \text{ v } (D^2 \supset P^2) \text{ v } (D^3 \supset P^3)] \cdot P^{2*}\} \supset D^2]$$

Nothing in the schema and what the schema represents casts doubt upon the notion that pleasure is a simple and indefinable concept. The reason the gourmet is to choose D^2 is that as a gourmet he *is* to choose the item that brings about the most pleasure. Why? Because that's what the gourmet *wants*; that's the sense to being a gourmet. Pleasurable meal-experiences *call* your choice, qua gourmet. It's evident.

The moral agent, according to G. E. Moore, becomes reflectively aware of alternatives for action: K^1, K^2, and K^3. The agent wonders which one of the actions he ought to do. When he wonders, in the context of (the moral) ought, his deliberation is governed by the general rule: Do the action that will bring more value into existence than any other that is open to you. Why that principle (for Moore)? It's self-evident! So, the moral agent investigates the alternatives to see what the likely consequences may be. They are C^1, C^2, and C^3. The agent, next, must try to assess the value of each set of consequences. They are: $C^1_v{}^1$, $C^2_v{}^2$, and $C^3_v{}^3$. $C^3_v{}^3$ is judged to be the most valuable, $C^3_v{}^{3*}$, and so, because K^3 is likely to promote the most valuable consequences, the moral agent is to choose K^3. The schema in Section 10 shows the reflective situation.

Value (good) remains a simple notion. The fact that good can be called 'ought to exist for its own sake' does not threaten good's simplicity. Needless to say, exist is a notion distinct from good and from ought. But 'ought to exist for its own sake' refers to good from the point of view of possible action in the world of experience. It is a way of cognizing, and therefore pointing to good. Possible action in the world is one of the elements that *define* or *constitute* the moral point of view. Persons think of producing good consequences when they are in situations in which 'what ought I to do?' becomes relevant.

Ought to do is a complex notion. It is a defined notion, as we know. It is when the question of value becomes embedded in the context of moral choice that value calls one to action. The point is that until a real situation arises, cognizing value as demanding to be actualized does not occur. The demand to be actualized, furthermore, occurs in the context already felt as moral. By *itself*, value does not demand. As exemplified in the world it makes no demands. As a possibility for qualifying things and events in the world in the future it makes no demands, *until and unless a person wonders to himself, What ought I to do?*

'What ought I do?' is the *reason* for *Principia Ethica*. It is also probably why Moore thought of the *Ethics*: "this book I myself like better than *Principia Ethica* because it seems to me to be much clearer and far less full of confusions and invalid arguments."[19] The entire moral philosophy is aimed toward action. *Principia* is, as he declared, a prolegomenon.

Moore's notion of the moral self, however, may be seen as having taken preliminary shape even before that prolegomenon was worked out. In the 1898 "Freedom"—one of the pieces that contain his early critique of Kant—Moore wrote:

> With this we seem to have arrived at the notion of a thing with a distinguishable self, having a distinct efficacy in virtue of that self. And in this conception of nature there is contained the Union of Determinism with Freedom, in its simplest form. Each thing marked by a simple qualitative nature, is no doubt determined in that it is the effect of some other thing, and, given that other thing, it was forced to appear. But also it is itself similarly the cause of something else, and free as far as its effect depends upon its own nature. It is nothing against this, that its own nature depends in its turn upon something else, for that something else could not by itself have produced the effect which it produces.[20]

It is in the nature of the human self to reflectively assess alternatives for action in terms of a criterion indicating which of the alternatives would maximize good. That alternative represents human duty. And so the agent ought to choose it rather than one of the other alternatives in his power. Since 'ought' implies 'can,' the agent has the power to do what he ought—even though, as Moore has said, it may be very difficult. The self has a distinct efficacy in virtue of its nature, and that is what I have endeavored to find in this chapter—some hints as to Moore's notion of the self.

CRITICAL BIBLIOGRAPHY: CHAPTER VIII

As we mentioned in the Introduction, Sylvester planned, but did not write, a chapter called Conclusions; the manuscript leaves off with Chapter VIII. We have reckoned that, in the absence of the projected final chapter, Chapter VIII serves handsomely as an appropriate conclusion to the book as a whole. For in it Sylvester reviews and brings to bear upon his topic virtually all the important arguments in his reading of Moore's ethics developed in the preceding chapters. By bringing all this material to bear upon a topic that Moore himself "chose not to study" (as Sylvester puts it), the chapter is highly original and fills a significant lacuna in Moore scholarship.

Sylvester addresses two distinct but related items of unfinished business in the chapter. He wants to make good on his earlier claim that Moore's ethics is not just a theoretical exercise in metaethics; that it includes a serviceable practical ethics as well, an ethics that can best be grasped in terms of a lived-through experience, as he puts it. Second, Sylvester wants to make good on the promissory note he left in Chapter VII; he wants to show how the *ontological* ought to be can be synthesized with the *practical* ought to do, that these distinct notions that Frankena has conflated in his treatment of Moore's naturalistic fallacy argument may be seen as essentially connected when studied in the ontological context that Moore himself provides, once that context in *Principia* is seen as organically linked to the practical context of the *Ethics*.

Sylvester approaches his twofold task through an account of the context of moral choice and the related concept of the moral self, which he finds implicit in Moore's philosophy. Developing the *Principia* distinction between possible actions and actions of which it is possible to think (in the sense of being likely to be thought of by the agent), Sylvester shows how Moore's account of ought to do is properly explicated in terms of the twin notions of ontological rightness and moral rightness. The former grounds the latter as a real ideal for the guidance of practical moral choice: real in the sense that there is a possible action that would maximize value; ideal in the sense that though it may be hopelessly unachievable in practical terms, it is nevertheless to be deliberately aimed at.

As Sylvester sees it, moral rightness is akin to the traditional concept of an agent's praiseworthiness. See, for example the treatment of praise and blame in Frankena's textbook analysis and Richard Brandt's as well (William Frankena, *Ethics* [Englewood Cliffs, N.J.: Prentice Hall, 1963], p. 44; Richard Brandt, *Value and Obligation* [New York: Harcourt, Brace & World, 1961], pp. 10–11 and 639–43). In Sylvester's use the concepts of moral rightness and the real ideal remove much of the paradox that is usually thought to becloud Moore's theory of obligation—for example, how can it be my duty to do that of which I lack cognizance, or to do that which I sincerely believe to be of great harm?

Regan points out that even Russell thought Moore's view of duty paradoxical—in his 1904 review of *Principia*—but that Moore himself, after almost forty years, while conceding the appearance of paradox, refused to concede that duty is anything else than the production of maximum good in the world (Regan, pp. 229–30; Schilpp, p. 558). It is also worth pointing out that the passages in Sylvester's copy of the Schilpp volume in which Moore considers this matter are thick with underlinings and marginalia. It is clearly evident that Sylvester tries to square his own interpretation of the relation between ought to be and ought to do with what Moore says about that relation in the several pages following the reference to Russell's review, in which the paradox was first mentioned. (See Schilpp, pp. 558 ff; also Kurt Baier's treatment of similar paradoxes in *The Moral Point of View* [Ithaca: Cornell University Press, 1958]. Russell works out his own solution of the paradox in 1910 in terms of subjective rightness and objective rightness. See the reprint of this article in Russell's *Philosophical Essays*.)

Utilitarians have often been charged with providing an analysis of moral action that strips the moral life of its essential subjective (or intentional) component, though Mill himself insisted that his doctrine left ample room for the consideration of the moral worth of persons, as distinct from the rightness of their actions. But where utilitarians may underplay the importance of motive, the Kantians have been accused of making far too much of it. It is an original feature of Sylvester's treatment of Moore's ethics that he shows how Moore manages to strike a balance here between the utilitarians and the Kantians, managing to retain the strong consequentialist emphasis of the utilitarians while he gives to the will of the individual moral agent a decisive role in maximizing value in the universe.

Sylvester argues that Moore's account of moral duty requires that there be free moral agents capable of choice. He takes it that Moore held, at least implicitly, a metaphysical doctrine of *persons* (selves) that could live through moral choices and freely make decisions, a doctrine made plausible by reference to Moore's early writings on sensation, cognition, and judgment. Moreover, Sylvester's case for this reading of Moore is strengthened by the fact that Russell—whose metaphysical, epistemological, and ethical views between 1903 and 1912 were heavily influenced by and very similar to Moore's—certainly *did* have such a doctrine. (See his *Problems of Philosophy* [New York: Oxford University Press, 1912/1959], pp. 50–51 and 158–60.) It is also clear that Sylvester's thesis concerning the necessity of personal freedom for Moore's conception of duty is borne out by what is still the most comprehensive comparative study of utilitarianism and the ethics of Kant: Donald Mackinnon's *A Study in Ethical Theory* (London: Adam & Charles Black, 1957). Mackinnon observes that Moore was "emphatic in insisting that duty and obligation were logically subordinate to goodness and excellence," however obscure and controversial that subordination might be, and that something like the Kantian notion of moral freedom is required to account for the "synthetic necessity" of the link between the ontological good and practical obligation (pp. 11–12 and Chapter 4, "The Notion of Moral Freedom").

In the light of such early references as these, it is at least arguable that the central questions addressed in this chapter—What does Moore advise people to do about moral choices? What freedom do people have to make their own moral choices?—are not as speculative as Sylvester takes them to be. Moreover, in what is surely the most important study of Moore's ethics published since Sylvester's manuscript was written, Tom Regan's *Bloomsbury's Prophet*, Regan argues that Moore's moral influence over the decidedly *un*conventional moral behavior of the so-called Bloomsberries was based on a perception of Moore's ethics as (to put it mildly) liberating its followers from the conventional morality of the Victorian age.

Regan portrays Moore as the liberator of the Bloomsbury group, and he gives that title to the chapter in which he considers Moore's conception of how individuals should reach their moral decisions, using as his main evidence for that conception Moore's convoluted arguments in Chapter 5 of *Principia* (Regan, pp. 217–50). However, as we mentioned in the bibliography for Chapter V above, Regan's thesis of a direct link between Moore's influence and the unconventional moral behavior of his alleged disciples in Bloomsbury has not gone unchallenged. As we noted there, Avrum Stroll finds Regan's evidence unconvincing and exiguous; Thomas Baldwin is scarcely more sanguine, concluding that Regan can make his case only by construing Moore's influence as stemming from a falsely alleged quasi-religious element in his thought.

We can only conjecture as to what Sylvester's response might have been to Regan's claims in *Bloomsbury's Prophet*. However, in the light of Sylvester's very evident concern that the usual interpretations of Moore's ethics had often missed the central nerve of Moore's arguments, it is at least plausible that he would have welcomed Regan's challenge to the not infrequent reading of Moore as a moral conservative, as both Stroll and Baldwin represent him to be.

Perhaps the most telling evidence that could be presented in favor of this conjecture derives from the use that Sylvester makes of Moore's "Freedom" (which Regan also makes use of) and the Kantian theme of moral freedom, which he may see as tempering the morally conservative (conformist) strain of *Principia*. The presence of this Kantian theme is generally neglected by critics, who take the view of Moore as arguing, *simpliciter*, for practical moral conformism. And it may be this neglect that is behind Stroll's insistence that Regan's evidence for Moore's influence upon Bloomsbury is exiguous.

Moral freedom (and the closely related idea of autonomy) is difficult to square with a thoroughgoing conformism, and one should not be surprised to find that Moore's conservatism leaves considerable room for non-conformity. Thus Regan sees, as apparently Stroll and Baldwin do not, that Moore's prescription to make our choices conform to societal rules is contingent upon those rules being generally practiced and generally useful *and* upon their utility being certain (*Principia*, pp. 156–57, 160). Yet as Sylvester clearly sees, Moore *did* believe that these conditions obtain in the case of *some* of society's conventional rules. (Simon Blackburn makes a point of this in his review of *Bloomsbury's Prophet* in the *Times Literary Supplement*, January 29–February 4, 1988.) But as Moore says, "a proof of general utility is so difficult, that it can hardly be conclusive *except in a very few cases*." (*Principia*, p. 165, emphasis added; even earlier, pp. 158–59, he suggests that "the rules comprehended under the name of Chastity" may not be among those "very few cases.") In the end, of course, most conventional rules of society turn out—like our own judgments in complex cases, on Moore's analysis—to be less than certain.

As Regan points out, this leaves ample room for the justification of the Bloomsberries' non-conformity. Moore himself concludes:

> It seems, therefore, that in cases of doubt, instead of following rules, of which he is unable to see the good effects in his particular case, the individual should rather guide his choice by a direct consideration of the intrinsic value or vileness of the effects which his action may produce. [*Principia*, p. 166]

This affirmation of the practical primacy of the moral agent's duty to "guide his choice by a direct consideration of the intrinsic value" reveals the intimate connection in Moore's thought between the idea of moral freedom and the moral liberalism that John Maynard Keynes, Lytton Strachey, and others of the Bloomsbury group professed to find in it. (For Moore's influence, in addition to *Bloomsbury's Prophet*, see Paul Levy, *Moore: G. E. Moore and the Cambridge Apostles*, New York: Holt, Rinehart & Winston, pp. 234–59.)

In the event, although their purposes and styles could hardly be at greater variance, it seems clear that Sylvester would be inclined to agree that Moore has earned the title of Bloomsbury's prophet with which Regan endows him. It is indeed striking that this should be so, since few of Regan's kind of arguments are used by Sylvester, and almost *none* of Sylvester's kind of arguments are used by Regan.

Nicholas Griffin has a useful review of Tom Regan's *Bloomsbury's Prophet* in *The Journal of the Bertrand Russell Archives*, n.s., 9 (1989), pp. 80–93. He sides with Regan on the "unconventional" interpretation of *Principia's* Chapter 5, though he concludes that the class of actions subject to individual discretion will be somewhat smaller than Regan thinks. If Griffin is correct in his reading of Moore, this would seem to add strength to Sylvester's claim. But in the same context Griffin also offers a review of another book that is unsympathetic to Moore's treatment of ontology in *Principia Ethica*: Hasna Begum, *Moore's Ethics: Theory and Practice* (Dhaka, Bangladesh: University of Dhaka Press, 1982). Begum's argument is that Moore's distinction between natural and non-natural properties is incoherent, and claims that Moore actually uses a trichotomy of qualities: natural, non-natural and supersensible. Griffin points out, however, that Begum sometimes refers to Moore's later work in order to clarify *Principia* and that she seems unmindful of changes that may have taken place in Moore's views over time. See also Ray Perkins, Jr., "Moore's Moral Rules," *Journal of the History of Philosophy* (forthcoming).

Notes

Chapter I

1. G. E. Moore, *Principia Ethica*, p. 6.
2. Ibid., pp. 6–7.
3. Ibid., p. 187. See also Moore, *Ethics*, p. 65, and "The Conception of Intrinsic Value," pp. 253–75
4. *Principia Ethica*, p. 180.
5. Ibid., p. 148.
6. Ibid., pp. 25–26.
7. *Ethics*, pp. 40–41. The first two chapters are devoted to the development of a pleasure utilitarian theory. Moore's strategy in argument through the remainder of the text is to criticize pleasure utilitarianism, extracting from the doctrine elements that are objectionable, but retaining features that are sound. He finds the central role ascribed to pleasure in the theory to be objectionable. He rejects it and substitutes intrinsic value.
8. Ibid., p. 143. See also Chapter III, Section 4, below.
9. Stephen Toulmin, *An Examination of the Place of Reason in Ethics* (Cambridge: Cambridge University Press, 1950), especially p. 28. Toulmin does not accurately capture Moore's view in his critique.
10. *Principia Ethica*, p. 210. The principle of organic unities is further examined in what follows.
11. Ibid., p. 191.
12. Ibid., p. 189.
13. Ibid., pp. 201–2.
14. Ibid., pp. 192–93.
15. Ibid., p. 202. See also Section 10, above.
16. Austin Duncan-Jones, "Intrinsic Value: Some Comments on the Work of G. E. Moore," *Philosophy*, 33, 126 (July 1958), p. 254.
17. Moore's article in *Philosophical Studies*, pp. 269–71.
18. *Principia Ethica*, pp. 6–7.

Chapter II

1. An important example can be found in P. H. Nowell-Smith's influential *Ethics* (Baltimore: Penguin, 1954), pp. 23–74. Moore is there

219

lumped together with other intuitionists such as David Ross and H. A. Pritchard.

2. There is a good discussion of Russell's early theory of propositions in Ronald Jager's *The Development of Bertrand Russell's Philosophy* (London: Allen & Unwin, 1972), pp. 36–37, "The Early Metaphysics," Chapter 2.

3. George Santayana, *Winds of Doctrine: Studies in Contemporary Opinion* (New York: Scribners, 1913), pp. 120–24.

4. G. E. Moore, *Principia Ethica*, p. 143.

5. Moore, "Experience and Empiricism," *Proceedings of the Aristotelian Society, n.s.,* 3 (1902–1903), p. 89.

6. *Principia*, p. x.

7. Ibid., p. 143.

8. Moore, "The Nature of Judgement," *Mind*, 8, 30 (1899).

9. Ibid., pp. 181–82.

10. James Mark Baldwin, *Dictionary of Philosophy and Psychology,* (London: Macmillan, 1902) vol. 2, p. 717.

11. Ibid.

12. Moore, *Some Main Problems of Philosophy* (London: Allen & Unwin, 1953), p. 261.

13. Stephen C. Pepper, *Ethics* (New York: Appleton-Century-Crofts, 1960), pp. 268–69.

14. *Principia*, p. 144.

Chapter III

1. "Experience and Empiricism" held that propositions and the objects of experience, called here the states of affairs, cannot actually be distinguished. I distinguish them here since I am talking from the context of *Principia Ethica*'s distinguishing the natural world from the reality proper to concepts or universals.

2. *Principia*, p. 75.

3. Ibid., p. 145.

4. Ibid., p. 89.

5. Ibid., p. 75.

6. Ibid., p. 90.

7. G. E. Moore, *Ethics*, p. 147.

8. Ibid., p. 143.

9. Ibid.

10. The exchange between Moore and C. D. Broad in the Schilpp volume on issues involving egoism and its claims should be consulted by the reader. I am not concerned with the Broad-Moore discussion for its own sake. The issue I am concerned with is one of contradictory intuitions and Moore's way of dealing with such contradiction instances.

11. A. C. Ewing, *Ethics* (New York: Macmillan, 1959).

12. *Principia*, pp. 148–49.
13. Ibid., p. 166. See also "The Conception of Intrinsic Value," p. 265.
14. Ibid., p. 187.
15. Ibid., pp. 4–5.
16. Ibid., p. 172.
17. Ibid.
18. Ibid., p. 173.

Chapter IV

1. G. E. Moore, "An Autobiography," in *The Philosophy of G. E. Moore*, ed. P. A. Schilpp (LaSalle, Ill.: Open Court, 1942), p. 24. See pp. 20–25.
2. Moore, *Principia Ethica*, p. 187.
3. Moore, "The Nature of Judgment," *Mind*, 7, 30 (1899), pp. 176–93. [This essay is reprinted in *G. E. Moore: The Early Essays*, ed. Tom Regan (Philadelphia: Temple University Press, 1986), pp. 59–80. The Regan edition gives the original page numbers used here parenthetically and adopts the American spelling of "judgment." Sylvester follows this practice.]
4. Moore, Ibid., p. 179.
5. Ibid.
6. Ibid., p. 181.
7. Ibid.
8. *Principia*, pp. 9–10.
9. Moore, review of F. Brentano, *The Origins of Our Knowledge of Right and Wrong*, in *International Journal of Ethics*, 14 (October 1903), p. 120.
10. Moore, "Identity," *Proceedings of the Aristotelian Society*, n.s., 1 (1900–1901), pp. 103–27.
11. Moore, *Some Main Problems of Philosophy*, (London: Allen & Unwin, 1953), pp. 52–71.
12. Moore, "Experience and Empiricism," *Proceedings of the Aristotelian Society*, n.s., 3 (1902–1903), p. 89.
13. *Principia*, p. 111.
14. "Judgment," pp. 182–83.
15. *Principia*, p. 127.
16. Brentano review, p. 121.
17. *Principia*, pp. 83–84.
18. Patrick Nowell-Smith, *Ethics* (Baltimore: Penguin, 1954), p. 74. Nowell-Smith, also says: "it is doubtful whether any sense can be given to the idea of something being good if there was no one to judge it good" (p. 130).
19. *Principia*, p. 83.

Chapter V

1. G. E. Moore, "The Nature of Moral Philosophy," in *Philosophical Studies*, pp. 310–39. See p. 319 for the distinction.

2. Ibid., pp. 320–21.

3. Moore, *Principia Ethica*, p. 149. See *Ethics* as well: "It is admitted that [the moral agent] cannot know for certain beforehand which [alternative] will actually have the best results" (p. 120).

4. *Principia*, p. 151.

5. I discuss "possible actions" in Chapter VIII. Moore distinguishes between a possible action and an action of which it is possible to think.

6. *Principia*, p. 157.

7. Ibid., pp. 162–63.

8. Ibid., p. 164.

9. *Ethics*, p. 119.

10. Ibid., p. 121.

11. Ibid., p. 188.

Chapter VI

1. G. E. Moore, "The Conception of Intrinsic Value," *Philosophical Studies*, p. 273, a collection of essays published in 1922. Moore indicates that the essay, one of the unpublished pieces appearing for the first time in the text, was written earlier than "The Conception of Reality," which appeared in 1917.

2. Ibid., p. 269. The italics are Moore's.

3. Moore, *Principia Ethica*, p. 41.

4. C. D. Broad, "Moore's Ethical Doctrine," Schilpp, p. 54.

5. *Principia*, pp. 110–11.

6. Herbert Hochberg, "Moore's Ontology and Non-natural Properties," *Review of Metaphysics*, 15, 3, 59 (1962) pp. 365–95; and Gustav Bergmann, "Inclusion, Exemplification and Inherence in G. E. Moore," *Logic and Reality* (Madison: University of Wisconsin Press, 1964), pp. 158–70.

7. Moore, "Identity," *Proceedings of the Aristotelian Society*, n.s., 1 (1900–1901), p. 115 [p. 133].

8. Schilpp, p. 588.

9. "Conception of Intrinsic Value," p. 268.

10. Moore, "A Reply," p. 153.

11. *Ethics*, p. 153.

12. *Principia*, p. 188.

13. A. C. Ewing, *Mind*, 71, 282 (1982), p. 251.

14. Moore, "Is Goodness a Quality?" *Proceedings of the Aristotelian Society*, supplementary volume II (1932), pp. 212–22.

15. *Principia*, p. 206.
16. Ibid., p. 27.
17. *Ethics*, pp. 151–52. Moore's italics.

Chapter VII

1. G. E. Moore, *Principia Ethica*, p. 10.
2. Ibid., p. 9.
3. Ibid., p. 59.
4. Ibid., p. 8.
5. Ibid., p. 13.
6. Ibid., p. 125.
7. William Frankena, "The Naturalistic Fallacy," *Mind*, 48 (October 1939), pp. 464–77. This quotation, 472.
8. Ibid.
9. Ibid., p. 474.
10. R. M. Hare, *The Language of Morals* (Oxford: Clarendon, 1952), p. 86.
11. *Principia*, p. 187.
12. Ibid., p. 188.
13. Ibid.
14. Ibid., pp. 208–9.
15. Ibid. On p. 14, further to the open question, "Why, if good is good and indefinable, should I be held to deny that pleasure is good?" Moore says "there is no meaning in saying that pleasure is good, unless good is something different from pleasure."
16. Ibid., p. 13.
17. Moore, Brentano review, p. 121.
18. Ibid.
19. Moore, "Mr. McTaggart's Ethics," *International Journal of Ethics*, 13 (April 1903), p. 342.
20. Frankena, "The Naturalistic Fallacy," p. 467.
21. *Principia*, p. vii.
22. Ibid., p. 17.
23. Ibid., p. 67. My colleague Ray Perkins pointed out that this argument needs clarification.
24. Frankena, Schilpp volume, p. 100.
25. Moore, Schilpp volume, p. 572.
26. Ibid., p. 525.
27. *Principia*, pp. 110–111.
28. Schilpp, p. 99.
29. Frankena, Schilpp volume, p. 97.
30. Moore, *Ethics*, p. 143. "It seems to me quite self-evident that it

must always be our duty to do what will produce the best effects on the whole."

Chapter VIII

1. G. E. Moore, *Principia Ethica*, p. x.
2. Ibid., p. 151.
3. Moore, *Ethics*, p. 140.
4. Ibid., p. 10–11. *Voluntary* actions are characterized as "if, just before we began to do them, we *had* chosen not to do them, we *should* not have done them."
5. Ibid., p. 121.
6. *Principia*, p. 201.
7. Ibid., p. 204. Emphasis added.
8. Moore, "The Value of Religion," *International Journal of Ethics*, 12 (October 1901), p. 83 [Regan, p. 104].
9. Moore, "The Subject Matter of Psychology," *Proceedings of the Aristotelian Society*, n.s., 10 (1909–1910), pp. 54–55.
10. Moore, "The Refutation of Idealism," *Mind*, 12 (1903).
11. Moore, "Are the Materials of Sense Affections of the Mind?" *Proceedings of the Aristotelian Society*, n.s., 17 (1916–1917), p. 429.
12. Moore, "Mr. McTaggart's 'Studies in Hegelian Cosmology,'" *Proceedings of the Aristotelian Society*, n.s., 2 (1901–1902), pp. 207–8 [Regan, pp. 177–78].
13. *Ethics*, p. 124.
14. Moore, "A Reply," p. 629.
15. *Ethics*, pp. 136–37.
16. Moore, "The Nature of Moral Philosophy," *Philosophical Studies*, p. 317. The essay was written probably in 1920. It appears ten years after the publication of *Ethics* and nearly 20 years after *Principia Ethica*. I think it faithfully represents Moore's view in the entire period. The notion that ought, duty, and right (*b*) could make moral sense without free choice would be *at best* peculiar for Moore.
17. See Moore, "Freedom," *Mind*, n.s., 7 (April 1898), pp. 179–204 [Regan edition, pp. 25–57]; and Moore, "Necessity," *Mind*, n.s., 9 (July 1900), pp. 289–304 [Regan pp. 81–99].
18. "Reply," in Schilpp, p. 616.
19. "An Autobiography," in Schilpp, p. 27.
20. "Freedom," p. 194 [Regan, p. 43].

Index